The Economics
of Private Pensions

Studies in Social Economics

TITLES PUBLISHED

STUDIES IN SOCIAL ECONOMICS

Alicia H. Munnell

The Economics
of Private Pensions

THE BROOKINGS INSTITUTION
Washington, D.C.

Copyright © 1982 by
THE BROOKINGS INSTITUTION
1775 Massachusetts Avenue, N.W., Washington, D.C. 20036

Library of Congress Cataloging in Publication data

Munnell, Alicia Haydock.
  The economics of private pensions.
  (Studies in social economics; 21)
  Includes bibliographical references and
index.
  1. Old age pensions—United States.
I. Title. II. Series.
HD7106.U5M83   331.25′2′0973   82-4223
ISBN 0-8157-5894-4   AACR2
ISBN 0-8157-5893-6 (pbk.)

9 8 7 6 5 4 3 2 1

THE BROOKINGS INSTITUTION is an independent organization devoted to nonpartisan research, education, and publication in economics, government, foreign policy, and the social sciences generally. Its principal purposes are to aid in the development of sound public policies and to promote public understanding of issues of national importance.

The Institution was founded on December 8, 1927, to merge the activities of the Institute for Government Research, founded in 1916, the Institute of Economics, founded in 1922, and the Robert Brookings Graduate School of Economics and Government, founded in 1924.

The Board of Trustees is responsible for the general administration of the Institution, while the immediate direction of the policies, program, and staff is vested in the President, assisted by an advisory committee of the officers and staff. The by-laws of the Institution state: "It is the function of the Trustees to make possible the conduct of scientific research, and publication, under the most favorable conditions, and to safeguard the independence of the research staff in the pursuit of their studies and in the publication of the results of such studies. It is not a part of their function to determine, control, or influence the conduct of particular investigations or the conclusions reached."

The President bears final responsibility for the decision to publish a manuscript as a Brookings book. In reaching his judgment on the competence, accuracy, and objectivity of each study, the President is advised by the director of the appropriate research program and weighs the views of a panel of expert outside readers who report to him in confidence on the quality of the work. Publication of a work signifies that it is deemed a competent treatment worthy of public consideration but does not imply endorsement of conclusions or recommendations.

The Institution maintains its position of neutrality on issues of public policy in order to safeguard the intellectual freedom of the staff. Hence interpretations or conclusions in Brookings publications should be understood to be solely those of the authors and should not be attributed to the Institution, to its trustees, officers, or other staff members, or to the organizations that support its research.

Foreword

Private pension plans have grown dramatically since the Second World War. Between 1945 and 1950 the proportion of the private nonfarm work force covered by such plans increased from 19 percent to 48 percent. By 1980 about 40 percent of retirees were receiving $35 billion of private pension benefits annually to supplement social security. Contributions to private plans amounted to $70 billion a year, or about 6 percent of wages and salaries, and aggregate assets exceeded $400 billion. Despite the importance of the development of private pension plans for workers, retirees, and corporations, little is known about the economic effects of the private pension system.

In this book Alicia H. Munnell explores the factors that have influenced the growth of the private pension plans, emphasizing the ways in which private plans affect the economy. She begins by describing the complicated interaction between social security and private pensions, both of which developed in the aftermath of the Great Depression. She evaluates the extent to which various tax provisions have not only affected the form in which savers accumulate assets, but have also stimulated increased retirement saving. She argues that the shift in control of $400 billion of pension assets influences the performance of the nation's financial markets. And the Employee Retirement Income Security Act of 1974, under which companies are liable for unfunded pension liabilities, has affected corporate financial policies.

The relation between private plans and the economy has been further complicated by inflation. Indeed, Munnell concludes that the ability of private plans to provide adequate benefits has been seriously diminished by rapidly rising prices, and that the future of private pensions depends on the capacity of plan sponsors to index benefits, at least partially. But even if all other difficulties are overcome, she warns, a potential problem will remain: only half the work force is currently covered by private pensions. For this and other reasons, the introduction of a universal private pension system may merit serious consideration.

Alicia H. Munnell, an economist and vice president of the Federal Reserve Bank of Boston, wrote this book, the twenty-first in the Brookings Studies in Social Economics series, as a member of the Brookings associated staff. She is grateful for the support of the Bank's president, Frank E. Morris, and its director of research, Robert W. Eisenmenger, and for the capable research assistance of Jennifer B. Katz, Laura E. Stiglin, and Kristine M. Keefe, of the Bank's staff.

She is also grateful to all those who read and commented on parts of the manuscript, among them Robert M. Ball, Randy Barber, Carolyn Shaw Bell, Gary Burtless, Constance Dunham, John A. Fibiger, Daniel I. Halperin, George A. Hambrecht, Daniel M. Holland, Francis P. King, Richard W. Kopcke, Dean LeBaron, Robert F. Link, William J. McDonnell, Dan M. McGill, Robert J. Myers, Joseph A. Pechman, James H. Schulz, and Irwin Tepper. She acknowledges the substantial contribution of John A. Brittain, who would have been a coauthor of this volume if illness had not intervened. And she is indebted to Diane E. Levin and Ellen W. Smith, who purged the manuscript of numerous errors; to Anna M. Estle, who typed the manuscript; to Caroline Lalire, who edited it, and to Florence Robinson, who prepared the index.

The views expressed are those of the author and should not be ascribed to the officers, trustees, and staff members of the Brookings Institution, to the Federal Reserve Bank of Boston, to the Federal Reserve System, or to any of those who were consulted or who commented on the manuscript.

BRUCE K. MACLAURY
President

April 1982
Washington, D.C.

Contents

Appendix Tables

Figures

chapter one Introduction

The rapid growth of organized retirement saving programs—social security, federal, state, and local plans, and the private pension system—is one of the most important structural changes in the U.S. economy since World War II. In recent years economists have begun to explore the economic impact of social security—which covers over 90 percent of the work force—on saving, labor force activity, and the income of the elderly. In contrast, the economic effects of private pension plans, which cover about half of total private employees and control over $400 billion in assets, have been virtually ignored.[1]

Such neglect is no longer possible because private plans affect the income security of millions of workers and their families, influence the employment and mobility of half the work force, constitute a significant claim on corporate profits, and play an important role in financial markets. Private plans are certainly a legitimate subject for public policy analysis, since they are regulated by the federal government under the Employee Retirement Income Security Act of 1974 (ERISA) and are nurtured by the favorable federal income tax provisions for covered workers. Moreover, recent social and economic developments—demographic shifts, high levels of inflation, and volatile stock market performance—affect the ability of private plans to provide adequate retirement income. The effectiveness of the private pension system and the impact of private plans on the economy must be known in order to determine rationally the appropriate share of retirement income to be provided by social security, private pensions, and individual saving initiatives.

1. Of the numerous task forces and commissions that examined retirement issues in the early 1980s, only the President's Commission on Pension Policy explicitly considered the status of private pension plans. See President's Commission on Pension Policy, *Coming of Age: Toward a National Retirement Income Policy* (Government Printing Office, 1981).

Scope of the Book

While the complexity of the private pension system and the lack of complete data preclude a comprehensive study of private plans, this book attempts to fill part of the void by exploring the impact of the social security system and the federal tax structure on the development of private plans, the macroeconomic effects of private pensions on saving and financial markets, the microeconomic effects of pensions on corporations and the income of the elderly, and, finally, the viability of the private pension system in an inflationary environment.

One major area not addressed in this study is the effect of pensions on the labor market—particularly the effect of pension coverage and vesting on labor mobility and the incidence of pension costs. These topics have been omitted not because they are unimportant but because so little evidence exists to support or refute the predictions of economic theory. Employers' willingness to supply pensions as part of a compensation package is presumably related to the perceived beneficial effects of pension plans on the stability of the work force. Low employee turnover reduces recruiting and hiring costs and may be valuable to employers who must invest heavily in teaching workers the skills that are specific to the firm. Pensions with delayed vesting may be used to induce workers to remain with the firm until training costs are recouped. It is difficult, however, to determine empirically the relation between pensions and turnover, since pensions generally play a minor role in the complex decision to quit a job. The one study that produced estimates of a detectable influence of vesting provisions on turnover patterns yielded predictable results.[2] Younger workers were found less likely to quit as the opportunity for vesting approached, and older workers' termination decisions increased once vesting occurred.

The extent to which workers pay for pension benefits through lower wages is also difficult to test empirically. According to economic theory, profit-maximizing employers try to assemble a qualified labor force to produce output at competitive prices. To attract qualified workers, the employer must offer total compensation roughly equivalent to that offered by other employers. An employer who offers much more will be unable to compete in the products market. An employer who offers much less than the market wage will not be able to attract qualified workers.

2. Bradley Schiller and Randall Weiss, "The Impact of Private Pensions on Firm Attachment," *Review of Economics and Statistics,* vol. 61 (August 1979), pp. 369–80.

This analysis implies that total compensation for workers of given skills will be equal across firms and that differences in pensions will be offset by differences in other forms of compensation. In other words, employees pay for their own pensions through lower wages.

To test empirically whether a pension-wage trade-off exists is a formidable task. It involves estimating the coefficient of pension accruals in a wage equation that contains variables to explain all other factors that could affect wage rates. Thus the data requirements include employer information on the actuarial cost of accruing pension benefits and the level of pension funding as well as such characteristics of persons in the sample as age, sex, race, education, and marital status. Not only are the data requirements considerable, but there is also a further complication: the technical relationship between the worker's wage and pension is positive, since pensions are normally calculated as some fraction of wages, whereas the hypothesized behavioral relationship is negative. Because of these difficulties, only two studies have attempted to estimate the wage-pension trade-off for workers in private industry.[3] Although their results are far from robust, both studies indicate that, other factors being equal, higher pensions will lead to lower wages. This finding is consistent with the results of studies for public employees and with a body of research indicating that in the long run the burden of the social security payroll tax rests on labor.[4] Thus a trade-off between pension accruals and wages is assumed throughout the book.

Organization of the Book

Even though the first private pension plan was established by the American Express Company in 1875, by 1930 only 15 percent of the

3. Bradley Schiller and Randall Weiss "Pensions and Wages: A Test for Equalizing Differences," *Review of Economics and Statistics*, vol. 62 (November 1980), pp. 529–38; and Ronald Ehrenberg and Robert Smith, "The Wage/Pension Trade-Off," in President's Commission on Pension Policy, *Coming of Age*, pp. 1200–18.

4. Ronald Ehrenberg, "Retirement System Characteristics and Compensating Wage Differentials in the Public Sector," *Industrial and Labor Relations Review*, vol. 33 (July 1980), pp. 470–83; Robert Smith, "Compensating Differentials for Pensions and Underfunding in the Public Sector," *Review of Economics and Statistics*, vol. 63 (August 1981), pp. 463–68; John A. Brittain, "The Incidence of Social Security Payroll Taxes," *American Economic Review*, vol. 61 (March 1971), pp. 110–25; Brittain, *The Payroll Tax for Social Security* (Brookings Institution, 1972), pp. 39–44, 55–57; Wayne Vroman, "Employer Payroll Tax Incidences: Empirical Tests with Cross-Country Data," *Public Finance*, vol. 29, no. 2 (1974), pp. 184–200; and Daniel Hamermesh, "New Estimates of the Incidence of the Payroll Tax," *Southern Economic Journal*, vol. 45 (April 1979), pp. 1208–19.

private nonfarm labor force was covered by private pensions and only 100,000 retirees were receiving benefits.[5] Most elderly persons depended on the nuclear family structure and the work apprenticeship system for an adequate income in old age. The Great Depression, however, plunged the elderly into poverty and undermined individual confidence in private provisions for old age. This environment created an urgent public demand for institutionalized retirement savings, which was partially met by the enactment of the social security program in 1935. However, while social security coverage expanded rapidly, benefits remained rather meager and actually declined during the 1940s from 27 percent to 15 percent of average earnings. Thus a heightened interest in private pension benefits as a supplement to social security was the natural outgrowth of the desire for guaranteed retirement income. On the one hand, then, the provision of a retirement income floor through social security increased the demand for private supplementary retirement benefits. On the other hand, private pensions and social security benefits are substitutes, and the expansion of one discourages the growth of the other. This complicated interaction of the nation's two retirement systems is discussed in chapter 2, and some econometric evidence is presented in appendix A. Appendix B summarizes the various charac-teristics of today's private pension system and develops a prototypal plan that is used as a basis for discussion throughout the book.

Chapter 3 examines the other main influence on the development of private plans—namely, the federal tax system. By clarifying the condi-tions under which corporations could deduct contributions to private plans from taxable income, the 1942 amendments to the Internal Revenue Code made pensions an attractive investment for employers. These amendments were introduced at a time when employers faced strict controls on the wages they could offer and were therefore eager to increase benefits to attract workers in the tight civilian labor force. The favorable tax treatment accorded employer contributions not only encouraged the growth of private pension plans but also influenced their structure. Allowing a deduction for employer contributions without treating these contributions as income to the employee has encouraged the growth of plans that are financed primarily by employers.

Chapter 4 shifts the focus of the book from those factors influencing the development of the private pension system to the macroeconomic

5. American Council of Life Insurance, *Pension Facts, 1978–1979* (Washington, D.C.: ACLI, 1979), pp. 34, 37.

effects of private pensions on the economy. It explores the impact of private pension plans on individual saving, comparing this impact with that of social security. Studies indicate that since covered workers tend to reduce other forms of saving in anticipation of private pension benefits, the increase in private pension assets represents a shift in the form of individual saving rather than an increase in the total amount of saving. At the same time, the available evidence on social security does not support the contention that the pay-as-you-go scheme has substantially reduced the saving rate in the economy. Thus neither the public nor the private pension system has had a dramatic effect on the nation's saving or capital accumulation.

Although private pensions do not appear to have altered aggregate saving, they could affect the economy in their role as financial intermediaries. Chapter 5 investigates the investment behavior of private pensions and summarizes the available evidence on their impact on financial markets. Because the increased demand for long-term assets by private pensions appears to be offset by a reduced household demand, the growth of the private pension system has probably not had much effect on relative yields. Moreover, there is little evidence to support the contention that speculative trading by institutional investors has caused the stock market to become more volatile.

While pension plans may have a minimal macroeconomic impact, they have important implications for covered workers, beneficiaries, and sponsoring corporations. Chapter 6 delves into the relation between pensions and corporate finance, highlighting the change in the status of unfunded vested benefits in the wake of ERISA and examining the implications of the Pension Benefit Guaranty Corporation's claim on corporate assets. The chapter also explores the anomaly that despite the strong tax incentive to fund (income earned on pension assets is exempt from the corporate income tax, whereas earnings on other corporate assets are fully taxable), some corporate pension plans are only partially funded. Partial funding has resulted in unfunded liabilities for these corporations, and the empirical work summarized in chapter 6 indicates that the future claims are reflected in lower market values of corporate equities. The chapter concludes with a discussion of the proper accounting for unfunded pension liabilities in light of the fact that a significant portion of benefits are now a legal liability of the corporation.

The last two chapters focus on the future of the private pension system. Chapter 7 addresses the problems created by the current high levels of inflation. Preserving the value of benefits over the employee's work life depends on how private plans are structured. Vesting, portability, and the nature of the compensation base determine whether the worker's initial benefit reflects inflation-induced wage increases. After retirement, protection hinges on whether pensioners are provided annual cost-of-living adjustments. The chapter summarizes the degree to which pension benefits keep pace with rising prices and evaluates whether private plans can provide fully indexed benefits while remaining actuarially sound. Although full cost-of-living indexing for private pension benefits is probably not feasible since returns on equities and fixed income securities do not keep pace with inflation, partial indexing is both possible and desirable. Without at least partial indexing, the relative role of private pensions in providing retirement income will decline in an inflationary environment.

Chapter 8 summarizes the other important factors influencing the future of private pension plans, including the impact of ERISA and the maturation of the private pension system. Finally, the chapter examines some of the major proposals for reform of the private pension system and appraises its future in light of the existence of social security and other public plans.

chapter two **The Development of Private Plans**
and Their Relation to Social Security

The development of the social security program and private pension system, in the wake of the Great Depression, reflected a shift in the nation's preference away from individual saving for retirement and toward organized savings plans. The two systems developed simultaneously, since neither program provided adequate retirement income. Yet they clearly are alternative ways to accomplish the same goal—namely, providing an adequate retirement income. In fact, many private plans are explicitly integrated with social security and so reduce private pension benefits as social security benefits are increased. Because of the substitutability of the two programs, as the gap between desired and actual retirement assets narrows, an expansion in either social security or private pensions will lead to a decline in the relative role of the other.

The recent expansion of social security, therefore, has profound implications for the development of private plans. In the 1970s social security benefits grew particularly fast as a result of ad hoc increases and automatic cost-of-living adjustments. Despite this growth, a substantial gap still exists—especially for workers with above-average earnings—between retirees' income needs and social security benefits. Whether the gap is filled by private pensions or a larger social security program will depend on the relative ability of the two programs to provide good retirement protection.

The Growth of Private Plans

Although private pension plans date officially from 1875, the early plans were financially vulnerable and most were bankrupted by the Great

Depression.[1] Contemporary U.S. pension plans, both public and private, are rooted in the desire for financial security that became part of the national psychology after the onset of the Depression. The expansion of private plans was stimulated by the inflation, tax changes, and wage controls of World War II.

The introduction of a few private plans by large industrial employers during the last quarter of the nineteenth century reflected the United States' transition from a rural agricultural society to an urban industrial economy. The large, prosperous, and heavily regulated transportation industry, which employed many workers in hazardous jobs, pioneered the establishment of private plans. In 1875 the American Express Company established the first pension plan, providing benefits for permanently disabled workers with twenty years of continuous service. The Baltimore and Ohio Railroad Company, noted for its enlightened labor policy, organized a contributory plan in 1880, and in 1900 the Pennsylvania Railroad established a noncontributory plan, which served as a model for other railways. By 1905 U.S. railroads had instituted twelve formal pension plans; by the end of the 1920s pension coverage had been extended to 80 percent of railroad workers.[2]

The early twentieth century witnessed the growth of pensions in other regulated and concentrated industries where price competition was not important and pension costs could be passed forward to consumers. By 1920 most banks, utility, mining, and petroleum companies as well as a sprinkling of manufacturers had established formal plans. These plans offered employers the impersonal and egalitarian option of retirement as a way to restructure the age composition of their work force.[3] In 1929, 397 of the 421 plans instituted since 1875 were still in operation; approximately 3.7 million workers—about 10 percent of the nonagricultural labor force—were employed by corporations offering pension plans, although not all employees were eligible for plan membership.[4]

1. The authoritative source on early pension movement is Murray W. Latimer, *Industrial Pension Systems in the United States and Canada,* 2 vols. (New York: Industrial Relations Counselors, 1932). For an excellent discussion of the historical evolution of private pension plans, see also William C. Greenough and Francis P. King, *Pension Plans and Public Policy* (Columbia University Press, 1976), pp. 27–58; and Bruno Stein, *Social Security and Pensions in Transition: Understanding the American Retirement System* (Free Press, 1980), pp. 68–76.

2. American Council of Life Insurance, *Pension Facts, 1978–1979* (Washington, D.C.: ACLI, 1979), p. 34.

3. William Graebner, *A History of Retirement: The Meaning and Function of an American Institution, 1885–1978* (Yale University Press, 1980), pp. 18–53.

4. Latimer, *Industrial Pension Systems,* pp. 42, 47; and Greenough and King, *Pension Plans and Public Policy,* p. 31.

While large industrial employers were establishing pension plans, a small number of trade unions were instituting their own schemes for retirement benefits. Mutual benefit societies for survivors, sickness, and disability were traditional among unions, but the first union old-age plan, established by the Granite Cutters' International Association of America, did not appear until 1905.[5] Under most of the early trade union plans, benefit payments were offered as gratuities and depended largely on the state of the union treasury and its ability to assess members; the first union plan to offer old-age benefits as a matter of right was established by the Brotherhood of Locomotive Engineers in 1912. By 1928 about 40 percent of trade union members belonged to unions that offered some form of old-age and permanent and total disability benefits.[6]

The Great Depression had a disastrous effect on both the industrial and trade union plans. Many railroads had become unprofitable during the late 1920s, and by the early 1930s they were operating in the red. Despite emergency measures to cut costs through reduction of wages and pension benefits, the railroads' financial situation continued to deteriorate. Approximately 25 percent of railway workers were approaching retirement, but the railroads, with virtually no reserves, were incapable of fulfilling benefit promises.[7] Because so many people were involved, strong pressure developed for legislative action to bail out the railroads. Thus the Railroad Retirement Act of 1935 was enacted, which rescued the failing pension plans by establishing a quasi-public retirement system for railway employees.

Employees covered by other industry plans were not so fortunate as the railroad workers. Beginning in 1929, as business activity declined, many companies were unable to meet both operating expenses and rising pension payments. In response, they made substantial cutbacks in pension benefits, ranging from tightening eligibility requirements and suspending pension credit accumulation to abolishing pension plans and terminating benefit payments even for retired employees.[8] The trade union plans also floundered; with high unemployment and competing demands on the union treasuries, it was impossible to increase dues enough to support the growing number of union retirees. Within a few

5. The plan of the Granite Cutters' association was the first trade union plan that actually functioned. Earlier trade union plans—those of the Pattern Makers' League of North America (1900) and the National Association of Letter Carriers (1902)—dissolved before paying any benefits. American Council of Life Insurance, *Pension Facts, 1978–1979*, p. 37.

6. Greenough and King, *Pension Plans and Public Policy*, p. 41.

7. Charles L. Dearing, *Industrial Pensions* (Brookings Institution, 1954), p. 24.

8. Ibid., pp. 24–25.

years after the Depression began, almost all union welfare plans had collapsed.

The Depression not only bankrupted most trade union and industrial pension plans but also undermined American confidence in the historic tradition of self-reliance and in the virtue of individual thrift as a way to provide for old age. By 1933 nearly 13 million people were unemployed and the lifetime savings of many were erased. The nation was therefore sympathetic to the need for the Social Security Act of 1935 and the subsequent development of negotiated funded private pension plans.

Although World War II initially consumed much of the nation's resources that might have been directed toward improved provisions for old age, two wartime factors—wage control policies and tax changes— greatly stimulated the expansion of private plans.[9] The wage stabilization program instituted during the war impeded employers' ability to attract and hold employees in the tight civilian labor market. However, the War Labor Board attempted to relieve the pressure on management and labor from the legal limitations on cash wages by permitting employers to bid for workers by offering attractive fringe benefits. The cost to the firms of establishing pension plans to attract workers was minimal in light of the tax deductibility of contributions and the wartime excess profits tax on corporate income. Moreover, the Revenue Act of 1942 specified the types of private plans that could qualify for favorable tax treatment and allowed a company to receive assurance from the Internal Revenue Service before its plan was put into operation that employer contributions would be tax deductible.[10] The deductibility of the contributions combined with the very high corporate tax rates meant that a major portion of pension contributions were financed by funds that would otherwise have been paid to the government in taxes. Thus in little more than two years—from September 1942 through December 1944—the IRS approved 4,208 pension plans, as against 1,360 plans approved during the previous twelve years.[11] Employer contributions to private plans increased from $180 million to $830 million a year between 1940 and 1945 (see table 2-1).

The rate of growth of new pension plans fell off markedly during the immediate postwar period as employees focused on cash wage increases

9. Ibid., pp. 36–37.
10. See Merton C. Bernstein, *The Future of Private Pensions* (London: Free Press of Glencoe, 1964), p. 198.
11. Dearing, *Industrial Pensions*, p. 37.

Table 2-1. Private Pension Plans: Coverage, Contributions, Benefits, and Assets, Selected Years, 1940–80

| Year | Workers covered (thousands)[a] | Contributions (millions of dollars) | | | Benefits | | Assets, end of year (billions of dollars)[b] |
		Total	Employer	Employee	Number of beneficia-ries (thousands)	Amount of payments (millions of dollars)	
1940	4,100	310	180	130	160	140	2.4
1945	6,400	990	830	160	310	220	5.4
1950	9,800	2,080	1,750	330	450	370	12.1
1955	14,200	3,840	3,280	560	980	850	27.5
1960	18,700	5,490	4,710	780	1,780	1,720	52.0
1965	21,800	8,360	7,370	990	2,750	3,520	86.5
1970	26,300	14,000	12,580	1,420	4,750	7,360	137.1
1975	30,300	29,850	27,560	2,290	7,050	14,810	212.6
1980	35,800[c]	68,970[d]	64,840[d]	4,130[d]	9,100[c]	35,177[e]	407.9

Sources: Alfred M. Skolnik, "Private Pension Plans, 1950–74," *Social Security Bulletin,* vol. 39 (June 1976), p. 4; Martha Remy Yohalem, "Employee-Benefit Plans, 1975," *Social Security Bulletin,* vol. 40 (November 1977), p. 27; ICF, Inc., *A Private Pension Forecasting Model,* submitted to the Department of Labor, Office of Pension and Welfare Benefits Programs (October 1979); American Council of Life Insurance, *Life Insurance Fact Book, 1981* (Washington, D.C.: ACLI, 1981), p. 54; Securities and Exchange Commission, *Monthly Statistical Review,* vol. 40 (May 1981), p. 10.

a. Includes active civilian wage and salary workers in private industry who are accruing pension credits in their present job. Excludes the self-employed, annuitants, and those who have vested pension credits but are no longer employed under a private plan. The series corrects for duplication for employees who are covered by more than one retirement plan.

b. Does not include individual retirement accounts or tax-sheltered annuities, and includes only 40 percent of Keogh plans, which are assumed to be established by self-employed people for their employees. Since the data in table 5-4 include IRAs, tax-sheltered annuities, and 100 percent of Keogh plans, the pension assets in that table exceed the figures shown above.

c. Estimate from ICF, Inc., *Private Pension Forecasting Model.* This figure may substantially understate the total number of participants. According to a recent study of 5500 forms filed by pension plans for the 1977 plan year, the Department of Labor concluded that there were 42.5 million active participants in 1977. See *Preliminary Estimates of Participant and Financial Characteristics of Private Pension Plans, 1977* (GPO, 1981). The ICF estimate was retained, however, for consistency with the earlier data provided by the Social Security Administration.

d. Author's projections, based on actual employer contributions of $54,899 million in 1979 as reported by the Department of Commerce, Bureau of Economic Analysis. Projections assume that employer contributions grew at the same rate from 1979 to 1980 as over the 1975–79 period and that, in 1980, employers made 94 percent of total contributions to private plans.

e. Author's estimate derived from the ICF, Inc., 1980 estimate of the ratio of benefits to contributions and the author's 1980 projection of employer contributions.

in an attempt to recover the ground lost during the period of wage stabilization.[12] By 1949, however, pension benefits again became a major issue of labor negotiation because of the increased resistance to further wage increases and a weak economy. The importance of pensions was highlighted by a presidential fact-finding board, which concluded that while a cash wage increase in the steel industry was not justified, the industry did have a social obligation to provide workers with pensions.[13]

12. Joseph J. Melone, "Management and Labor Considerations in the Establishment of Private Pension Plans," in *Old Age Income Assurance,* A Compendium of Papers on Problems and Policy Issues in the Public and Private Pension System, submitted to the Subcommittee on Fiscal Policy of the Joint Economic Committee, pt. 4: *Employment Aspects of Pension Plans,* 90 Cong. 1 sess. (Government Printing Office, 1967), p. 8.

13. *Inland Steel Co.* v. *United Steelworkers of America,* 77 NLRB 4 (1948).

This decision was based in part on the obvious inadequacy of social security benefits, which averaged $26 a month at the time. Labor's drive for pension benefits was aided further when the Supreme Court confirmed a 1948 ruling of the National Labor Relations Board that employers had a legal obligation to negotiate the terms of pension plans.[14] Both the United Steelworkers of America and the United Automobile Workers then launched successful drives for pension benefits under the influence of the 1949 recession.

The main expansion of today's private pension system, then, actually began during the 1950s. Private pension coverage grew rapidly during this period, not only in union plans but also among nonunionized industries. The economic impact of the Korean War further stimulated the pension movement as employers once again competed for workers in the face of wage and salary controls and excess profits taxes. The mid-1950s marked the beginning of substantial collective bargaining gains in multiemployer pension plans. These plans were established in industries containing many small companies and involving frequent job changes that prevented employees from remaining with a single employer long enough to qualify for pensions. The multiemployer pension movement, encouraged by the success of the United Mine Workers of America, spread to such industries as construction, food, apparel, and transportation.[15]

The growth of private pensions continued into the 1960s. But much of the increase in coverage during that decade was due to an expansion of employment in firms that already had pension plans, in contrast to the growth during the 1950s, which resulted primarily from the introduction of new plans. Coverage under multiemployer plans grew more than twice as fast as single-employer plans during the 1960s, owing in part to the merging of single-employer plans into multiemployer ones.[16]

The growth of private pension plans since 1940 is summarized in table 2-1. By 1980 approximately 36 million wage earners and salaried employees were covered by private retirement plans financed either by the employer alone or jointly by employers and employees. Coverage under private plans nearly doubled between 1950 and 1980, from 25 percent of

14. *Inland Steel Co.* v. *National Labor Relations Board,* 170 F. 2d. at 247, 251 (1949).

15. See Walter W. Kolodrubetz, *Multiemployer Pension Plans under Collective Bargaining, Spring 1960,* Department of Labor, Bureau of Labor Statistics Bulletin 1326 (GPO, 1962).

16. Harry E. Davis and Arnold Strasser, "Private Pension Plans, 1960 to 1969—An Overview," *Monthly Labor Review,* vol. 93 (July 1970), p. 45.

the private nonfarm labor force to 48 percent. Annual contributions to private pension funds increased almost thirty-five times, from $2 billion in 1950 to $69 billion in 1980. On the benefit side, an estimated 9 million retirees and survivors were receiving periodic payments from private pension plans in 1980. These beneficiaries received a total of $35 billion, an average of almost $3,870 per recipient.

The Interaction of Social Security and Private Pensions

Once the Depression had created the psychological environment for institutionalizing retirement saving, the initial resolution was to provide old-age income primarily under public auspices. With the Social Security Act of 1935 the federal government assumed responsibility for maintaining a floor of income protection for the retired elderly. Yet social security failed to keep pace with the growth in wages, perhaps because of the diversion of resources for World War II. Thus the average monthly benefit for a retired worker, which equaled $22.71 in 1940, was only $29.03 in early 1950, declining from roughly 27 percent to 15 percent of average earnings. Much of the union pressure for private pension plans was a response to the growing inadequacy of social security benefits. Furthermore, union leaders believed that the creation of private plans would encourage employers to support increases in OASI (old-age and survivors insurance) benefit levels to reduce the burden on private industry of providing retirement income.[17]

At first glance, the simultaneous expansion of public and private programs during the last thirty years seems to imply that social security has not infringed on the development of private pension plans. For instance, despite a major increase in social security benefits in 1950, private pension plans continued to grow rapidly. Many argue that social security has actually encouraged the growth of private pensions by establishing sixty-five as an acceptable retirement age and by providing a basic retirement benefit that permits workers to plan for an independent future. However, the simultaneous expansion of social security and private plans can also be explained as society's attempt to close the large gap between actual and desired retirement assets. Social security and private pensions are alternative vehicles to achieve a targeted level of guaranteed retirement benefits. That these two mechanisms are substi-

17. Bernstein, *Future of Private Pensions,* p. 13.

tutes is suggested not only by anecdotal evidence from union leaders that employer contributions to private plans are implicitly considered in contract negotiations but also by the existence of integrated private pension plans under which the worker's social security benefit is explicitly factored into the calculation of his private pension benefit.

Integration

The concept of integration is based on the notion that public and private retirement programs should function as a unified system. Congress incorporated this reasoning into the tax code in the Revenue Act of 1942 by including the proviso that public and private retirement benefits would be considered together in determining whether or not a plan discriminates against low-wage workers. Since the social security program is weighted in favor of low-income workers, integrated private plans favor high-income workers, so that all workers receive about the same ratio of their preretirement earnings when they retire.

While most plans were integrated with social security in the early 1950s, after 1960 the number of integrated plans declined. Nevertheless, integration remains characteristic of many plans. A 1974 study by the Congressional Research Service found that 60 percent of the 412,376 active corporate-type pension plans were integrated, although integration affected only about 25 to 30 percent of the 30 million participants covered by private pensions. The discrepancy arises because small plans with fewer than twenty-six participants are more than twice as likely to be integrated with social security than large plans. Thus an estimated 64 percent of small plans were integrated, whereas only 29 percent of plans with twenty-six or more workers were integrated.[18]

Integrated plans are usually categorized as "excess" plans or "offset" plans. The former allow the employer to provide either contributions or benefits only on earnings in excess of some level specified by the plan. Under an excess plan an employer can contribute up to 7 percent of compensation above the social security taxable wage base without providing any pension contributions for earnings below the base. Or an excess plan can provide a pension benefit of up to 37.5 percent of average

18. Raymond Schmitt, "Integration of Private Pension Plans with Social Security," in *Studies in Public Welfare,* paper 18: *Issues in Financing Retirement Income,* studies prepared for the Subcommittee on Fiscal Policy of the Joint Economic Committee, 93 Cong. 2 sess. (GPO, 1974), pp. 174–75.

pay in excess of the social security taxable wage base without providing a benefit for wages below that point. Very few workers are actually covered by either of these pure forms of excess plans, which provide no benefits below the compensation level. Rather, the typical form is a step-rate plan in which benefit accrual rates are somewhat higher above the compensation level than below it.

Offset plans are the most popular method for integrating social security and private pension benefits. Under an offset plan, the pension provided by the employer may be reduced by as much as 83.33 percent of the employee's social security benefit. In actual practice, however, the maximum offset is usually 50 percent.[19] Once the employee retires or terminates his employment with a vested benefit, however, the dollar amount of the offset is frozen, since the plan is not permitted to consider further increases in social security benefits.

Under an integrated pension scheme, then, employees receive reduced private pensions in response to increased social security benefits. This substitutability of private pensions and social security is also evident in the following, more general model of the interaction of the two systems in the provision of retirement income.

Empirical Evidence

An analysis was undertaken to test the hypothesis that social security and private pensions have acted as almost perfect substitutes in the provision of retirement income.[20] This analysis was based on a stock-adjustment model according to which people were assumed to alter their accumulations in private pension plans and other savings so that their combined retirement assets (including social security) would ensure a desired level of retirement income.[21] The model and results are summarized in appendix A. But the importance of the empirical study for those concerned about the future of private pensions is that, for a large part of the population, the two systems are alternative ways to accomplish the

19. Dan M. McGill, *Fundamentals of Private Pensions*, 4th ed. (Irwin, 1979), p. 181.

20. Although social security and private pensions both provide retirement income, each has distinct advantages. Social security offers benefits indexed to inflation, universal coverage, and portability. Private pensions, in their various forms, can adapt to the specific characteristics of an industry.

21. Although this assumption may not hold for individual workers, it seems reasonable that over time workers in the aggregate would alter their accumulations in private savings plans so that combined assets plus projected social security income met a specific goal.

same objective. For any level of income, wealth, and retirement patterns, an additional dollar of social security taxes implies about a dollar less in private pension fund reserves. The presence of a large gap between desired and actual retirement assets would allow the two programs to grow rapidly even if they were perfect substitutes. As the gap narrows, however, a major expansion of social security would lead to a relative decline in saving through private plans. Therefore, it is crucial to examine recent changes in the social security program and their implications for the private pension system.

The Role for Private Pensions

In view of the relative substitutability of the two programs, the potential role for private pensions is determined by the gap between the income requirements of the elderly and the benefits provided by social security. Estimating the size of this gap is complicated somewhat by social security's transitional benefit provisions, which have led to a bulge in benefit levels.[22] Although social security benefits as a percentage of preretirement earnings are projected to decline slightly, they will remain higher than they were at the beginning of the 1970s. Therefore, given the substitutability of the two benefit systems, private pensions will have a relatively smaller role than they would have had without the expansion of social security. Nevertheless, as the following discussion reveals, ample room still exists for supplementary private pension benefits—especially for workers with above-average earnings.

22. The temporary bulge in replacement rates, popularly referred to as the "notch" problem, arises because the decoupled benefit formula introduced by the Social Security Amendments of 1977 applies only to those workers who reach age sixty-two in 1979 or later; those who became sixty-two before 1979 continue to use the previous overindexed method. The 1977 amendments attempted to phase in the new decoupled or average monthly indexed earnings method by introducing an alternative (if more favorable) computation for those reaching sixty-two in the period 1979–83. But this transitional computation procedure, based on the previous coupled benefit formula, contained two important limitations: (1) the benefit table was frozen at its December 1978 level until the year the worker attained age sixty-two, and (2) earnings in and after the year of attaining age sixty-two were not used in the benefit computation. These restrictions, especially the second one, eliminated the advantage of the alternative computation procedure (sometimes referred to as the transitional minimum guaranty) very rapidly; in fact, the transitional provision was probably widely effective only for retirements in 1979 and 1980. The result is that significantly different benefits are payable to those who reached age sixty-two before 1979 and those who reach that age in and after 1979. The discrepancy becomes even greater as retirement is delayed beyond age sixty-two. For instance, consider people who have

The Expansion of Social Security

After three decades of relatively minor changes in the OASI program, the 1970s brought a significant expansion in retirement benefits.[23] A succession of ad hoc benefit increases in the early 1970s, followed by the automatic cost-of-living adjustments introduced by the Social Security Amendments of 1972, raised social security benefits by 205 percent between February 1968 and June 1981 (see table 2-2). The near tripling of benefits during the 1970s is especially striking when compared with the 59 percent benefit increase between 1950 and 1968. The recent benefit increases have resulted in a major adjustment in replacement rates, from 31 percent of preretirement earnings in 1969 to over 50 percent in 1980 for the worker with average earnings (see table 2-3). As a result of the Social Security Amendments of 1977, which eliminated the flaw in the benefit computation method, replacement rates are now scheduled to decline slightly, stabilizing at about 43 percent for the average worker. But despite this reduction, social security benefits will continue to replace a considerably higher proportion of preretirement earnings than during the 1960s.

As social security benefits have grown, the taxable wage base has also risen sharply. In 1969 taxes and benefits were calculated on earnings up to a maximum of $7,800; after ad hoc adjustments in the early 1970s the base was linked to the growth in average wages, so that by 1978 taxes

---

always had maximum covered earnings and who retire at sixty-five. A person who reached that age at the end of 1981 receives a monthly benefit of $719, whereas someone who reached age sixty-five at the beginning of 1982 receives only $617—more than $100 less per month and 14 percent less relatively. This discrepancy is smaller for retirees under sixty-five and greater for those retiring after sixty-five. These figures were computed by Robert J. Myers on the basis of the intermediate economic assumptions in the *1979 Annual Report of the Board of Trustees of the Federal Old-Age and Survivors Insurance and Disability Insurance Trust Funds*, H. Doc. 96-101, 96 Cong. 1 sess. (GPO, 1979). For a clear description of the notch problem and proposals to eliminate the inequity, see Robert J. Myers, "Certain Technical Issues of the Social Security System," in *Employer Payment of Social Security Taxes; Benefit Formula Differential*, Hearings before the Subcommittee on Social Security of the House Committee on Ways and Means, 96 Cong. 1 sess. (GPO, 1979), pp. 25–30.

23. The social security program as a whole did expand during the 1940s, 1950s, and 1960s through broader coverage, the introduction of disability and health insurance, and provisions for early retirement. Moreover, during that period OASI benefits generally kept pace with wages, yielding a replacement rate that hovered around 30 percent. In addition, ad hoc adjustments usually ensured that retirees' benefits kept pace with price increases after retirement.

Table 2-2. **Cumulative Effect of Statutory and Automatic Increases in Primary Insurance Benefits under the Social Security Program, 1959–81**
Percent

Base date	Effective date of increase														
	January 1959	January 1965	February 1968	January 1970	January 1971	September 1972	June 1974	June 1975	June 1976	June 1977	June 1978	June 1979	June 1980	June 1981
September 1950	31.0	41.0	59.0	83.0	101.0	142.0	168.0	190.0	202.0	214.0	234.0	267.0	319.0	366.0
January 1959	...	7.0	21.0	39.0	53.0	84.0	104.0	120.0	134.0	148.0	164.0	190.0	231.0	268.0
January 1965	...	...	13.0	30.0	43.0	72.0	90.0	106.0	119.0	132.0	147.0	171.0	210.0	245.0
February 1968	...	...	...	15.0	27.0	52.0	68.0	82.0	94.0	105.0	118.0	140.0	174.0	205.0
January 1970	...	...	...	...	10.0	32.0	47.0	58.0	68.0	78.0	90.0	109.0	139.0	166.0
January 1971	...	...	...	...	...	20.0	33.0	44.0	53.0	62.0	73.0	90.0	117.0	141.0
September 1972	...	...	...	...	...	...	11.0	20.0	28.0	35.0	44.0	58.0	81.0	101.0
June 1974	...	...	...	...	...	...	...	8.0	15.0	22.0	30.0	42.0	62.0	80.0
June 1975	...	...	...	...	...	...	...	...	6.4	13.0	20.0	32.0	51.0	68.0
June 1976	...	...	...	...	...	...	...	...	...	5.9	13.0	24.0	42.0	58.0
June 1977	...	...	...	...	...	...	...	...	...	...	6.5	17.0	34.0	49.0
June 1978	...	...	...	...	...	...	...	...	...	...	...	9.9	26.0	40.0
June 1979	...	...	...	...	...	...	...	...	...	...	...	...	14.3	27.0
June 1980	...	...	...	...	...	...	...	...	...	...	...	...	...	11.2

Sources: *Social Security Bulletin: Annual Statistical Supplement, 1974*, p. 25, and *1980*, p. 33.

and benefits were calculated on the first $17,700 of earnings. Under the 1977 amendments Congress further accelerated the rate of growth of the wage base by prescribing three ad hoc increases—to $22,900 in 1979, $25,900 in 1980, and $29,700 in 1981—after which the taxable wage base is once again increased automatically in line with the growth in average wages. The 1981 base represented a 36 percent increase over the projected level of $21,900 that would have resulted from the automatic increases. While the 1978 base of $17,700 covered the full wages of 85 percent of all workers, the 1982 base of $32,400 covered 92 percent (see table 2-4). Because of the increase in replacement rates and the expansion of the earnings base, social security is now a substantial source of retirement income for a large part of the population.

The Adequacy of Social Security Benefits

The extent to which social security benefits meet the income goals of the elderly can be assessed against two alternative measures: an absolute standard of living and the maintenance of preretirement living standards. Income standards for the elderly are published by both the Bureau of the Census and the Bureau of Labor Statistics. The Census Bureau calculates the income needed to live at the poverty level in a nonfarm area. In 1980 the Census Bureau estimated the poverty threshold as $4,983 for a retired couple and $3,949 for a retired individual.[24] Because these figures represent such a meager existence, the definition is sometimes expanded to include a "near poor" threshold—equal in 1980 to $6,229 for a retired couple and to $4,936 for a retired individual.

A poverty index, however, is probably not the most useful measure of adequate living standards for retired workers. Since 1960 the Bureau of Labor Statistics has issued an intermediate-level retired couple budget and, more recently, has designed two additional budgets, one at a somewhat lower and one at a somewhat higher standard. These budgets represent the cost of hypothetical lists of goods and services for retired couples at those three relative levels of living and are updated on the basis of changes in the consumer price index and in consumer expenditure patterns. In 1981 the low, intermediate, and high budgets for a retired

24. Bureau of the Census, *Current Population Reports,* series P-60, no. 127, "Money Income and Poverty Status of Families and Persons in the United States: 1980" (Advance Data from the March 1981 Current Population Survey) (GPO, 1981), p. 28.

Table 2-3. Social Security Replacement Rates for Three Earning Levels for Males Retiring at Age Sixty-Five, Selected Years, 1940–90[a]

	Earning level		
Year	Low ($7,636 in 1982)	Average ($15,116 in 1982)	Maximum ($32,400 in 1982)
1940[b]	. . .	0.292[b]	. . .
1945[b]	. . .	0.222[b]	. . .
1950[b]	. . .	0.192[b]	. . .
1955	0.496	0.346	0.328
1960	0.438	0.333	0.297
1965	0.400	0.314	0.329
1966	0.400	0.314	0.332
1967	0.405	0.299	0.247
1968	0.414	0.323	0.281
1969	0.370	0.308	0.247
1970	0.427	0.343	0.292
1971	0.475	0.366	0.328
1972	0.512	0.377	0.355
1973	0.583	0.392	0.355
1974	0.638	0.409	0.330
1975	0.595	0.423	0.301
1976	0.579	0.437	0.321
1977	0.572	0.448	0.335
1978	0.627	0.467	0.347
1979	0.604	0.481	0.361
1980	0.640	0.511	0.325
1981	0.685	0.544	0.334
1982	0.646	0.492	0.290
1983[c]	0.625	0.473	0.283
1984[c]	0.588	0.446	0.267
1985[c]	0.573	0.434	0.261
1986[c]	0.569	0.431	0.256
1987[c]	0.564	0.429	0.252
1988[c]	0.562	0.427	0.250
1989[c]	0.558	0.425	0.248
1990[c]	0.556	0.424	0.246

Source: Social Security Administration, Office of the Actuary, unpublished data, November 1981.

a. Replacement rates are the ratio of the average primary insurance amount (the monthly amount payable to a worker who retires at sixty-five) at award to average monthly taxable earnings in the year just before retirement. Replacement rates given are for the beginning of each calendar year.

b. Replacement rates for 1940–50 were approximated by the ratio of average benefit award to average taxable wages. For later years this ratio is similar to the actual replacement rate. The figure for 1950 pertains to January through August; a legislated benefit increase became effective in September.

c. Replacement rates are estimates and may vary depending upon the rate of growth of prices and wages.

Table 2-4. Percentage of Workers with Total Annual Earnings below the Annual Maximum Taxable Earnings, by Sex, Selected Years, 1940–82[a]

Year	Maximum taxable earnings (dollars)	Percent of workers with earnings below maximum		
		Total	Men	Women
1940	3,000	96.6	95.4	99.7
1945	3,000	86.3	78.6	98.9
1950	3,000	71.1	59.9	94.6
1955	4,200	74.4	63.3	95.9
1960	4,800	72.0	60.9	93.5
1965	4,800	63.9	51.0	87.3
1966	6,600	75.8	64.4	95.6
1967	6,600	73.6	61.5	94.2
1968	7,800	78.6	68.0	96.3
1969	7,800	75.5	62.8	96.0
1970	7,800	74.0	61.8	93.5
1971	7,800	71.7	59.1	91.7
1972	9,000	75.0	62.9	93.9
1973	10,800	79.7	68.9	96.2
1974	13,200	84.9	76.2	97.8
1975	14,100	84.9	76.3	97.5
1976	15,300	85.0	76.2	97.5
1977	16,500	85.2	76.4	97.5
1978	17,700	85.3	76.4	97.5
1979	22,900	90.4	81.0[b]	98.6[b]
1980	25,900	91.6	82.1[b]	98.8[b]
1981	29,700	92.6	83.0[b]	99.0[b]
1982	32,400	92.3	82.7[b]	99.0[b]

Sources: *Social Security Bulletin: Annual Statistical Supplement, 1977–79*, p. 88; and Social Security Administration, Office of Research and Statistics, unpublished data.

a. The figures for 1978–82 are author's projections.

b. Assumes that the percentage of men with earnings below the taxable maximum will grow at the same rate as the percentage of total workers with taxable earnings. The percentage of women with taxable earnings is assumed to increase to 98.6 percent because of the large increase in the taxable wage base in 1979, and thereafter to level off at approximately 99 percent.

couple were $7,315, $10,387, and $15,329, respectively.[25] Even though these budgets may be too high as a level for welfare support, the intermediate budget was designated by the 1981 White House Conference on Aging as the minimum standard for aged couples in the United States and may therefore be considered a reasonable goal for combined social

25. Because the most recent retired couple budgets available are for 1980, the 1981 budget projections are the author's own calculations. These projections assumed a 10.1 percent increase in the budgets for 1981. For 1980 budgets, see Department of Labor, Bureau of Labor Statistics, "Three Budgets for a Retired Couple, Autumn 1980," BLS *News* (August 10, 1981), p. 1.

Table 2-5. Social Security Benefits for Retired Couple, January 1982, as a Percentage of Three Bureau of Labor Statistics Budgets[a]

1981 earnings of retired worker and spouse, both sixty-five	Low budget ($7,315)	Intermediate budget ($10,387)	High budget ($15,329)
Low earnings ($6,968)	0.875	0.616	0.418
Average earnings ($13,783)	1.318	0.929	0.629
Maximum earnings ($29,700)	1.673	1.178	0.798

Sources: Author's calculations based on Department of Labor, Bureau of Labor Statistics, "Three Budgets for a Retired Couple, Autumn 1978," BLS News, August 20, 1978; BLS, "Three Budgets for a Retired Couple, Autumn 1979," BLS News, August 25, 1980; "Three Budgets for a Retired Couple, Autumn 1980," BLS News, August 10, 1981; and Social Security Administration, Office of the Actuary, unpublished data, November 1981.

a. Budgets are projected to autumn 1981. The projections assume an 11.3 percent increase in 1981.

security and private pension benefits for a worker with a history of average earnings and steady employment.[26]

As shown in table 2-5, social security benefits in 1982 for a retired couple with average earnings amount to about 93 percent of the intermediate budget. For those with a history of earnings at the taxable maximum, benefits exceed the intermediate budget by 18 percent; and benefits for low-wage workers equal 62 percent of the intermediate budget. However, the diagonal elements of the table may be the most relevant, since it is difficult to argue that a low-wage worker earning $6,968 in 1981 should receive a social security benefit of $10,387 in order to attain the intermediate budget. In fact, the diagonal percentages indicate that social security benefits to workers with low, average, and maximum earnings amount to approximately 87 percent of the low, intermediate, and high budgets, respectively. Although the benefits in table 2-5 include the 50 percent supplement for a nonworking spouse, the percentages would be identical for retired individuals, assuming that the cost of supporting a couple is 50 percent greater than it is for an individual.

Social security benefits can also be evaluated in terms of preretirement living standards rather than against a monetary standard, in which case replacement rates rather than benefit levels are the relevant measure of benefit adequacy. Once a minimum level of income support is assured, a replacement rate—the ratio of benefits to preretirement earnings—is actually a more appropriate criterion against which to assess wage-related benefit programs.

26. 1981 White House Conference on Aging, "Committee Recommendations from White House Conference on Aging" (November 30–December 3, 1981), Recommendation 23, p. 3.

Retirees require considerably less than 100 percent of their preretirement income to maintain their standard of living. First, whereas preretirement earnings are subject to the federal income tax, the social security payroll tax, and state and municipal income taxes, a large portion of retirement income is not taxed.[27] Second, work-related expenses, such as transportation, clothing, and meals purchased away from home, are reduced during retirement. Finally, expenditures will also be lower for services, such as cleaning and cooking, that were purchased while a person worked but that retirees can perform for themselves.[28] Owing to lower taxes, lower expenditures for household services, and reduced work expenses, retirees require 50 to 80 percent of preretirement earnings to maintain their preretirement living standards (see table 2-6).[29]

Social security replacement rates for various types of beneficiaries are presented in table 2-7. These data are calculated for workers retiring at the beginning of 1982; the new benefit formula is used to eliminate most of the effects of the temporary replacement rate increase of the late 1970s and more accurately reflect the long-run provisions of the social security program. As illustrated, a worker aged sixty-five earning $13,783 (average wage) in 1981 receives a benefit in early 1982 equal to 47 percent of preretirement earnings; to maintain his preretirement standard of living, he would need approximately 68 percent of prior earnings (table 2-6). The replacement rate for a couple with average earnings eligible for the 50 percent supplementary spouse's benefit approximates that required to maintain a preretirement standard of living. A low-income worker aged sixty-five earning $6,968 in 1981, who needs about 78 percent of prior earnings to maintain his preretirement living standard, has 61 percent of his wages replaced by social security. In contrast, a

27. Social security benefits, which constitute the bulk of retirement income, are not taxable.

28. Some would argue that the availability of medicare reduces out-of-pocket medical expenses for the elderly as well. Medicare, however, requires certain out-of-pocket expenditures. Moreover, many retired workers have had health insurance during their working years, so that their pre- and post-retirement out-of-pocket medical expenses may remain fairly constant.

29. For earlier estimates of the percentage of preretirement earnings to maintain preretirement living standards, see Peter Henle, "Recent Trends in Retirement Benefits Related to Earnings," *Monthly Labor Review*, vol. 95 (June 1972), p. 18; and Jane L. Ross, "Maintenance of Preretirement Standards of Living after Retirement," Technical Analysis Paper 10, Office of Income Security Policy, Office of the Assistant Secretary of Planning and Evaluation, Department of Health, Education, and Welfare (August 1976).

Table 2-6. Retirement Income Needed to Keep Preretirement Standard of Living for Persons Retiring in January 1981, Selected Income Levels
Amounts in dollars

Gross preretirement income	Preretirement taxes		Disposable preretirement income	Reductions in expenses at retirement			Net preretirement income	Post-retirement taxes[d]		Equivalent retirement income	
	Federal[a]	State and local[b]		Work-related expenses[c]	Savings and investments			Federal income	State and local[b]	Amount	Ratio
					Amount	Percent					
Single person											
6,000	786	79	5,135	308	0	0.0	4,827	0	0	4,827	0.80
8,000	1,272	149	6,579	395	99	1.5	6,085	0	0	6,085	0.76
10,000	1,785	223	7,992	480	240	3.0	7,272	0	0	7,272	0.73
15,000	3,259	444	11,297	678	678	6.0	9,941	0	0	9,941	0.66
20,000	5,055	728	14,217	853	1,280	9.0	12,084	166	32	12,282	0.61
30,000	9,550	1,513	18,937	1,136	2,272	12.0	15,529	1,077	205	16,811	0.56
50,000	19,655	3,433	26,912	1,615	4,037	15.0	21,260	3,153	599	25,012	0.50
Married couple											
6,000	449	85	5,466	328	0	0.0	5,138	0	0	5,138	0.86
8,000	860	163	6,977	419	105	1.5	6,453	0	0	6,453	0.81
10,000	1,311	249	8,440	506	253	3.0	7,681	0	0	7,681	0.77
15,000	2,550	485	11,965	718	718	6.0	10,529	0	0	10,529	0.70
20,000	3,965	753	15,282	917	1,375	9.0	12,990	0	0	12,990	0.65
30,000	7,173	1,363	21,464	1,288	2,576	12.0	17,600	53	10	17,663	0.59
50,000	16,366	3,110	30,524	1,831	4,579	15.0	24,114	1,651	314	26,079	0.52

Source: Author's calculations based on President's Commission on Pension Policy, *An Interim Report* (GPO, November 1980), pp. 11–12.
a. 1980 federal income and social security taxes.
b. Based on state and local income tax receipts, which were 19 percent of federal income tax receipts from 1970 to 1980. Does not include property tax.
c. Estimated as 6 percent of disposable income.
d. Post-retirement taxes are on income in excess of social security benefits, which are nontaxable. Retirees without social security benefits would need higher replacement ratios.

sixty-five-year-old worker with a history of maximum earnings, who needs about 56 percent of previous earnings to prevent a decline in his living standard, receives a social security benefit equal to 28 percent of past wages. The social security benefit for a couple with a maximum earning history would also fall substantially short of that needed to maintain a preretirement living standard, even if one spouse were eligible for the 50 percent supplementary benefit. Moreover, as noted earlier, replacement rates are scheduled to decline from the 1982 levels, so that a worker with a history of average earnings will receive 42 percent of preretirement earnings rather than the 47 percent used in the example.

Reassessing the Role for Private Plans

Although the preceding analysis implies that despite social security a substantial gap remains to be filled by private pensions, the size of this gap must be interpreted carefully. Before conclusions are drawn about the potential for private plans, two additional factors should be considered—one that understates and the other that exaggerates the apparent need for private pensions. First, an analysis of social security benefits that focuses on replacement rates for the average earner will exaggerate the size of social security benefits, thereby underestimating the gap to be filled by private plans. Second, and more important, defining the need for private pension benefits as the gap between social security and full replacement of preretirement income may seriously overstate the role of private plans.

Focusing on the average earner replacement rates in order to judge the adequacy of social security benefits and, therefore, the gap to be filled by private pensions can be misleading.[30] Even though the "average earner" designation implies that replacement rates are being measured for retiring workers in the approximate middle of the earnings distribution of all retiring workers, that is simply not the case. Rather, the concept of average earnings is based on a composite of earnings for all workers at all stages in their careers and does not reflect the fact that the earnings of retiring workers are usually higher than those of their younger counterparts.[31] For instance, in 1979 average earnings for all workers was

30. The following discussion is based on work by James H. Schulz. For a recent statement of this argument, see "Assessing the Adequacy of Pension Income," testimony before the President's Commission on Pension Policy, January 11, 1980.

31. See Nancy D. Ruggles and Richard Ruggles, "The Anatomy of Earnings Behavior," in F. Thomas Juster, ed., The Distribution of Economic Well-Being, National Bureau of Economic Research Studies in Income and Wealth, vol. 41 (Ballinger for NBER, 1977), pp. 115–58.

Table 2-7. Monthly Benefits, Replacement Rates, and Family Benefit as a Percentage of Primary Insurance Amount, by Type of Beneficiary, Early 1982 [a]

Age and type of beneficiary	Family benefit as percent of primary insurance amount	Monthly benefit by preretirement income level (dollars) [b]			Replacement rate by preretirement income level (percent) [b]		
		Low ($6,968) [c]	Average ($13,783) [d]	Maximum ($29,700) [e]	Low ($6,968) [c]	Average ($13,783) [d]	Maximum ($29,700) [e]
Single worker							
Sixty-five	100.0	356	536	680	61.3	46.7	27.5
Sixty-two	80.0	285	429	544	49.1	37.4	22.0
Worker sixty-five, with spouse							
Sixty-five	150.0	534	804	1,020	92.0	70.0	41.2
Sixty-two	137.5	489	737	935	84.2	64.2	37.8
Worker sixty-two, with spouse							
Sixty-five	130.0	462	697	884	79.6	60.7	35.7
Sixty-two	117.5	418	630	799	72.0	54.9	32.3
Widow sixty-five, spouse retired at							
Sixty-five	100.0	356	536	680	61.3	46.7	27.5
Sixty-two	82.9	295	444	561	50.8	38.7	22.7

Source: Author's calculations based on unpublished data from Social Security Administration, Office of the Actuary, November 1980.
a. Monthly benefits and replacement rates are projections based on the following economic assumptions for 1980 and 1981: wage increases of 9.64 percent and 9.50 percent, respectively, and benefit increases of 14.30 percent and 11.30 percent, respectively.
b. Income level in 1981.
c. Assumes an annual income slightly below the minimum wage.
d. Assumes an annual income equal to the average of total wages in each year in the past.
e. Assumes income equal to the maximum taxable amount each year in the past.

$11,835, whereas the average for full-time men and women workers in their late fifties and early sixties was $17,662 and for full-time men near retirement was $20,825. The "average" preretirement man in 1979 was actually earning close to the taxable maximum ($22,900 in 1979), and the long-run "average" replacement rate should therefore not be viewed as 42 percent but rather as 30 to 35 percent of preretirement earnings.[32] In short, conventional replacement rate analyses exaggerate the extent to which social security replaces preretirement income and consequently underestimate the need for private pensions.

Conversely, the assumption of full replacement of preretirement earnings through organized savings plans probably overstates the gap to be filled by private pensions. Full replacement is an extremely ambitious goal in an economy with numerous demands on its resources. It simply may not be possible or desirable for organized savings plans to ensure that no one experiences a decline in living standards on retirement.

Both social security and private pensions face severe economic constraints. Demographic changes will place increasing financial pressure on the social security system as the ratio of aged to working population rises in response to a lower fertility rate and increased life expectancy. Since these factors will greatly increase the burden on future workers anyway, transferring additional resources to retirees would be too oppressive. The ability of private plans to aim at full replacement of preretirement income is also limited. Insofar as employer contributions to private pensions are actually paid by the employee through lower wages, higher pension benefits will result in reduced income for today's workers.[33] Most people are already under some financial pressure from declining real wages in the face of accelerating inflation and would be reluctant to trade current consumption for future retirement income.

Moreover, full replacement of preretirement earnings through organized savings plans may not be necessary, since people usually accumulate some assets before retirement. According to data for 1975 from the Social Security Administration's Retirement History Study, 71 percent of those aged sixty-three to sixty-nine owned homes with a median equity of $21,609 ($54,000 in 1981 dollars). Almost 80 percent of homes owned by persons sixty-three and older were mortgage free. Nearly 80 percent of respondents aged sixty-three to sixty-nine also had

32. Bureau of the Census, *Current Population Reports,* series P-60, no. 129, "Money Income of Families and Persons in the United States: 1979" (GPO, 1981), pp. 220, 224.

33. The question of who actually pays for the employer's contribution to private pension plans is discussed in chapter 7.

some type of financial assets, although the median value was only $4,703 ($11,700 in 1981 dollars).[34] A more recent survey would probably reveal a significant increase in the number owning homes and holding other assets.

Implications for the Private Plan System

The foregoing analysis has two important implications for the future of the private pension system. First, the great increases in social security benefits over the past forty years have mitigated the need for supplementary benefits from private plans. Second, despite the expansion of social security, the role of private plans in providing retirement income remains viable. This is particularly true once the myth of the "average" worker's replacement rate is dispelled and when one considers the large number of workers who retire before age sixty-five and thus receive actuarially reduced social security benefits. While there is clearly room for private pensions to supplement social security, the complete replacement of preretirement income through these two retirement programs is probably an unrealistic standard by which to project the future role of private plans.

The Trade-off between Social Security and Private Pensions

The simultaneous expansion of social security and private pensions since 1940 reflected the United States' desire to accumulate a large stock of retirement assets to ensure adequate income in old age. But since social security and private pensions are substitutes, the recent increase in social security benefits, to levels that prevent poverty for most new retirees, reduces the need for supplementary benefits from private pensions.[35] Despite the implied reduction in the relative role for private

---

34. See Joseph Friedman and Jane Sjogren, "The Assets of the Elderly as They Retire" (Cambridge, Mass: ABT Associates, 1980), pp. 30, 34, 35, 46.

35. That social security benefits have reached adequate levels was highlighted in a recent statement by Bert Seidman of the AFL-CIO: "In the past, the labor movement generally felt that the most important steps to improve the social security system were to effect across-the-board increases in benefits plus even more sizable boosts in the minimum benefit. Overall benefit increases may be needed again at some time in the future, but this is not where we place our priority today. . . . Instead, we would like to see the SSI floor raised immediately to at least the poverty level and, in time, to the BLS lower level budget amount." Seidman, "Concepts of Balance between Social Security (OASDI) and Private

plans, however, a gap still exists between the income goals of retirees and their current benefits from social security.

Determining the appropriate roles for social security and private pensions remains one of the most crucial issues facing policymakers and will require careful analysis of the advantages and disadvantages of social security and private pensions. Social security provides wide coverage, portability, and benefits that keep pace with inflation.[36] These characteristics are extremely important in the current inflationary environment and will be described at length in chapter 7. While some people argue that increases in payroll taxes add to business costs and thereby create inflationary pressure, the same can be said of provisions for private pensions. Potential expansion of the social security program, however, raises the philosophical issue of the government's right to infringe on individual freedom beyond assuring a basic retirement benefit.

Private pensions offer variety and flexibility but do not provide fully indexed benefits. However, the ability to provide fully indexed benefits is only one criterion by which to evaluate the relative merits of private pensions and social security. Because private plans are funded while social security is financed on a pay-as-you-go basis, it has usually been claimed that private pensions have a favorable impact on capital formation and that social security does not. Although the empirical evidence on this topic is inconclusive, the relative impact on saving of the two programs will be explored in chapter 4.

The most compelling practical argument against replacing private pensions with an expanded social security program is that the welfare of high-income workers cannot be well served by a program that is heavily weighted with redistribution toward the lower end. Nevertheless, if the federal government were called upon to assist private plans in providing indexed benefits, an expanded and nonredistributive social security program would be an alternative way to provide retirement benefits to workers with incomes above the median.

Pension Benefits," in Dan M. McGill, ed., *Social Security and Private Pensions Plans: Competitive or Complementary?* a compilation of papers presented at the 1976 Symposium for Institutional Members of the Pension Research Council of the Wharton School, University of Pennsylvania (Irwin for the Pension Research Council, 1977), p. 86.

36. Social security covers over 90 percent of the paid labor force, including almost all private civilian workers and approximately 70 percent of state and local government employees. Federal civil servants, the military, and the remaining 30 percent of state and local government workers are not covered under the present system.

chapter three Federal Tax Provisions and the Development of Private Plans

The federal income tax laws have been instrumental in both encouraging the growth of private pension plans and influencing the way they developed. Favorable tax provisions, which consist of current deductions of pension contributions for employers, exclusion of the contributions from employee income, and tax exemption of income earned by the pension trust, have been part of the Internal Revenue Code since the 1920s.[1] But the value of these provisions increased dramatically during World War II in the face of sharp rises in corporate and personal income taxes and the imposition of an excess profits tax. The deductibility of employer contributions combined with corporate tax rates of 85.5 percent permitted firms to establish pensions at a very low net cost. This low cost made private pensions attractive to employers who, hampered by wartime wage controls, were eager to expand fringe benefits to attract workers in the tight civilian labor force. The reimposition of wage controls and an excess profits tax during the Korean War added further impetus to the development of private pension plans.

In addition, the tax laws have influenced the structure of these plans. For instance, to qualify for favorable tax treatment, private pension plans must satisfy certain coverage, participation, and vesting requirements. Moreover, the tax provisions have influenced the financing of private plans by encouraging the establishment of pensions that are paid for almost entirely by employer contributions.

The favorable tax treatment accorded pension contributions is extremely costly to the Treasury in terms of forgone revenues. According to Treasury estimates, the special tax provisions for private pension

1. These tax benefits are also available to members of the civil service retirement system and participants in most state and local pension plans.

30

plans amounted to $14.7 billion in 1981, with most of this benefit accruing to higher-paid employees.[2] These tax provisions have seldom been questioned, since saving for retirement has generally been considered worthy of support. Yet the extent to which they have encouraged a net increase in retirement saving is debatable.

This chapter examines the tax provisions for private pension plans, their distributional implications, and their effectiveness in achieving the goals for which they were intended.

Legislative Background

Before the passage of the Revenue Act of 1921, payments to cover current pension liabilities were usually deductible as ordinary business expenses from the employer's gross income for tax purposes, but payments to fund liabilities for past service credits were not. The interest income from a pension or profit-sharing trust was taxable to the employer, the employee, or the trust, depending on the provisions of the specific plan. Employer contributions were taxed as income to the employee unless his chance of receiving a benefit seemed too uncertain.[3]

The 1921 Revenue Act exempted from current taxation the interest income on trusts for stock bonus or profit-sharing plans, and by administrative ruling pension trusts were awarded the same treatment. Under the new law, trust income was taxed as it was distributed to employees and then only to the extent that it exceeded the employee's own contributions.[4]

The 1921 act, however, did not authorize deductions for past service contributions, so many employers began to carry balance sheet reserves against their pension obligations, although credits to these reserves were not tax deductible. The increase in the number and size of these reserves finally led to the passage of the Revenue Act of 1928, which permitted

2. Revised estimates indicate a tax expenditure of $23.6 billion in fiscal 1981. See *Special Analyses, Budget of the United States Government, Fiscal Year 1982*, Special Analysis G, p. 229. The $14.7 billion estimate is used here in order to be consistent with the data in table 3-1, the only series for which historical data are available.

3. Jacob Mertens, Jr., *The Law of Federal Income Taxation*, vol. 4A, 1979 rev. (Callagan, 1979), sec. 25B.02.

4. The income of pension trusts was exempt from current taxation by statute under the Revenue Act of 1926. Dan M. McGill, *Fundamentals of Private Pensions*, 4th ed. (Irwin, 1979), p. 23.

employers to deduct reasonable amounts paid to trusts in excess of the amount required to fund current liabilities. Employers were then able to transfer their balance sheet reserves to trust funds or to make payments to finance past service liabilities. However, deductions for these contributions were required to be amortized over a ten-year period.[5]

Provisions for deducting contributions to a pension trust contained two major loopholes that effectively permitted pensions to be used as tax-avoidance schemes. First, the law did not require that the pension trust be irrevocable. Employers, effectively, were allowed to take large deductions for contributions made to a trust during years of high earnings and to recapture those earnings by revoking the trust in poor years. Such manipulation not only deprived the Treasury of revenue but was also detrimental to the welfare of the employees. Second, pension trusts were eligible for favorable tax treatment as long as they were created for the benefit of "some or all of the employees." This provision allowed employers to establish trusts for small groups of officers and key employees in high-income brackets.

To prevent the use of trust funds for purposes other than the exclusive benefit of the employees, a "nondiversion rule" was included in the Revenue Act of 1938. While this legislation required that trusts be irrevocable, no attempt was made to broaden participation. But with the proliferation of new plans after the sharp increases in corporate taxes in 1940 and the imposition of wage controls during World War II, Congress was faced with the problem of ensuring employee welfare while preventing pension trusts from being used as tax-avoidance schemes for high-paid persons. Through the Revenue Act of 1942, therefore, the definition of an exempt pension, profit-sharing, or stock bonus trust was completely revised, and participation was broadened by requiring that the plan be nondiscriminatory to qualify for tax-exempt status.

The provisions of the Revenue Act of 1942 were reenacted in the Internal Revenue Code of 1954, which, with successive refinements and extensions, still provides the statutory base for the tax treatment of private pension plans. The 1954 code and implementing regulations

5. This was a reasonable requirement when the past service liability was liquidatd in one year, but became unduly burdensome and complicated when only a part of the liability was funded each year and each part had to be spread out over a ten-year period. This limitation on past service liabilities did not apply to plans funded through group annuities. The discrepancy was eliminated in 1942, when all plans became subject to the limitations of section 23(p) of the Internal Revenue Code.

divide private plans into two categories—qualified plans and all other plans. For a pension or profit-sharing plan to qualify for the favorable tax provisions it must satisfy four requirements:

—The plan must be for the exclusive benefit of the employees and/or their beneficiaries.

—The sole purpose of the plan must be either to give the employees a share of the employer's profits or to provide them with retirement income.

—The plan must be a permanent one, made in writing and communicated to the employees.

—The plan must not discriminate in favor of corporate officers, stockholders, or highly compensated employees.

The nondiscrimination requirement, the heart of the qualification conditions, applies to coverage, contributions, and benefits. In determining whether a plan operates for the benefit of the majority of employees, pension coverage is evaluated either on the basis of certain percentage guidelines or, more commonly, under the so-called discretionary rule, whereby reasonable classifications of employees can be approved by the commissioner of Internal Revenue. In each case, the code provides for less than total coverage of all employees. The percentage guidelines allow part-time and seasonal employees as well as 20 to 30 percent of otherwise eligible employees to be excluded from coverage.[6] Under the discretionary rule the commissioner may approve any classification of employees that does not discriminate in favor of officers, stockholders, or highly compensated employees, so that it is possible to have a plan for only salaried workers or for workers in a particular division.

The nondiscrimination requirements for contributions and benefits also allow considerable flexibility in plan design. Because discrimination is measured in terms of combined private pension and social security benefits, a plan that includes only those employees whose compensation exceeds the social security taxable wage base is not considered discriminatory. In fact, the Treasury "integration" guidelines allow explicit

6. The requirements under section 410(b)(1) of the Internal Revenue Code are as follows: 70 percent or more of all active employees or 80 percent or more of the eligible employees (provided that 70 percent of all employees are eligible) must participate in the plan. The second alternative is provided for contributory plans because employees may have to elect coverage. In effect, the rule states that when participation is optional, 80 percent of the eligible employees must elect to participate.

recognition of social security provisions by permitting the benefit structure of private plans to offset the exclusion of earnings above the social security taxable wage base and the weighting of the social security benefit formula in favor of low-wage workers.

The conditions for plan qualification were further extended by the Employee Retirement Income Security Act of 1974.[7] While ERISA made the coverage requirements more rigorous by introducing age and service standards, these changes were aimed primarily at fostering the accrual of benefits rather than at preventing discrimination. As a result of this concern about the accrual and preservation of benefits, vesting standards also have been introduced as preconditions for tax exemption.[8] Therefore, to qualify for tax exemption, plans now must satisfy two additional requirements:

—The plan must permit any employee who is at least twenty-five years old and has had at least one year of service to participate.

—The plan must meet one of the following three minimum vesting standards: (1) 100 percent vesting after ten years of covered service; (2) gradual vesting with 25 percent after five years of covered service, increasing by 5 percent annually over the next five years and 10 percent annually for five more years; or (3) gradual vesting with 50 percent attained when the employee's age and years of service total forty-five, increasing by 10 percent annually over the next five years.[9]

7. The structure of ERISA is complex because it is enforced by both the Labor and the Treasury departments. Title I, which applies to all pension plans, is concerned with the protection of employee benefits and includes sections on (1) reporting and disclosure, (2) participation and vesting, (3) funding, and (4) fiduciary responsibility. The reporting, disclosure, and fiduciary provisions replace the Welfare and Pension Plans Disclosure Act of 1958 and are enforced primarily by the Department of Labor. The Treasury has primary jurisdiction over participation, vesting, and funding. Title II contains the same provisions as Title I with respect to participation, vesting, and funding, but in the context of conditions that must be satisfied for qualification of a plan, Title II is in effect an amendment to the Internal Revenue Code of 1954. But while failure to meet the participation or vesting standards may result in tax disqualification, the funding requirements are enforced by financial penalties. If the minimum contributions have not been made, the account shows an "accumulated funding deficiency." The plan sponsor is charged interest on this deficiency at the rate assumed in the plan's valuation and, in addition, is subject to a nondeductible excise tax of 5 percent (100 percent if not corrected within 90 days of IRS demand). For a more complete discussion, see McGill, *Fundamentals of Private Pensions,* pp. 30–58.

8. Vesting refers to the provision that an employee covered by a private pension plan will, after meeting certain requirements, retain a right to the benefits he has accrued even though his service with the employer terminates before retirement.

9. However, regardless of the employee's age, he must be at least 50 percent vested after ten years of service and fully vested after fifteen years of service.

In addition to these participation and vesting requirements for qualification, ERISA established new standards in virtually every area of pension administration, including reporting and disclosure, funding, and fiduciary responsibility. Thus, for the first time, a single law regulates all aspects of private pensions. This represents a considerable expansion of the earlier regulatory environment in which legislation was restricted to Internal Revenue Code provisions designed to prevent pensions from being used as tax-avoidance schemes.[10] The advantages of complying with the ERISA and IRS requirements are substantial, as can be seen by the differences in the tax treatment of contributions to qualified and nonqualified plans.

Taxation of Qualified and Nonqualified Plans

While all observers agree that the tax treatment of qualified and nonqualified plans differs greatly, there is considerable controversy over whether the tax provisions for qualified plans should be viewed as a subsidy. This section describes the tax treatment of both qualified and nonqualified plans. Then, in an effort to decide whether qualified pension plans are in fact subsidized, the opposing sides of the subsidy debate are examined.

Qualified Plans

Compensation in the form of employer contributions to qualified plans is deductible by the employer when contributions are made, but not taxed to the employee until benefits are distributed from the plan.[11]

10. Before ERISA, private plans were also regulated by the Welfare and Pension Plans Disclosure Act, passed in 1958 and substantially amended in 1962 (Welfare and Pension Plans Disclosure Act Amendments of 1962). This legislation was designed to provide plan participants with enough information to detect any malpractices and then to seek relief for themselves under existing federal or state laws. Originally the secretary of labor was not authorized to prescribe the forms on which information was to be reported, nor was he given authority to enforce the act. The 1962 amendments remedied these deficiencies and shifted the burden of protecting plan assets from plan participants to the federal government. But the legislation continued to pursue the limited goal of preventing poor administration or outright fraud rather than the broader one of preserving the rights of participants.

11. Under federal corporate income tax regulations employers can deduct contributions to a pension plan as ordinary business expenses, but taking such a deduction would require taxing the contribution as ordinary income to the employee. In contrast, employer contributions to a qualified plan are exempted specifically from taxation to the employee. This provision allows the employer to put aside money in advance of future benefit

Moreover, income earned on accumulated contributions is not taxable until distributed to beneficiaries. By allowing the worker to defer the taxes until retirement, qualified plans (including employer-sponsored pensions as well as individual retirement accounts [IRAs] and Keogh plans) offer three main advantages over nonqualified plans. First, the full dollar of contribution, without any reduction for income tax, is available for investment during the employee's working years—in sharp contrast to the situation in which a dollar is paid in current compensation and the employee has only the after-tax dollar to invest. Second, no tax is currently paid on the investment income from funds held by trustees or insurance companies under qualified plans, whereas income earned by the employee on his investment is subject to tax as income accrues.[12] Finally, when benefits are distributed, either in the form of periodic payments or as a lump sum, they are likely to be taxed at a lower marginal rate than if they had been taxed as they accrued to the employee.[13] The

---

payments and to take advantage of the tax-exempt status of investment income of a qualified pension plan. Accruing investment income tax-free is a great advantage to the employer, since, at current corporate rates, the employer would have to earn roughly double the return before taxes on assets accumulated outside the pension trust to end up with the same after-tax return.

12. These two provisions, which permit tax deferral on both employer contributions and the earnings on those contributions, are equivalent to exempting from taxation the earnings on the amount of money that would ordinarily be available after tax, assuming the employee remained in the same tax bracket. Sunley explains the equivalence with the following example: "Assume t is the employee's marginal tax rate, and r is the annual rate of earning on the pension fund. If the employer contributes $1,000 to the fund, then after n years the fund will have grown to $1,000(1 + r)^n$. When the money is paid out, both the employer contribution and the earnings are taxable. The income after tax is therefore $1,000(1 - t)(1 + r)^n$. But this is the same amount of after-tax income the employee would have if he had paid tax on the $1,000 and then had invested the after-tax proceeds, $1,000 (1 - t)$, in a tax-exempt account at rate r for n years." See Emil M. Sunley, Jr., "Employee Benefits and Transfer Payments" in Joseph A. Pechman, ed., *Comprehensive Income Taxation* (Brookings Institution, 1977), p. 77n.

13. If a retiring employee receives pension benefits in the form of periodic payments, these payments are taxed like ordinary income. However, any contributions made to the pension plan by the employee are exempt from taxation when benefits are being received, since the employee has already paid taxes on the contributions. This exemption does not apply to benefits derived from investment earnings attributable to previously taxed employee contributions. If the employee's contributions can be recouped within three years, tax payments are deferred until the employee's contributions are recovered completely. The specific tax treatment depends on the length of time required for the employee to receive an amount equal to his contributions. If the employee will receive within three years total benefits that exceed his contributions, then all benefits will be excluded from taxable income until the employee contributions are recovered. For instance, if the employee had contributed $5,400 under the employer's retirement plan and

employee's income is usually lower after retirement, and double exemptions for persons over sixty-five and the credit for the elderly further reduce the tax rate applicable to retired persons.[14]

If an employee's accumulated pension benefits are distributed to him in one year, further tax concessions are available. Originally, all lump-sum distributions of funds attributable to employer contributions were treated as long-term capital gains. This provision was designed to avoid very high marginal tax rates on benefits that had accumulated over the employee's entire working life and were distributed in one year. In effect, however, high-income employees were able to receive deferred compensation at the capital gains rate without regard to the actual level of their income. This provision encouraged employees to accept lump-sum payments and thus, in some cases, an inadequate retirement income.[15]

---

would receive an annual payment of $2,400, he would not have to report any part of the payments as taxable income for the first two years. In the final year, having recovered $4,800 of contributions, the employee would exclude $600 ($5,400 less $4,800) from taxable income, reporting only $1,800 as income subject to taxation. Thereafter, the full $2,400 would be taxed each year as ordinary income.

If it will take longer than three years to recover the employee's contributions, then an exclusion ratio (the ratio of employee's contributions to total expected benefits) is calculated to determine the portion of each benefit payment to be excluded from taxable income. For example, consider a sixty-five-year-old male employee who had contributed $9,000 under the employer's plan and is now entitled to an annual benefit of $2,400. First, the employee's total expected benefits are calculated by multiplying his life expectancy—fifteen years—by the annual benefit, yielding total expected benefits of $36,000. Second, the exclusion ratio is determined by dividing the employee's contributions of $9,000 by total expected benefits of $36,000, which yields a ratio of 25 percent. Consequently, $600 of each year's benefit would be excluded from the employee's taxable income, and the balance of $1,800 would be subject to tax as ordinary income. The exclusion percentage, once calculated, applies to all future benefit payments regardless of how long the employee lives. If retirement payments are made under some form of joint-and-survivor annuity, the total expected benefits are adjusted to reflect the value of the survivorship option.

14. The Tax Reform Act of 1976 replaced the retirement income credit with the credit for the elderly. This credit equals 15 percent of the initial amount of income for credit computation reduced by the total of certain nontaxable pensions and annuities plus one-half of adjusted gross income in excess of $7,500 for a single person and $10,000 for a married couple.

15. A new provision that is increasingly encouraging participants to elect lump-sum distributions is the availability of a rollover individual retirement account. If an employee in a qualified plan transfers all or part of the lump-sum distribution, exclusive of his own contributions, to a rollover IRA within 60 days, he is not taxed on the portion of the distribution that is rolled over. Under the Revenue Act of 1978 the rollover provision has been extended to an employee's spouse. Between the ages of fifty-nine and one-half and seventy and one-half withdrawals made by an employee or his spouse from the rollover IRA are taxed as ordinary income. Distribution from the IRA, however, must commence no later than the taxable year in which the person attains age seventy and one-half. See 26 U.S.C. 402(a)(7).

The code has now been revised to phase out the capital gain treatment of lump-sum distributions by separating these payments into two parts— the part attributable to the employee's participation in the plan before 1974 is treated as a long-term capital gain, and the part based on participation after 1974 is taxed as ordinary income under a ten-year averaging rule.[16] One further favorable provision is extended to that part of a lump-sum distribution consisting of employer securities. Any unrealized appreciation of these securities is not taxed at the time of distribution but, rather, is included in taxable income at the time the securities are sold.

The treatment of pension benefits under the gift and estate taxes includes additional concessions, which are particularly beneficial to high-income employees. Upon the death of a plan participant, any beneficiary payments that are attributable to employer contributions are excluded from the decedent's gross estate for federal estate tax purposes.[17] Similarly, under the federal gift tax, an annuity that becomes payable to a beneficiary upon the plan participant's death is not considered a transfer. Without this provision, a participant choosing a joint-and-survivor annuity would incur some federal gift tax liability under that option.

Besides the favorable provisions for qualified plans, the IRS allows certain tax advantages for persons covered under retirement plans for the self-employed and individual retirement savings plans. The Self-Employed Individuals Tax Retirement Act of 1962, more popularly known as H.R. 10 or Keogh, enabled the self-employed to establish

16. The share of the distribution to be taxed under each method is calculated in the following way. To determine the portion of the lump-sum distribution to be treated as long-term capital gains, the sum of the employee's years of participation before 1974 is divided by the employee's total years of participation and the resulting percentage is applied to the total lump-sum distribution. To determine the amount of tax under the ten-year averaging rule for such an employee, the tax is first calculated as if the entire distribution were subject to the ten-year rule. Under this rule the ordinary income tax is calculated on one-tenth of the lump-sum payment, using the rates applicable to single taxpayers and assuming no exemptions, deductions, or other income. The actual tax is then determined by multiplying this amount by ten. The actual amount of tax is determined by dividing the years of participation after 1973 by total years of participation and applying the resulting percentage to the tax first determined as though the total distribution were being taxed under the ten-year rule.

17. This is true only if the pension benefit is not a lump-sum distribution or payable to the estate. Also, the actuarial value of payments attributed to the employee's own contributions are included in his gross estate.

retirement plans and to deduct their contributions from current income.[18] Initially, the annual contributions to a Keogh plan were limited to the lesser of $2,500 or 10 percent of earned income. These limits have since been liberalized. Under Title II of ERISA the taxpayer could deduct the lesser of 15 percent of his income or $7,500 per year. Under the Economic Recovery Tax Act of 1981 the maximum deductible contribution was increased from $7,500 to $15,000, effective January 1, 1982. Like other qualified plans, income produced by funds held under a Keogh plan accumulates tax free until benefits are distributed to the participant.

The 1974 ERISA legislation also authorized a new form of retirement plan, namely an individual retirement account. Beginning in 1975, persons not covered by either an employer plan or a Keogh plan could set up an IRA and make tax-deductible contributions equal to 15 percent of their income, up to a maximum of $1,500.[19] In 1977 the maximum IRA contribution limit was increased to $1,750 for participants with an eligible nonemployed spouse. The Economic Recovery Tax Act of 1981 substantially liberalized the provisions by expanding eligibility to include all workers, even those currently covered by private pension plans. The 1981 legislation also increased the maximum deductible contribution for an individual from $1,500 to $2,000, up to 100 percent of annual earnings, and raised the maximum for a spousal IRA from $1,750 to $2,250. Again, the return obtained from the accumulated fund is not currently taxable.[20]

18. This legislation represented the culmination of a decade of considering alternative proposals to eliminate the discrimination against the self-employed who could not avail themselves of the tax deferral benefits open to participants in private pension plans. This discrimination was particularly inequitable because state laws allowed business proprietors, but not professional people, to qualify for pension plans by incorporating their businesses and paying themselves salaries. For a discussion of earlier proposals, see Leslie M. Rapp, "The Quest for Tax Equality for Private Pension Plans: A Short History of the Jenkins-Keogh Bill," *Tax Law Review*, vol. 14 (November 1958), pp. 55–83.

19. The Revenue Act of 1978 liberalized eligibility requirements for establishing IRAs by allowing employers in some instances to contribute to IRAs for their employees. If the contributions were made under a definite, written allocation formula that was nondiscriminatory and if the employee's right to the contribution was 100 percent vested, the employer could contribute the lesser of $7,500 or 15 percent of the employee's compensation. Under the Economic Recovery Tax Act of 1981 the maximum deductible contribution for this provision was increased to $15,000. See American Council of Life Insurance, *Pension Facts, 1980* (Washington, D.C.: ACLI, 1980), p. 72.

20. Contributions may be deducted from adjusted gross income regardless of whether the taxpayer itemizes personal deductions or elects the standard deduction.

Nonqualified Plans

The importance of the tax concessions granted to qualified plans becomes clear when one considers the tax treatment of plans that do not satisfy the qualification requirements. The principal disadvantage incurred by these plans is that pension contributions deducted by the employer are taxable in the same year to the employee. In addition, the investment income of a nonqualified trust is not tax exempt, and the federal gift and estate tax concessions do not apply to distributions from nonqualified plans.

For nonqualified plans, the availability and timing of employer deductions and the employee's tax liability hinge on the extent to which the employee's pension rights are forfeitable. The code permits a deduction by the employer if the rights of the employee are nonforfeitable (that is, vested) at the time the contribution is made. But if the employee's rights are vested and employer contributions are deducted for tax purposes, the employee must include the employer's contribution as part of his taxable income. Conversely, if the employee's rights are not vested, employer contributions are neither deductible nor included in the employee's taxable income.

The treatment of prior employer contributions once the employee becomes vested has changed over time. Until 1969 the employer's prior contributions did not represent reportable income until the employee received a distribution from the pension fund. At that time, the income would be taxable to the employee and the prior contributions deductible by the employer. Under the Tax Reform Act of 1969, however, employer contributions to nonqualified plans are treated as income to the employee and are deductible by the employer as soon as the employee's rights are no longer subject to much risk of forfeiture.

The Subsidy Argument

The indisputable tax advantages for qualified plans have led to a controversy over whether this preferential treatment should be considered a subsidy. The argument hinges on the way in which a subsidy is defined. On the one hand, opponents of the subsidy argument contend that the current tax treatment of pensions does not deviate from the general principles of income taxation that would have applied in the absence of statutory provisions governing private plans.[21] On the other hand, proponents of the subsidy argument base their case on a comparison of the tax treatment of employer pension contributions and the tax treatment of other forms of employee compensation. Since a worker who receives part of his compensation through employer pension contributions will pay lower taxes over his lifetime than a worker paid entirely in cash wages, proponents conclude that compensation through pension plans is subsidized by the federal tax laws. The two opposing arguments are summarized here.[22]

Private plans are not subsidized. Opponents of the subsidy argument emphasize that under general principles of tax law most employers who sponsor funded retirement plans would be allowed a current deduction for their contributions without any current tax on the employee. The employer's contribution to a pension trust constitutes an irrevocable payment and, as such, is an allowable deduction without any special statutory provisions. Pension contributions were always considered ordinary and necessary business expenses, even though the rights of particular employees to benefits from the trust were forfeitable.

These opponents hold that since employee payrolls are almost universally on the "cash receipts and disbursements" method of accounting, participants in private plans do not receive any special tax concessions. They argue that the two major exceptions to the cash accounting rule—constructive receipt and economic benefit—are not applicable to employer contributions to pension plans. The concept of constructive receipt was incorporated into the IRS regulations to prevent manipulation in the timing of the receipt of income. Under this regulation, income is taxable to the individual if it has been "credited to his account, set apart for him, or otherwise made available so that he could have drawn upon it during the taxable year."[23] Constructive receipt is, however, dependent on the right of possession. Even when an employee's rights

---

21. See Robert R. Frie and James G. Archer, "Taxation and Regulation of Pension Plans under the Internal Revenue Code," *University of Illinois Law Forum,* vol. 1967 (Winter 1967), pp. 691–737; and Raymond Goetz, *Tax Treatment of Pension Plans: Preferential or Normal?* (Washington, D.C.: American Enterprise Institute for Public Policy Research, 1969).

22. While the following discussion may appear to treat defined benefit plans as if they were funded on an individually allocable defined contribution basis, that is not so. Rather, employers make pension contributions in light of their total anticipated future pension liabilities.

23. 26 C.F.R. 1.451-2(a).

are vested, he still does not have an unrestricted right to immediate payment.

It could be argued, however, that while the employee does not have a right to immediate payment, he has received an economic benefit. The concept of economic benefit is closely related to constructive receipt, but in this case the taxpayer receives something of value that may be equivalent to cash but that is not immediately convertible into cash. Most would agree that if a pension contribution was not vested, its receipt would be too contingent to constitute a significant economic benefit. Opponents of the subsidy argument maintain, however, that the economic benefit doctrine is not even applicable for vested contributions, because the employee may not survive to retirement age and may therefore never receive any payment. A further argument they use, less compelling since the passage of ERISA, is that the pension fund could become insolvent and unable to pay benefits despite the vesting status of the employee's rights. Therefore, they conclude that since employer pension contributions do not constitute either constructively received income or an economic benefit, deferring taxation until the person receives payment is consistent with the general principles of income taxation.

Similarly, on the basis of general tax principles, opponents argue that the interest income on the pension fund should not be taxable to beneficiaries who have only a contingent right to receive the income at some future time or on the employer who has irrevocably surrendered all right to receive it. Without some special statutory provision, the earnings would be considered the income of the pension trust and subject to taxation. In most cases, however, the resulting tax liability would be more than offset by a deduction for the amounts distributed by the trust to retired employees in the form of benefits. In the event that benefit payments did not exceed trust income, the tax rate applicable to the nondistributed income would vary drastically from one pension trust to another, since trusts are taxable at the same progressive rates applicable to individuals.

In short, those who argue that the tax treatment of qualified plans does not constitute a tax subsidy claim that this treatment results from the application of relevant accounting rules to business and individuals. That is, wages and other forms of employee compensation are deductible from the employer's gross income on an accrual basis and income is recognized only on a cash basis for the employee.

Private plans are subsidized. While the legal and accounting arguments constitute an interesting area of debate, many believe that they do not justify the differences in tax treatment of pension contributions and other forms of employee compensation. According to this view, whether the generally accepted tax accounting principles would permit the current deductibility of employer contributions accompanied by the deferral of tax on the part of the employee is irrelevant in considering whether qualified plans are subsidized. The issue is that contributions to qualified plans are treated more favorably than other types of compensation, such as cash wages. The tax treatment of current wages is therefore regarded as the appropriate benchmark, and the relevant comparison is the difference in tax liabilities between a situation in which all compensation is in the form of cash wages and a situation in which the employer pays workers both in wages and through contributions to a qualified pension plan. Clearly, the worker who receives part of his compensation in the form of deferred pension payments will have a higher after-tax income over his lifetime. On this reasoning, the reduction in lifetime taxes for those persons covered by qualified plans constitutes a subsidy.

The Tax Expenditure for Private Pensions

The Department of the Treasury prepares estimates of the revenue loss or tax expenditure resulting from the favorable provisions accorded qualified pensions and individual retirement plans. The distribution of this tax expenditure by income class not only provides an indication of who gains from the subsidy but also allows a comparison with the tax expenditure surrounding the treatment of social security contributions and benefits. But while the Treasury estimates are invaluable for this type of analysis and are consistent with the cash basis accounting of the expenditure side of the federal budget, they fail to capture the essential nature of the favorable provisions accorded qualified plans. Hence an alternative approach to estimating the tax expenditure is discussed in this section.

Treasury Estimates

In calculating the tax expenditure for private pensions, the Treasury attempts to measure the revenue loss arising from the current treatment of pension contributions and pension fund earnings. The benchmark for comparison is a comprehensive income tax, under which the increase in the present value of expected retirement benefits (approximately the sum of employer contributions and pension earnings) would be included in the employee's income and pension benefits would not be subject to taxation in retirement. Thus the Treasury estimate consists of two parts—the revenue loss from exempting employer contributions and pension fund earnings from current taxation, and the revenue gain from currently taxing private pension benefits. For these calculations, contributions to pension funds and pension fund earnings are assumed to be substitutes for wages and salaries that would have been taxed at a marginal rate of 23 percent—the rate applicable to the typical worker covered by a private plan. Private pension benefits are assumed to be

Table 3-1. Tax Expenditures for Employer-sponsored Pension Plans, Fiscal Years 1968–82
Billions of dollars

Fiscal year	Revenue loss at 23 percent rate		Revenue gain at 11.5 percent rate on benefit payments	Net cost of employer pension plans
	Employee contributions	Earnings on reserves		
1968	2.2	1.2	0.6	2.8
1969	2.5	1.3	0.7	3.1
1970	2.8	1.2	0.8	3.2
1971	3.3	1.4	0.9	3.7
1972	3.8	1.6	1.1	4.3
1973	4.3	1.6	1.2	4.7
1974	5.0	1.6	1.4	5.3
1975	6.0	2.0	1.6	6.4
1976	7.0	2.5	1.9	7.6
1977	8.1	2.8	2.2	8.7
1978	9.3	3.2	2.5	9.9
1979	10.7	3.5	2.9	11.3
1980	12.3	4.0	3.3	12.9
1981	14.1	4.4	3.8	14.7
1982	16.2	4.9	4.4	16.8
Revised estimates[a]				
1980	. . .	. . .	. . .	19.8
1981	. . .	. . .	. . .	23.6
1982	. . .	. . .	. . .	27.9

Sources: Department of the Treasury, Office of Tax Analysis, unpublished data. For revised estimates, *Special Analyses: Budget of the United States Government, Fiscal Year 1982* (GPO, 1981), Special Analysis "G," p. 229. Figures are rounded.

a. Revised estimates employ higher, and therefore more realistic, marginal tax rate assumptions. These indicate a substantially larger tax expenditure for private plans. The earlier series is used above since it provides historical data.

Table 3-2. Tax Expenditures for Employer and Individual Pension Plans, by Expanded Gross Income Class, Fiscal Year 1977[a]

Expanded income class (thousands of dollars)	Estimated returns filed		Tax expenditures			
			Employer pension plans		Individual pension plans	
	Number (thousands)	Cumulative percent distribution	Amount (millions of dollars)	Cumulative percent distribution	Amount (millions of dollars)	Cumulative percent distribution
0–5	25.474	100.0	38	100.0	2	100.0
5–10	20,109	71.1	416	99.6	32	99.9
10–15	16.106	48.2	1,030	94.8	76	97.6
15–20	11,824	29.9	1,515	83.0	115	92.1
20–30	9,907	16.5	2,608	65.6	266	83.8
30–50	3.347	5.2	1,672	35.7	349	64.7
50–100	985	1.4	912	16.5	420	39.6
100–200	198	0.3	375	6.0	112	9.4
200 and over	49	0.1	149	1.7	18	1.3
Total	87,998	. . .	8,715	. . .	1,390	. . .

Source: *Tax Notes*, vol. 6 (March 13, 1978), pp. 275, 278.

a. Expanded gross income includes adjusted gross income plus the untaxed portion of capital gains, percentage depletion in excess of cost depletion, and other tax preferences that are subject to minimum tax. It excludes the deduction of investment interest up to the amount of investment income.

currently taxed at a marginal rate of 11.5 percent, a rate intended to reflect the typical worker's lower income in retirement. At these marginal rates, the Treasury in 1981 would have gained $14.1 billion by taxing employer contributions and $4.4 billion by taxing earnings on pension reserves and would have forgone $3.8 billion from eliminating the taxation of pension benefits (see table 3-1). Thus Treasury revenues would have been $14.7 billion higher if employer contributions and pension fund earnings had been taxed currently to the employee. This $14.7 billion tax expenditure for qualified employer-sponsored plans is not only large but is expected to increase by two-thirds, to $24.9 billion, by fiscal 1985. Moreover, the tax expenditure for Keogh plans and IRAs amounted to an additional $2.1 billion in fiscal 1981 and is projected to rise, as a result of the liberalization in the Economic Recovery Tax Act of 1981, to $5.5 billion in fiscal 1985.[24]

Most of the benefits of the tax expenditures for employer plans accrue to higher-paid employees. As indicated in table 3-2, in 1977 (the last year for which data are available) 66 percent of the tax benefits for employer

24. Congressional Budget Office, *Tax Expenditures: Current Issues and Five-Year Budget Projections for Fiscal Years 1981–1985*, A Report to the Senate and House Committee on the Budget, pt. 3 (Government Printing Office, 1980), p. 33; data for IRAs and Keoghs from Department of the Treasury, Office of Tax Analysis.

plans went to the 16 percent of employees with incomes over $20,000.[25] Among persons with IRAs and Keogh plans, those with incomes above $20,000 received an even larger share of the tax benefits—almost 84 percent.

There are several reasons why higher-paid workers receive most of the benefits of the tax expenditure from private pensions. First, coverage is concentrated in unionized industries, where average earnings tend to be above the median. Second, many workers who are not covered are relatively young and lower paid, even though they may be covered and earning more later in their working careers. Finally, through the pre-scribed integration guidelines, the Treasury permits plans to provide lower benefits to workers whose earnings fall below the social security taxable wage base.

An Alternative Perspective

The Treasury's tax expenditure estimates are computed on a cash-flow basis consistent with the expenditure side of the federal budget. Essentially the calculation is designed to measure how much higher federal revenues would be in a given year if a particular subsidy had not been enacted.[26] Although this approach is meaningful for permanent deductions and exclusions, it does not properly account for tax conces-sions in those cases where tax payments are deferred. Its limitations for qualified pension plans are seen clearly by considering a situation in which (1) annual contributions to private plans exactly equal benefit payments during the year, and (2) workers face the same marginal tax rate in retirement as they do during their working years. Under these assumptions the revenue loss would equal zero, according to the Trea-sury calculations of tax expenditures. Yet individuals covered by private plans would continue to enjoy the advantage of deferring taxes on employer contributions and investment income until after retirement. Clearly, such tax deferral is equivalent to an interest-free loan from the Treasury and reduces the present value of taxes to be collected from an individual over his lifetime.

25. These figures are based on expanded gross income, which is a broader concept than adjusted gross income as defined in the tax law. Expanded gross income comprises adjusted gross income, the untaxed portion of capital gains, percentage depletion in excess of cost depletion, and other tax preferences that are subject to the minimum tax. But it excludes the deduction of investment interest up to the amount of investment income.

26. For a discussion of the rationale and justification for the current method of calculating tax expenditures, see *Special Analyses, Budget of the United States Govern-ment, Fiscal Year 1980*, Special Analysis G, pp. 189–93.

A better estimate of the annual revenue loss resulting from deferral would be the difference between (1) the present discounted value of the revenue from current taxation of employer contributions and pension fund earnings as they accrue over the employee's working life, and (2) the present discounted value of the taxes collected when the employer's contributions and investment returns are taxable to the employee after his retirement. To estimate the annual tax expenditure for employer-sponsored plans in this way requires assumptions about the average age of covered workers, the typical retirement age, life expectancy at retirement, the rate of earnings on pension reserves, the appropriate discount rate, and marginal tax rates for workers and retirees. In the following calculations the typical retirement age is assumed to be sixty-two and the participants' life expectancy upon retirement is assumed to be seventeen years.[27] For consistency with assumptions underlying the Treasury estimates, employer contributions to private plans in fiscal 1981 are assumed to be $61.3 billion, the marginal tax rate for workers covered by a pension plan is 23 percent, and the marginal tax rate for pension plan beneficiaries is 11.5 percent. Because of the sensitivity of the calculations to the other assumptions, a range of estimates is presented based on alternative values for the average age of a covered worker and on differences between the rate of return on pension reserves and the discount rate.[28]

27. Retirements tend to be clustered around age sixty-two, when workers become eligible for actuarially reduced social security benefits. Life expectancy at age sixty-two is 16.97 years, according to life insurance mortality tables for the U.S. total population for 1969–71. See American Council of Life Insurance, *Life Insurance Fact Book, 1981* (ACLI, 1981), p. 109.

28. Since the estimate is designed to measure the cost of the tax subsidy to the Treasury, the discount must reflect the opportunity cost of funds for the government. Long-term government bond yields of approximately 10 percent overstate the cost, since the Treasury recoups approximately 30 percent (the assumed marginal rate for purchases of long-term government securities) through taxes. Thus the discount rate is assumed to be 7 percent, reflecting the after-tax opportunity cost of funds to the Treasury.

The rate of earnings on pension fund revenues is calculated to reflect both their stock and bond holdings. The dividend price ratio for corporate equities is assumed to remain at 5 percent, and stock prices are assumed to keep pace with a long-run rate of inflation of about 5 percent. The yield on pension fund bond holdings is assumed over the forty-five-year period to reflect current levels of 10 percent. Thus the overall yield on pension reserves is projected to be about 10 percent.

Since the cost to the Treasury largely depends on the difference between the yield on reserves and the discount rate, the estimates in table 3-3 hold the discount rate constant and vary the return on assets. This format does not indicate any more confidence in one estimate than another but is an arbitrary decision. For dividend–price ratios and yields on government and corporate bonds, see *Federal Reserve Bulletin,* vol. 66 (February 1980), p. A27.

Table 3-3. Alternative Estimates of Cost to the Treasury of Favorable Tax Provisions for Private Pension Plans, Fiscal Year 1981
Billions of dollars

Rate of return on plan assets (percent)	Average age of covered worker			
	Thirty	Thirty-five	Forty	Forty-five
Estimate A[a]				
8	29.3	26.7	23.8	20.9
9	31.8	28.6	25.3	21.9
10	34.1	30.5	26.7	22.9
11	35.7	32.0	27.9	23.7
Estimate B[b]				
8	21.4	19.3	17.0	14.6
9	20.5	18.6	16.5	14.2
10	17.9	16.8	15.3	13.3
11	12.7	13.4	13.1	11.9

Source: Author's estimates. In all cases, the discount rate is 7 percent.
a. Tax rate is 23 percent during working years and 11.5 percent during retirement.
b. Tax rate is 23 percent during working years and retirement.

As shown in estimate A of table 3-3, the effect of deferring taxes on employer contributions and pension fund earnings until retirement, combined with a significantly lower marginal tax rate in retirement, implies a considerably larger tax expenditure than that estimated by the Treasury. For instance, if the typical worker covered by a pension plan were forty, and if the earnings on reserves were 10 percent and the discount rate 7 percent, then for fiscal 1981 the tax expenditure calculated on the present-value basis would be $26.7 billion, as opposed to the Treasury estimate of $14.7 billion. However, it could be argued that the tax benefit for private plan participants should be limited to the value of deferral, and the rate effect that results from the progressive tax structure ignored. Focusing solely on the revenue loss from deferral, the comparable tax expenditure becomes $15.3 billion (see estimate B in table 3-3). Similarly, eliminating the rate effect from the Treasury estimate—that is, assuming benefits are taxed at 23 percent rather than at 11.5 percent—reduces the estimated tax expenditure to $10.9 billion. While eliminating the rate effect from both calculations yields two figures that are somewhat closer, the present-value estimate still exceeds the cash-basis calculation prepared by the Treasury. Moreover, the discrepancy between the two figures will increase over time as the private pension system matures and benefits grow relative to contributions.

Although data on the distribution of deferral benefits by income class are not available, the very nature of the tax deferral on employer contributions and pension fund earnings makes pension coverage more beneficial to those in high-income brackets. Deferral is equivalent to an interest-free loan from the Treasury to the employee: the higher the tax bracket, the greater the loan. For example, if an employee is in the 25 percent bracket, the annual interest-free loan from the Treasury amounts to 25 cents for each dollar of employer contribution, while for an employee in the 50 percent bracket the loan is 50 cents per dollar of employer contribution.

Not only is the Treasury loan per dollar of contribution greater for high-wage workers, but because larger pension contributions are made on behalf of such workers, the absolute amount of their dollar loan is much greater. For example, a plan that calls for a pension equal to 50 percent of pay would provide a person earning $20,000 with $10,000 a year in retirement. If he were in the 25 percent bracket, the annual contribution of $2,000 would result in a loan of $500. For a person covered by the same plan earning $60,000 a year, the annual cost of his $30,000 pension would be $6,000. At a marginal tax rate of 50 percent this constitutes a loan of $3,000, six times as large as the one for the person in the 25 percent bracket.[29] Even if the loan is measured as a percentage of annual income, the person in the 50 percent bracket receives the greater benefit. The $3,000 loan is equal to 5 percent of his income, whereas the person in the 25 percent bracket receives a loan equal to 2.5 percent of his earnings.

A more direct approach to analyzing the distributional implications of the tax deferral on employee contributions and pension fund earnings is to consider the equivalence of this deferral to the exemption of the earnings on after-tax employer contributions.[30] The value of a tax-exempt rate of return is certainly greater for employees in higher tax brackets. Thus, regardless of how the tax expenditure is calculated, the conclusions remain that (1) the revenue loss from the preferential treatment of employee contributions and pension fund earnings is very large, and (2) the tax treatment of qualified plans favors higher-paid rather than lower-paid persons.

29. See statement by Daniel I. Halperin, in *General Tax Reform,* Panel Discussions before the House Committee on Ways and Means, pt. 7: *Pensions, Profit Sharing, and Deferred Compensation,* 93 Cong. 1 sess. (GPO, 1973), pp. 1126–39.
    30. See note 12.

A Comparison with Social Security

It would be misleading to imply that private pension benefits are the only form of retirement income that is given special tax concessions. Social security benefits have been exempt from the personal income tax since the institution of the program. While it would be unfair to tax benefits in full, since a portion represents the return of the employee's after-tax contribution, exempting the portion of benefits that represents employer contributions and interest on both employer and employee contributions is not consistent with comprehensive income taxation. Because workers now entering the labor force will make payroll tax payments totaling no more than 17 percent of the benefits they can expect to receive, some argue that 83 percent of social security benefits should be taxable.[31] However, the more commonly suggested solution has been to require recipients to pay taxes on one-half their benefits, since employees and employers each contribute equal shares.[32] Using this standard, Treasury estimates of the forgone revenue from the existing favorable tax treatment of social security benefits for retired workers, their dependents, and their survivors amounted to $9.9 billion in fiscal 1981.[33] But in sharp contrast to private pensions, the bulk of this tax expenditure benefits low- and middle-income people.[34]

The Effectiveness of Tax Expenditures

The special tax concessions to private pension plans cause a loss to the Treasury of nearly $15 billion annually, an expenditure that cannot be taken for granted. The use of these public resources must be considered carefully to ensure that the benefits are reasonably commensurate with those that might be obtained by using the funds for other purposes. Whether the tax concessions are justifiable depends on their effectiveness in achieving the desired results.

31. *Report of the 1979 Advisory Council on Social Security,* Committee Print, House Committee on Ways and Means, 96 Cong. 1 sess. (GPO, 1980), p. 75.
32. The latest recommendation of this proposal is contained in ibid., p. 74.
33. Congressional Budget Office, *Tax Expenditures,* p. 32.
34. The Treasury estimates that in 1977 (the most recent year for which data are available) approximately 80 percent of this tax expenditure benefited people with incomes under $20,000. See *Tax Notes,* vol. 6 (March 13, 1978), p. 278.

The most obvious goal of the favorable provisions for private plans is to encourage saving for retirement. The rationale for subsidizing this form of saving probably lies with the uncertainty involved in making adequate provision for retirement income. People are unsure about how long they will be able to work, how long they will live after retirement, and how much it will cost them to provide for themselves in their old age. Because of these uncertainties, people tend to emphasize present consumption and, on their own, fail to save adequately for the time when they will no longer be working. The historically high incidence of poverty among the elderly has supported the contention that people are unable to save on their own for retirement. Certainly, these considerations led to the adoption and dramatic expansion of social security.

The fact that favorable tax provisions are available only to plans that do not discriminate in favor of stockholders, officers, or other highly compensated individuals implies that the purpose of the subsidy is to encourage plans that include lower-paid employees, who are unlikely to amass private savings for retirement. The rationale for the favorable treatment of qualified plans, then, seems to be that these tax incentives will induce higher-paid employees to save through a mechanism that will also benefit the rank and file.

This section explores the extent to which the tax provisions achieve their intended results. First, the growth of private pensions is examined to determine whether the tax provisions have in fact encouraged the growth of organized savings plans. Second, data on coverage are analyzed to see whether broad-based participation has been achieved under private plans. Finally, the integration of private pension and social security benefits is discussed to show which participants benefit most from private plan coverage.

Impact of the Tax Subsidy

Private pension plans have grown tremendously since World War II, and in that sense the tax provisions have been extremely successful. In fact, the exclusion from the worker's income of employer contributions for all types of employee benefit plans has encouraged the growth of compensation in the form of fringe benefits rather than cash wages. A dramatic expansion has occurred in a variety of employer-financed benefit plans, such as life insurance, medical insurance, disability, and, of course, retirement. As illustrated in table 3-4, between 1950 and 1980

Table 3-4. **Private Employer Contributions for Employee Benefits as a Percentage of Private Sector Wages and Salaries, Selected Years, 1950–80**

Amounts in millions of dollars

Contribution or benefit program	1950 Amount	1950 Percent of wages	1955 Amount	1955 Percent of wages	1960 Amount	1960 Percent of wages	1965 Amount	1965 Percent of wages	1970 Amount	1970 Percent of wages	1975 Amount	1975 Percent of wages	1980[a] Amount	1980[a] Percent of wages
Pension and profit-sharing	1,713	1.4	3,377	1.9	4,866	2.2	7,646	2.6	13,050	3.0	28,253	4.5	63,453	5.8
Group health insurance	1,030	0.8	1,706	1.0	3,374	1.5	5,890	2.0	12,099	2.8	24,043	3.8	48,072	4.4
Group life insurance			561	0.3	1,080	0.5	1,651	0.6	2,891	0.7	4,368	0.7	6,947	0.6
Workers' compensation	791	0.6	1,150	0.7	1,529	0.7	2,177	0.7	3,786	0.9	6,695	1.1	16,118	1.5
Supplemental unemployment	0	0.0	51	*	120	0.1	121	*	111	*	236	*	682	0.1
Total	3,534	2.8	6,845	3.9	10,969	4.9	17,485	6.0	31,937	7.4	63,595	10.1	135,272	12.4

Sources: *The National Income and Product Accounts, 1929–76, Statistical Tables*, Supplement to the *Survey of Current Business*, vol. 61 (September 1981), tables 1.11, 6.15; and *National Income and Product Accounts, 1976–79*, Special Supplement to the *Survey of Current Business*, vol. 61 (July 1981), tables 1.11, 6.15.

* Less than 0.05 percent.

a. Author's estimates based on the assumption that the 1980 distribution of "other labor income" among benefit programs is the same as the 1979 distribution.

employer contributions for fringe benefits rose from 2.8 percent to 12.4 percent of private sector wages and salaries. Over the same period, employer contributions for pension and profit-sharing plans increased from 1.4 to 5.8 percent of employees' cash compensation. Similarly, because each dollar of the tax-deductible employer contribution yields more benefits than an employee dollar (which is first taxed as income and then contributed to the plan), the trend away from employee contributions for private pensions has been widespread. Employee contributions have dropped from 42 percent of total contributions in 1940 to 6 percent in 1980 (see table 2-1).

Coverage

The widespread introduction of new pension plans between 1940 and 1960 led to a large increase in the percentage of workers covered by such plans. During this period pension coverage rose from 14.6 to 40.8 percent of wage and salary workers in private nonagricultural establishments (see table 3-5). The continued growth of private pension plan contributions in the 1960s and 1970s reflected the growth of employment in firms that already had pension plans, liberalization of qualification for pension coverage, and increased benefit provisions. After 1960 the percentage of workers covered by private pensions increased very slowly, rising to only 48.1 percent in 1980.

Table 3-5. Growth in Pension Coverage, Selected Years, 1940–80
Thousands

Year	Workers covered by private pension plans	Workers in private nonagricultural establishments	Covered workers as percent of total
1940	4,100	28,159	14.6
1945	6,400	34,429	18.6
1950	9,800	39,171	25.0
1955	14,200	43,727	32.5
1960	18,700	45,836	40.8
1965	21,800	50,691	43.0
1970	26,300	58,326	45.1
1975	30,300	62,260	48.7
1980	35,800	74,481	48.1

Sources: Alfred M. Skolnik, "Private Pension Plans, 1950–74," *Social Security Bulletin*, vol. 39 (June 1976), p. 4; Martha Remy Yohalem, "Employee-Benefit Plans, 1975," *Social Security Bulletin*, vol. 40 (November 1977), p. 27; *Economic Report of the President, January 1981*, p. 273; and ICF, Inc., *A Private Pension Forecasting Model*, submitted to the Department of Labor, Office of Pension and Welfare Benefit Programs (October 1979).

Coverage statistics like these are subject to considerable controversy; experts argue that very young, part-time, or mobile workers would not be expected to participate in a company's pension plan. Because of the controversy, two surveys were conducted in 1979 to determine the extent of pension plan coverage. The President's Commission on Pension Policy found that 48.1 percent of all active workers eighteen and older were participants in some type of employment-based pension, profit-sharing, or retirement plan in their current jobs.[35] Nearly identical results were found in a similar survey of private pension plans conducted by the Census Bureau for the Department of Labor and the Social Security Administration.[36] Analysis of that survey, however, indicated that the coverage picture did improve as the definition of the eligible population was narrowed. For full-time private sector workers, coverage rose to 50 percent; for those full-time workers over twenty-five with one or more years of service with their current employer, coverage increased to 61 percent.[37]

Regardless of the coverage figure selected, the fact remains that a large part of the U.S. work force is not covered by a private pension plan. In most industries the employees who are not covered are heavily concentrated in small companies that tend to be at the lower end of the wage scale.[38] The concentration of coverage among higher-paid workers is shown in table 3-6. Even though this table describes coverage in public as well as private pension plans, it nevertheless shows the strong correlation between income class and pension plan coverage.

35. President's Commission on Pension Policy, "Preliminary Findings of a Nationwide Survey on Retirement Issues" (May 1980), p. 2.

36. Daniel J. Beller, *Patterns of Worker Coverage by Private Pension Plans,* Department of Labor, Labor-Management Services Administration, Pension and Welfare Benefit Programs (GPO, 1980). For a summary of survey results, see Beller, "Coverage Patterns of Full-Time Employees under Private Retirement Plans," and the companion article by Gayle Thompson Rogers, "Vesting of Private Pension Benefits in 1979 and Change from 1972," *Social Security Bulletin,* vol. 44 (July 1981), pp. 3–11, 47, and 12–29, respectively.

37. This figure must be interpreted cautiously because only 58 percent of the private sector work force fell into the category of full-time, over twenty-five, more than one year of service with current employer, and over 1,000 hours of work a year. President's Commission on Pension Policy, "Preliminary Findings of a Nationwide Survey on Retirement Issues," p. 3.

38. Coverage has been shown to be directly related to both wage rates and firm size. In 1972 only 18 percent of private nonfarm workers earning less than $3 an hour were in firms with retirement plan expenditures. The comparable figure for those earning $7 or more an hour was 88 percent. Similarly, only 38 percent of firms with under 100 employees provided retirement benefits as against 93 percent of firms with 500 or more employees. See Donald R. Bell, "Prevalence of Private Retirement Plans," *Monthly Labor Review,* vol. 98 (October 1975), p. 18.

Table 3-6. Distribution of Participants in Public and Private Retirement Systems, by Income Level, 1977[a]

Income level (thousands of dollars)[b]	Wage earners (millions)	Percentage distribution of wage earners		
		Covered by public or private plan	IRA	Nonparticipants
0– 5	20.7	15.0	0.2	84.8
5–10	19.0	30.0	0.9	69.1
10–15	17.5	40.0	2.0	58.0
15–20	16.3	54.6	2.5	42.9
20–50	24.9	75.1	5.4	19.5
Over 50	1.4	71.4	15.0	13.6

Source: President's Commission on Pension Policy, *An Interim Report* (GPO, May 1980), p. 22.

a. Social security payments are excluded from income.

b. Family-adjusted gross income.

In passing ERISA, Congress recognized that a large segment of the working population was ineligible for the tax advantages associated with private pension plans. Therefore, ERISA established individual retirement accounts and liberalized contribution limits on Keogh plans for the self-employed. But while the ERISA provisions broadened the group eligible for tax-deferral retirement plans, most of the benefits accrued to higher-income persons. Thus the problem remains. Although the substantial tax concessions offered higher-paid workers have encouraged the growth of private plans, these concessions have not led to widespread coverage among lower-paid workers. Moreover, the adverse effects of coverage are reinforced by IRS integration guidelines for qualified plans, which permit significantly reduced benefits for lower-paid workers.

Integration

Although private pension plans must be nondiscriminatory to qualify for the favorable tax treatment described above, an employer is permitted to consider its contributions to social security in determining whether its plan discriminates in favor of officers, shareholders, or high-paid executives. This approach is based on the premise that public and private retirement programs should function as a unified system. Thus if the social security program is weighted in favor of low-income workers, the private pension system should favor high-income workers so that all workers will have the same ratio of their earnings replaced when they retire. Congress incorporated this reasoning into the tax code in 1942 by including the proviso that public and private retirement benefits would be considered together in determining whether a plan was discriminatory.

Basically, as long as the ratio of combined benefits to earnings is no higher for employees whose wages exceed the taxable wage base than for those whose wages are fully covered, a plan is held to be nondiscriminatory.

Employers defend integration on the ground that without it they would have to provide more than 100 percent of preretirement pay to lower-paid workers to ensure adequate benefits (as a percent of pay) to higher-paid ones. Employers contend that the cost of these excessively high benefits for lower-paid workers would result in much lower wages for these workers and an unnecessary reduction in their preretirement standard of living. Furthermore, employers point out that the cost of reducing the permitted integration differentials would be substantial.

The problem with the integration guidelines is that they allow or encourage the payments of tax-subsidized benefits to higher-paid workers while permitting the denial of benefits to some lower-paid ones. During its deliberations on ERISA, Congress recognized inequities that existed under the IRS integration guidelines. Subsequently both the House Committee on Ways and Means and the conference committee between the House and the Senate voted a freeze on further integration pending full consideration of the integration issue. In the face of last minute opposition by employers and pension practitioners, however, the freeze was canceled. In the spring of 1978 the Treasury proposed replacing the existing complex integration guidelines with new rules designed not only to ensure greater benefits for low-wage workers but also to simplify plan provisions and make them more easily comprehensible to plan participants.

Although any detailed discussion of integration is necessarily complex, a comparison of existing procedures with the Treasury proposal provides a clearer understanding of the problems and possible solutions surrounding integration.[39] The current guidelines include provisions for integration through either an "excess" or "offset" method. Under a pure excess plan, the employer can limit benefits to that portion of an employee's final average pay in excess of the "integration level." The integration level is a career average of the social security wage base

39. The following discussion is based on the statement of Daniel I. Halperin, Tax Legislative Counsel, Office of the Assistant Secretary of Treasury for Tax Policy, in *National Pension Policies: Private Pension Plans,* Hearings before the Subcommittee on Retirement Income and Employment of the House Select Committee on Aging, 95 Cong. 2 sess. (GPO, 1978), pp. 43–50, 228–50.

Table 3-7. Integrated Excess Plan Benefits as a Percentage of Earnings at Retirement under Present and Proposed Plans, 1982

Plan	Final average pay[a]					
	$5,000	$15,000	$30,000	$50,000	$75,000	$100,000
Present[b]						
Private pension benefits only	0	10	23	28	31	32
Private pension and social security benefits[c]	54	46	42	39	39	38
Proposed[d]						
Private pension benefits only	20	24	30	32	34	34
Private pension and social security benefits[c]	74	60	49	43	42	40

Source: Department of the Treasury, Office of Tax Analysis, unpublished data, January 25, 1978.

a. Assumes employees retire at sixty-five in 1982 after thirty-five years of service with employer. Final average pay is assumed to be average over the last five years; earnings are assumed to increase at 6 percent a year.

b. Pension benefit is 0 percent of final average pay up to $11,004 and 36 percent of final average pay above $11,004.

c. The social security benefits do not include the special "transitional guaranty" benefits available primarily for retirees in the early 1980s. Thus the numbers reflect patterns of replacement that will be in effect under the Social Security amendments of 1977 after the transition period.

d. Pension benefit is 20 percent of final average pay up to $11,004 and 36 percent of final average pay above $11,004.

applicable to a particular employee. For instance, an employee reaching retirement age in 1982 would face an integration level of $11,004, and an integrated plan could pay benefits in 1982 up to 37.5 percent of final pay in excess of $11,004 without providing any benefits below that level.[40] Thus an employee with final average pay below $11,004 would not receive any benefits. The top part of table 3-7 shows the effect of integration under a pure excess plan at various income levels and the employee's combined replacement rate from social security and the private plan. Under the offset method of integration, an employer can reduce a worker's pension benefit by as much as 83.33 percent of a worker's social security benefit.[41] Thus a plan that provides a pension equal to 50 percent of final average pay but uses the maximum offset provides almost no benefits to low-paid workers (see table 3-8).

The goal of the Treasury proposal is to ensure some benefits for low-income persons. For excess plans this goal is accomplished by limiting the disparity between benefits above and below the integration level.

40. The maximum differential for benefits above and below the integration level is 37.5 percent. Therefore, if the plan pays 50 percent of final pay above the integration level, it must pay benefits of 12.5 percent below that level.

41. The offset is limited to the worker's primary insurance amount received from social security. Thus additional benefits received for a nonworking spouse are not included in the offset calculation.

Table 3-8. Integrated Offset Plan Benefits as a Percentage of Earnings at Retirement
under Present and Proposed Plans, 1982

Plan	Final average pay[a]					
	$5,000	$15,000	$30,000	$50,000	$75,000	$100,000
Present[b]						
Private pension benefits only	5	20	34	40	44	45
Private pension and social security benefits[c]	59	56	53	52	52	51
Proposed[d]						
Private pension benefits only	23	32	40	44	46	47
Private pension and social security benefits[c]	77	68	59	55	54	53

Source: Same as table 3-7.

a. Assumes employees retire at sixty-five in 1982 after thirty-five years of service with employer. Final average pay is assumed to be average over the last five years; earnings are assumed to increase at 6 percent a year.

b. Pension benefit is 50 percent of final average pay, offset by 83.33 percent of primary insurance amount from social security.

c. The social security benefits do not include the special "transitional guaranty" benefits available primarily for retirees in the early 1980s. Thus the numbers reflect patterns of replacement that will be in effect under the Social Security Amendments of 1977 after the transition period.

d. Pension benefit is 50 percent of final average pay, offset by 50 percent of primary insurance amount.

Specifically, the original proposal suggested that the percentage of earnings replaced above the integration level not exceed 1.8 times the percentage replaced below that level.[42] Thus in terms of the example in table 3-7, if the plan pays 36 percent of final average pay above $11,004, it must pay 20 percent of final pay below $11,004. The effect of this restriction would be to substantially improve benefits for lower-paid workers. For offset plans the Treasury proposed that the offset percentage be limited to a plan's replacement rate. This means that a plan providing a benefit of 50 percent of final average pay could not reduce the pension by more than 50 percent of the worker's social security benefit. The effect of this proposal would be to raise the benefits of lower-paid employees (see bottom part of table 3-8).

In addition to the controversy that surrounds the precise ratio of benefits above and below the integration level and the appropriate magnitude of the offset, the existing integration procedures raise some troubling basic issues. If workers in fact pay for pension benefits throughout their working lives through reduced wages, then it seems difficult to justify provisions that can deny lower-paid employees any

42. In response to comments on the original proposal, the Treasury subsequently revised its permissible ratio to 2.1. This increase was also designed to achieve greater parity between offset and excess plans. See appendix B of statement by Daniel I. Halperin, in *Oversight on ERISA, 1978*, Hearings before the Subcommittee on Labor Standards of the House Committee on Education and Labor, 95 Cong. 2 sess. (GPO, 1979), p. 414.

benefits. Integration also seems to be based on the faulty assumption that social security fully replaces the preretirement earnings of low- and middle-income workers. Yet, as discussed in chapter 2, this is not the case.

In short, although the favorable tax provisions have encouraged the growth of private pension plans, the provisions have not been wholly successful in achieving their objective of broad-based benefit protection. The private pension system has failed to extend benefits to lower-paid workers, coverage is far from universal, and lower-paid workers can be denied benefits through the integration provisions. The more basic question of whether the growth in pension plan assets should be viewed as a net increase in saving for retirement or merely a change in the form of saving is discussed in chapter 4.

Conclusion

The tax concessions for private retirement plans represent a loss to the Treasury of roughly $15 billion annually. Whereas all taxpayers must pay higher taxes to make up those forgone revenues, only half the private work force is covered by a private plan. Furthermore, the benefits of the tax concessions accrue primarily to higher-paid workers because coverage is concentrated in unionized industries, the value of deferral increases with the worker's marginal tax bracket, and integration permits greater benefits for higher-paid workers.

The tax treatment of private pension plans could be made more equitable in one of two ways. Either the tax concessions to private plans could be eliminated, or coverage could be made universal so that all workers would enjoy the advantages of deferral. Since the tax incentives alone have clearly been an inadequate incentive to encourage participation in a voluntary system, perhaps the desirability and feasibility of a compulsory private system should be explored. In fact, the President's Commission on Pension Policy has recommended the establishment of an employer-financed minimum universal pension system.[43] According to the commission's plan, a 3 percent payroll contribution would be set as a minimum benefit standard and all benefits would be vested immediately.

43. See President's Commission on Pension Policy, *Coming of Age: Toward a National Retirement Income Policy* (GPO, 1981), pp. 42–45. The advantages and disadvantages of such a compulsory private pension system is discussed more extensively in chapter 7.

Without universal coverage it is difficult to justify a system that allows half the workers to be compensated in a form subject to extremely favorable tax treatment. However, to devise an appropriate and workable reform is difficult. Under a Haig-Simons definition of income the increase in the present value of expected pension benefits would be included in the employee's taxable income each year.[44] Were this definition adopted, the increase in the present value of expected benefits for each employee could either be estimated by actuaries or approximated as an apportioned share of employer contributions and pension fund earnings.[45] For nonintegrated plans, the value of employer contributions and fund earnings could be allocated in proportion to wages and salaries, but for integrated plans a more complex allocation formula would be required.

Taxing all employees on their share of employer contributions and fund earnings would clearly not be fair, since for many the pension benefits may never materialize. A more reasonable approach would be to limit taxation to vested employees. Even this scheme might not be desirable, however, because allocating pension fund earnings might have adverse effects. Allocating only realized earnings might act as a disincentive to realize gains, and allocating accrued earnings would lead to substantial fluctuations in the employee's income, reflecting swings in the stock market. Hence one possible solution might be to tax vested employees on their share of employer contributions, continue to allow deferral of interest on fund earnings, and in retirement tax the portion of the pension benefit attributable to fund earnings. But even this proposal raises problems. First, taxing only vested employees might provide an incentive to delay vesting. Second, in the year the employee becomes vested he would experience a significant increase in his income.[46] Finally, under ERISA vesting is not a cut-and-dried issue, since two of the options permit degrees of partial vesting.

An alternative solution was suggested by the Treasury during the Ford administration.[47] Under this scheme both employee and employer contributions would be deductible, benefits would be taxed when received, and earnings of pension plans would be included currently in the

44. The following discussion is based on Sunley, "Employee Benefits and Transfer Payments," pp. 76–84.

45. The apportioned share of employer contributions and fund earnings would differ from the increase in the present value of benefits if part of the contribution was made to service past unfunded liabilities.

46. Presumably this increase could be modified by income averaging.

47. Department of the Treasury, *Blueprints for Basic Tax Reform* (GPO, 1977), pp. 56–58.

income of vested employees.[48] Earnings not assignable to employees would be included in the income of the employer. This proposal is equivalent to taxing employees currently on pension plan contributions and earnings, assuming that earnings, benefits, and contributions are all taxed at the same rate.[49] While it might provide a disincentive for funding, it would eliminate most of the subsidy and mitigate the bias in favor of pensions completely financed by employers.

The incentive for employer-financed plans has significantly affected employee rights in private pensions. Under a noncontributory plan a worker who changes jobs before his pension is vested does not receive any compensation for the wages forgone in order to be covered by the company's plan. But if the plan were financed by tax-deductible employee contributions, the worker could at least reclaim his contributions with interest upon separation and deposit them either in the pension plan of his new employer or in an IRA. In view of the potential advantages of the Treasury scheme, both in terms of the equity of the tax structure and the rights of participants, the approach certainly merits further exploration.

Any proposal for reform of the tax treatment of private pension plans will meet with considerable resistance from covered workers, employers, and those who invest pension fund money. More recently, many academic economists have joined this coalition. The economists' resistance stems from their preference for taxation based on consumption rather than on income. Since the current treatment of pensions is consistent with consumption taxation, which excludes saving from the tax base, those in favor of a consumption tax would oppose any change. But even though a consumption tax may indeed be preferable, income is currently the designated basis for taxation, and ad hoc exclusions from a comprehensive income tax base result in serious inequities.

One of the principal arguments for a consumption tax is that it would stimulate capital formation. To examine this argument, the following chapter discusses evidence of the relative effects of the private pension system and social security on saving and capital accumulation.

48. Of course, employers' defined benefit plan contributions would have to be assigned appropriately to employees. This process would be somewhat complicated by the fact that different defined benefit plans use different funding methods.

49. If t is the tax rate and r is the annual rate of earnings on the pension fund and both contributions and earnings are taxed currently, a \$1,000 contribution would grow to $(1 - t)(\$1,000)[1 + (1 - t)r]^n$ after n years. This is equivalent to what would result if earnings were taxed currently and benefits were taxed in full regardless of any tax previously paid on earnings. See Sunley, "Employee Benefits and Transfer Payments," p. 84n.

chapter four **Pensions and Saving**

In recent years sentiment has been growing to move some of the responsibility for providing retirement income from social security to private pensions. Advocates of such a shift in financial responsibility contend that increased reliance on private plans not only would reduce the payroll tax burden but also would increase saving and capital accumulation. Their argument stems from the commonly held belief that the pay-as-you-go social security system reduces aggregate saving, whereas the funded private pension system encourages saving. Therefore, some have supported introducing additional tax benefits to encourage employers to strengthen pension plans, and the President's Commission on Pension Policy has even recommended introducing a mandatory universal private pension system.

This chapter summarizes evidence on the relative effects of private pension plans and social security on personal saving to determine if a shift of financial responsibility between the two would increase capital accumulation. The first part focuses on private pensions and examines whether the enormous growth in private pension plan reserves constitutes a net increase in asset accumulation or merely a shift in the form in which people accumulate assets. The second part evaluates the contention that the pay-as-you-go social security program has dramatically reduced saving. The third part examines the interaction of social security and private pensions. The chapter's conclusion is that both the positive effect of private pensions and the negative effect of social security on saving have been grossly exaggerated.

The Impact of Private Pensions on Saving

The total assets held by private pensions increased from $2.4 billion at the end of 1940 to over $400 billion at the end of 1980. Although it is

62

Figure 4-1. Effect of Pensions in a Simplified Life-Cycle Model

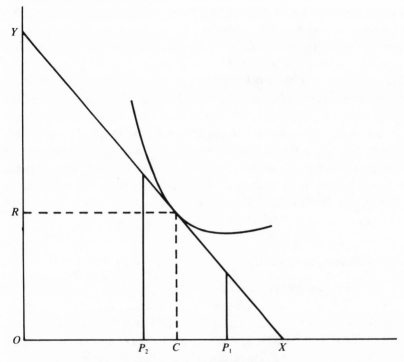

Income for retirement consumption

Income for current consumption

often assumed that the growth in these assets represents a net increase in saving, economic theory suggests that it may simply reflect a shift in the form of saving. This assumption rests on the traditional life-cycle saving model, according to which people try to allocate their resources so as to maintain a steady stream of consumption over their lifetimes.[1] During their working years they do not consume all their income but rather set aside positive saving, which they later dissave in retirement. The life-cycle model predicts that, in an ideal world characterized by perfect labor and capital markets, no taxes, and no uncertainty, people would view pension contributions as a substitute for their own saving.

The neutrality of pensions in this idealized world is shown in figure 4-1. Current and future consumption are measured along the horizontal

1. Albert Ando and Franco Modigliani, "The 'Life-Cycle' Hypothesis of Saving: Aggregate Implications and Tests," *American Economic Review*, vol. 53 (March 1963), pp. 55–84.

axis and vertical axis, respectively, so that under a comprehensive income tax a worker faces a lifetime budget constraint of XY. For the worker represented in the figure, the optimal allocation of income between present and future consumption would be at the point of tangency of his highest indifference curve to the budget constraint. Thus he would consume OC and save CX, which would allow him to consume OR in retirement. If the worker were to receive part of his compensation in the form of pension contributions (P_1X) rather than wages,[2] he would simply reduce his own saving to restore the desired allocation of resources between current and future consumption. If pension contributions were to exceed his desired level of saving—for instance, if pension contributions equaled P_2X—he could dissave from existing assets or borrow an amount equal to P_2C to regain his initial position.[3] In other words, according to the traditional life-cycle model, in an ideal world pension plans would have no effect on saving.

Theoretical Considerations in the U.S. Economy

The U.S. economy deviates substantially from the model described above, and these deviations introduce some ambiguity about the probable effect of private pensions on saving. Favorable tax provisions, imperfect capital markets, and induced retirement may cause pension plans to increase saving. Uncertainty about benefit receipt and amount may either increase or reduce saving, depending on whether people overestimate or underestimate their future pension receipts. The fact that pensions are paid as annuities and that private plans are less than fully funded should mean there is less aggregate saving than under the simple life-cycle saving model. An examination of all these factors indicates that the net effect of private pensions on aggregate saving is theoretically indeterminate.[4]

2. With perfectly competitive labor markets the worker's compensation would equal his marginal revenue product. Moreover, perfect capital markets and no uncertainty would ensure that both the firm and the worker consider a dollar of wages equivalent to a dollar of pension contributions.

3. With perfect capital markets people could borrow all they wanted at a given interest rate, r. If the worker were to borrow P_2C over his working years, he would owe $P_2C(1 + r)^{R-t}$ in retirement (R). However, at that time he would receive a pension equal to $(P_2C + CX)(1 + r)^{R-t}$. He could simply pay off his loan with his unwanted pension and thus would be restored to his optimal consumption path.

4. The following discussion is based in large part on the analytical framework of Blinder, Gordon, and Wise, although my analysis and conclusions differ from theirs in some important respects. See Alan S. Blinder, Roger H. Gordon, and Donald E. Wise, *An*

FAVORABLE TAX PROVISIONS. Compensation in the form of deferred pension benefits is treated favorably under the federal income tax. Workers can defer taxation on employer contributions and pension fund earnings until retirement, when they usually have lower marginal tax rates. Since these advantages raise the net rate of return on saving through pension contributions, they would be expected to stimulate individual saving. But this intuitive conclusion may not be correct. Rather, the impact of the favorable tax provisions on aggregate saving depends on two additional considerations. First, does the government reduce expenditures to offset the revenue loss from the tax breaks or does it recoup the revenue loss by raising taxes? Second, to what extent, in each of these situations, does the higher net rate of return enter into people's saving decisions?

No increase in taxes. Increasing the rate of return on saving without raising taxes to compensate for the forgone revenues will have two effects. First, lower overall taxes will increase a person's lifetime income. This increase induces an income effect—that is, because the person can afford to buy more of every good over his lifetime, he will increase both current and future consumption. Second, a person for whom pensions exhaust the desired level of saving—that is, the pension accounts for his last dollar of saving—will receive an increased rate of return at the margin, creating a substitution effect. The higher rate of return makes current consumption more costly relative to future consumption, inducing him to trade some current consumption for greater future consumption. Hence the income effect, which encourages greater consumption, and the substitution effect, which induces increased saving, work in opposite directions. Their net effect cannot be determined on theoretical grounds. But the most common finding among studies on the effect of interest rates on saving seems to be that the substitution effect outweighs the income effect, leading to a net increase in saving.[5]

Empirical Study of the Effects of Pensions and the Saving and Labor Supply Decisions of Older Men, prepared for the Department of Labor (Princeton, N.J.: Mathtech, Inc., 1981).

5. George M. von Furstenberg and Burton G. Mackiel, "The Government and Capital Formation: A Survey of Recent Issues," *Journal of Economic Literature*, vol. 15 (September 1977), pp. 840–42. Moreover, saving elasticities have probably been underestimated by focusing on two-period models. Compounding small differences in interest rates will become significant in a multiperiod setting. See David F. Bradford, "The Economics of Tax Policy Toward Savings," in George M. von Furstenberg, ed., *The Government and Capital Formation* (Ballinger, 1980), pp. 59, 60.

Figure 4-2. Effect of Favorable Tax Provisions for Private Plans, without Compensating Tax Increase

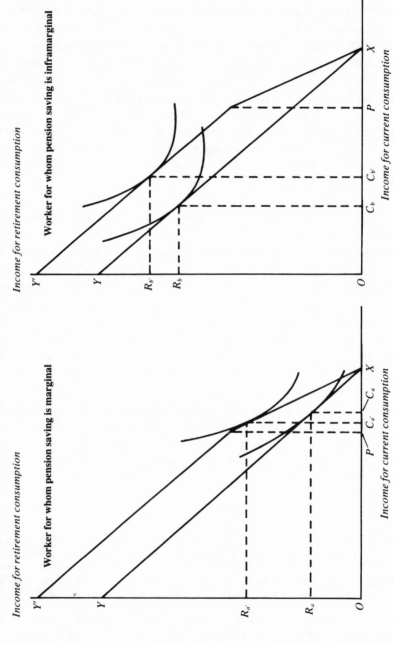

The case in which the substitution effect outweighs the income effect, leading to a net increase in saving, is depicted in the left half of figure 4-2. Since the worker's allocation of income between consumption and saving is determined by the tangency of the highest indifference curve to the budget constraint (XY), initially he consumes OC_a and saves C_aX, which would provide him with OR_a of consumption in retirement. The introduction of favorable tax provisions for pension saving rotates the budget constraint outward to form the new, kinked constraint, XY'. The kink is attributable both to a change in the slope of the budget constraint because of the higher rate of return available on that portion of disposable income saved through a pension plan and to a parallel shift in the budget constraint because of the windfall increment to the worker's lifetime income. Because the pension exceeds desired saving, this shift in the budget constraint not only increases his income but also alters the marginal rate of return on saving. The worker therefore moves to a higher indifference curve tangent to the kinked portion of the new budget constraint, increasing saving from C_aX to $C_{a'}X$ and retirement consumption from OR_a to $OR_{a'}$.

Workers for whom pension saving is inframarginal—that is, their desired levels of saving exceed that provided by private plans—will experience no change in the rate of return on saving at the margin. In other words, since the trade-off between current and future consumption remains unchanged, such workers will not be induced to increase their current saving. For them the introduction of the favorable tax treatment for pension saving induces an income effect, but no offsetting substitution effect. Since current consumption increases while current income remains unchanged, they will reduce their current saving.

This outcome is illustrated in the right half of figure 4-2, where the person initially consumed OC_b, saves C_bX, and has OR_b of consumption in retirement. Again, the introduction of favorable tax provisions for pension saving introduces a kink in the budget constraint and shifts it outward. But since desired saving exceeds pension levels, the worker does not face an increased rate of return at the margin. Rather, the new tangency between the individual's indifference curve and budget constraint occurs on that part of the new budget constraint that is parallel to the original budget constraint. This worker experiences an income effect but no offsetting substitution effect and therefore reduces saving from C_bX to $C_{b'}X$. Nevertheless retirement consumption increases from OR_b to $OR_{b'}$ because of higher lifetime income.

Figure 4-3. Effect of Favorable Tax Provisions for Private Plans, with Compensating Tax Increase

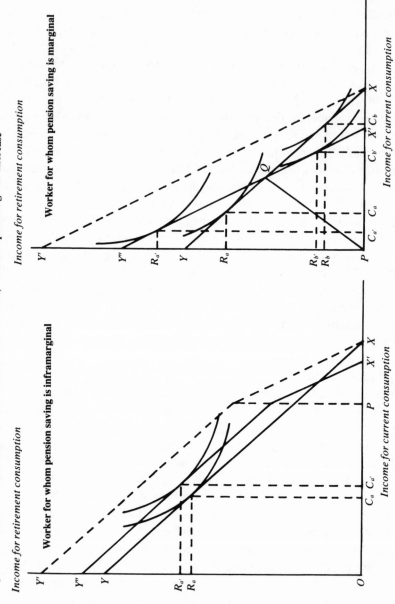

On balance, then, in the absence of compensating tax increases, favorable tax provisions for pension plans will lead to a net increase in saving when pension levels exceed the amount of saving workers would have done on their own and will lead to a reduction in saving when pension levels are less than workers' desired levels of saving.

Offsetting tax increases. In this case those workers for whom pension saving is inframarginal still experience an upward shift in their lifetime disposable income and will therefore increase consumption and reduce current saving. For example, in the left half of figure 4-3 consumption is increased from OC_a to $OC_{a'}$ as a result of the upward shift in the budget constraint. Since current period income is reduced (from OX to OX') by the higher taxes, saving will decline more in this case than if there are no compensating tax increases. Clearly, if desired saving, $C_{a'}X'$, were to exceed pension saving, PX', for everyone, the introduction of the tax incentives would reduce saving.

When pension saving is marginal, the results are again ambiguous because of the offsetting income and substitution effects. Nevertheless, the most likely outcome is for saving to increase. The right half of figure 4-3 focuses on this situation by expanding the relevant portion of the budget constraint from the left half of the figure. For those workers whose indifference curves were tangent to the original budget constraint at points above the ray PQ, the shift in the budget constraint will yield both higher income and an increase in the rate of return on saving. While the net effect of the income and substitution effects is indeterminate here, the indifference curves are drawn to depict the most likely outcome—namely, an increase in saving. Workers whose indifference curves are initially tangent below the ray PQ will experience a reduction in lifetime income along with an increased rate of return on saving. For them almost any outcome is possible. For instance, higher taxes in the current period could reduce both current consumption and current saving, while the increased return on saving could produce greater retirement income. Alternatively, the income and substitution effects could reinforce one another and current saving could be increased, as shown in the right half of figure 4-3.

The foregoing analysis implies that, contrary to one's intuitive assumption, the tax advantages for pension saving do not necessarily increase people's incentive to save. To the extent that pension saving falls below desired saving, the higher net return will not encourage any additional asset accumulation. In fact, the windfall increment to lifetime income from the tax advantages may actually reduce current saving. The favorable tax provisions will have the most stimulative effect when pension saving exceeds desired saving and people face a higher rate of return at the margin. In short, the effect that an increased rate of return for pensions will exert on the flow of saving is theoretically indeterminate.[6]

ILLIQUIDITY OF PENSION RIGHTS. The neutrality of pensions with respect to saving in the simplified life-cycle model hinges on the ability of workers to borrow at the market interest rate against excessive future benefits. Imperfect capital markets, however, often prevent people from borrowing freely, thereby forcing them to save more than they otherwise would. Such forced saving is most likely to occur among lower-paid workers, who are assured a relatively adequate benefit from social security. These workers may not want to trade current consumption for future retirement benefits, but they have little savings to reduce in order to offset excessive pension accumulation. Since workers cannot borrow against future benefits to increase present consumption, lower-paid workers may be forced to accumulate more for retirement than they would like. In this case pension plans may increase capital accumulation.

Even those workers whose desired levels of savings equal pension levels may not wish to do all their saving through pension plans. A future pension is an illiquid asset that, unlike other forms of saving, cannot be drawn on before retirement. This illiquidity reduces the substitutability of pensions for other private saving. People may therefore reduce their own saving by less than one dollar for each dollar of pension accumulation, and so contribute to a net increase in aggregate saving.

INDUCED RETIREMENT. The retirement provisions accompanying private plans also may have stimulated aggregate saving. Since most private pensions are available only when a worker retires from his job, the introduction of pension plans has encouraged many workers to retire earlier than they otherwise would. This early retirement would be expected to stimulate saving, since people who retire early are

6. Unfortunately, the conclusion is actually more complicated because while the tax incentives may not increase the *flow* of saving, workers will probably have a larger stock of assets just before retirement, owing to the increased rate of return on pension saving. Thus private pensions may have increased asset accumulation in the United States rather than saving flows.

forced to save at a higher rate over a shorter working life in order to finance a longer retirement. The magnitude of the effect of increased savings will depend on the rates at which both the population and incomes grow. With a stable population and no income growth, the higher rate of saving of workers will be exactly offset by the greater dissaving of retirees. In a growing population, savings would increase to the extent that the savers outnumber the dissavers. Similarly, if incomes were rising, the amount saved by workers would exceed that dissaved by retirees. In the past, both the population and real per capita income have tended to increase each year. Thus the trend toward earlier retirement that has accompanied the growth of private plans would be expected to have increased the rate of saving in the economy.

UNCERTAINTY. Because of the very many complicated pension provisions it is difficult for workers to be certain about receiving a pension or to know the magnitude of their benefits. Insofar as they are unaware of or underestimate future retirement benefits, they will not reduce their own saving to offset their share of pension asset accumulation. In this case, pensions would lead to a net increase in saving.

On the other hand, workers could just as easily overestimate future pension benefits by ignoring stringent vesting requirements, by assuming portability of accumulated pension credits in case of job changes, and by discounting the likelihood of being laid off. An inflationary environment further hinders an accurate assessment of pension benefits, because the true worth of a vested pension from a previous employer will depend on the future level of prices. A worker may tend to overvalue benefits that are, in fact, tied to an outdated wage level. Thus uncertainty about pension provisions could induce workers to reduce other saving either by more or less than pension asset accumulation, depending on whether they overestimate or underestimate their future benefits.

PENSIONS AS ANNUITIES. Because pensions are usually paid in the form of annuities—guaranteed benefit payments for the remainder of the employee's life—total saving may be less than if each worker saved for his own retirement.[7] Without pension annuities, most workers would be forced to accumulate sufficient assets to finance an extended retirement. While some would live to be very old and exhaust

7. The favorable tax provisions encourage the payment of benefits in the form of annuities, since interest on accumulated pension assets is allowed to accrue tax free until dispersed as benefits to retirees.

accumulated assets, others would die early and leave unplanned bequests. By pooling risk, gearing retirement saving to the average life expectancy, and offering annuities, pension plans reduce the total saving required to ensure workers a continuous stream of benefit payments during their retirements.

UNFUNDED BENEFITS. The previous discussion was based on the assumption that a dollar of accrued pension benefit was equivalent to a dollar increase in pension reserves. Thus if each worker were to reduce his saving by a dollar, the effect of pensions on saving would be neutral, since the reduction in individual saving would be offset by the increase in pension reserves.[8] In reality, firms do not always set aside assets for future pension benefits, and to the extent that pensions are not fully funded, a dollar reduction in savings by individuals will not be offset by increases in pension assets. Some argue, therefore, that with unfunded pension liabilities a reduction in individual saving leads to a decline in aggregate saving.

However, any negative effect of unfunded pensions on saving could be mitigated by the saving behavior of the shareholders of the firms. Recent studies indicate that each dollar per share of a firm's unfunded liability reduces the share price by approximately one dollar.[9] As the share price declines, shareholders' wealth will also decline; they would therefore be expected to reduce consumption and increase saving. Increased saving by shareholders could completely offset the lack of funding in the pension plan. In that case, the degree of funding would be expected to have no impact on aggregate saving.

Empirical Evidence

Although basic economic theory suggests that employees would respond to an increase in private pension benefits by reducing other

8. This is based on simplified assumptions that do not account for the time value of a dollar. In reality, the firm would set aside the present value of a dollar of accrued pension benefit, an amount that would vary depending on interest rates and the date on which the benefit became payable. According to the life-cycle saving model, employees would be expected to reduce their savings by the same amount.

9. George S. Oldfield, "Financial Aspects of the Private Pension System," *The Journal of Money, Credit and Banking,* vol. 9, pt. 1 (February 1977), pp. 48–54; Martin S. Feldstein, "Do Private Pensions Increase National Saving?" Discussion Paper 553 (Harvard Institute of Economic Research, 1977), pp. 20–21; Mark Gersovitch, "Economic Consequences of Unfunded Vested Pension Benefits," Working Paper 480 (National Bureau of Economic

direct saving by an equivalent amount, the preceding discussion enumerated several reasons why a dollar-for-dollar substitution may not occur. In fact, it is impossible to determine a priori whether the growth in private pension plans has fostered a net increase in saving or merely a shift in the form in which assets are held. Therefore, conclusions must rest on the existing empirical evidence.

Despite the widespread acceptance of the life-cycle theory, the conclusion that people are likely to reduce their saving in anticipation of pension benefits is relatively new. Until recently, most experts argued that participation in any pension plan would encourage personal saving. The 1968 Brookings study by Pechman, Aaron, and Taussig concluded, "The available evidence suggests that, over the long run, individuals covered by government and industrial pension plans tend to save more [in other forms] than those who are not covered."[10] This view, which was based in part on the historical stability of the saving rate, was buttressed by the results of two cross-sectional studies of the relation between private pension coverage and saving behavior.

In a 1965 study, Phillip Cagan analyzed the saving response of over 15,000 members of Consumers Union in 1958–59 and found that those covered by private pension plans actually saved more in other forms than those not covered.[11] Cagan's explanation of the surprising results is that pension coverage calls attention to retirement needs and prospects and thereby fosters a "recognitition effect" that counteracts any disinclination to plan for the future.

A study by George Katona, which was based on personal interviews conducted by the Survey Research Center of the University of Michigan with representative samples of American families in 1962–63, also concluded that pension plans stimulate voluntary saving.[12] Katona added a second explanation for his results, hypothesizing a "goal feasibility" effect, wherein people intensify their saving efforts as they approach

---

Research, 1980); Martin Feldstein and Stephanie Seligman, "Pension Funding, Share Prices and National Saving," Working Paper 509 (National Bureau of Economic Research, 1980).

10. Joseph A. Pechman, Henry J. Aaron, and Michael K. Taussig, *Social Security: Perspectives for Reform* (Brookings Institution, 1968), p. 186.

11. Phillip Cagan, *The Effect of Pension Plans on Aggregate Saving: Evidence from a Sample Survey*, Occasional Paper 95 (Columbia University Press for the National Bureau of Economic Research, 1965).

12. George Katona, *The Mass Consumption Society* (McGraw-Hill, 1964), chap. 19.

their retirement goal. Katona's results must be interpreted cautiously, however, since he focused on a narrow concept of saving—namely, changes in financial assets. Since the self-employed and farmers, who, in Katona's sample, account for 25 percent of those not covered by a pension plan and only 4 percent of those who are covered, would usually save through investment in their own businesses, the narrow definition of saving biases the results. Moreover, both the Cagan and Katona explanations of their results contradict the life-cycle model of consumer behavior by implying that a person's preference for present income over future income is modified by participation in a pension plan.

As part of a larger study, I reanalyzed a subsample of the Consumer Union survey and found that the results directly contradicted Cagan's earlier conclusions.[13] Separate saving equations were estimated for three age groups (30–39, 40–54, and 55–64); they included variables for home ownership, education, savings preference, income, wealth, family size, and pension coverage. The pension variable consistently entered with a negative sign, indicating that people covered by private pension plans tended to save less on their own, and, predictably, the size and significance of the coefficient increased with the age of the group. Additional equations were estimated for those aged 55–64, including the value of expected benefits and the value of vested benefits instead of the simple pension-coverage variable. Both benefit variables entered with a negative sign, but the size and significance of the coefficient of the vested benefit variable was substantially greater.[14]

A study I made in 1976 further supports the predictions of the life-

13.. Alicia H. Munnell, *The Effect of Social Security on Personal Saving* (Ballinger, 1974), chap. 5.

14. Three factors seem to explain the contradictory results of Cagan's and my analyses of the Consumer Union survey. First, the subsample I used contained more information; it included all four rounds of the Consumer Union questionnaires, whereas Cagan undertook his study when only three rounds had been completed. In my subsample the saving data were constructed from detailed balance sheet information rather than from estimates by respondents of "approximate changes" in broad categories of assets. The subsample was also subject to considerably more elaborate screening and consistency checks than Cagan's sample. Second, because his sample was so large, Cagan was not able to standardize for a large number of socioeconomic variables simultaneously. Multiple regression analysis made it possible in my study to isolate in the same equation the impact of pension coverage from that of education, family size, income, age, and other factors. Finally, my analysis of the subsample emphasized people whose saving is primarily for retirement, that is, people aged fifty-five to sixty-five. See Cagan, *Effect of Pension Plans on Aggregate Saving*, and Munnell, *Effect of Social Security on Personal Saving*.

cycle model—that saving in the form of future retirement benefits leads to a reduction in other forms of individual saving. This study examined the relation between private pension coverage and saving for a sample from Department of Labor surveys of men in their preretirement years over the period 1966–71.[15] The Labor Department data were particularly useful, since they included information on expected retirement age. Cagan's and Katona's surprising results may have arisen, in part, because pension coverage is usually accompanied by compulsory retirement and covered employees may simply have increased their saving in anticipation of that event. Fortunately, the Labor Department data provided information for constructing a fully specified life-cycle model, allowing for differences in expected retirement age between those who are covered by pension plans and those who are not. The results of the study indicate that coverage by private pension plans discourages saving in other forms, at least for the older men included in this survey, for whom retirement was the primary motivation to save.

Precise estimates of the substitution of pensions for other forms of saving were impossible, since the Labor Department survey included only the information about whether or not individuals had private pension rights rather than precise data about expected future benefits. Nevertheless, by extrapolating the behavior of the sample to the entire country for 1973 and assuming that if the 27.5 million workers covered under private retirement plans in that year expected to retire at sixty-five with an annual pension of $1,830 (the average benefit in 1973), it was found that the reduction in annual aggregate saving in 1973 because of future private pension benefits would have been about $13 billion.[16] Since total contributions to private pensions amounted to $21 billion in

15. Alicia H. Munnell, "Private Pensions and Saving: New Evidence," *Journal of Political Economy*, vol. 84 (October 1976), pp. 1013–32.

16. The calculation assumed that for each age group the propensity to save out of expected pension benefits was equal to the ratio of expected retirement span to life expectancy. This result is derived from the Ando-Modigliani life-cycle model:

$$C_t = \frac{1}{LE}[Y_t + (D - T)Y^e + A_{t-1}],$$

where D = age at death = $T + LE$; T = age in period t; Y_t = actual income in period t; Y^e = expected income in subsequent periods; A_{t-1} = asset holdings at beginning of period t; and LE = life expectancy. The expected future income expression can be rewritten as the sum of future earned income plus expected pension benefits after retirement. Assuming

1973, the results indicate that workers reduce their direct saving by 62 cents for every dollar of pension saving.[17]

The most recent study of individual saving behavior, by Diamond and Hausman, identified substantial substitution between individual asset accumulation and pension benefits provided through organized savings programs.[18] Using the data from the National Longitudinal Survey of Men Aged 45–59, the authors ran a unique regression designed to test the impact of a dollar per year of pension benefits on individual wealth accumulation. Their results indicated that family wealth is decreased by $5.84 for each dollar of annual pension benefits a family expects to receive after retirement. To use these results as a basis for calculating the actual offset between pension saving and individual saving, information would be needed on the cost of an equivalent annuity. However, a rough estimate might be that each dollar saved through private pensions reduces individual savings by 58 cents.

This rough estimate is consistent with Feldstein's results from time-series regressions based on aggregate consumption functions.[19] Feldstein estimated an equation of private saving, with real disposable income, the unemployment rate, private wealth, social security wealth, corporate retained earnings, and pension saving as explanatory variables. Owing to the usual problems of time-series analysis, the standard errors of the estimated coefficients were very large and therefore the coefficients of

---

future earned income is equal to income in period t (or that the rate of growth of earnings is equal to the discount rate), then total expected income can be written as

$$(D - T)Y^e = (R - T)Y_t + (D - R)PEN,$$

where R = expected retirement age, and PEN = expected pension benefits. Therefore,

$$C_t = \frac{1}{LE}[Y_t(1 + R - T) + (D - R)PEN + A_{t-1}]$$

$$S_t = Y_t - C_t$$

$$S_t = Y_t - \frac{1}{LE}[Y_t(1 + R - T) + (D - R)PEN + A_{t-1}]$$

$$= \frac{(D - R - 1)}{LE}Y_t - \frac{(D - R)}{LE}PEN - \frac{A_{t-1}}{LE}.$$

17. Total contributions to private plans is the relevant figure for comparison, since the original study focused on workers' response to contributions made on their behalf.

18. Peter Diamond and Jerry Hausman, "Individual Savings Behavior," paper prepared for the National Commission on Social Security, May 1980.

19. Feldstein, "Do Private Pensions Increase National Saving?"

pension saving and most of the other variables were not statistically significant. Nevertheless, his point estimates of the impact of pension saving on private saving ranged from 0.32 to 0.40 for the postwar period (1947–74), implying that for every dollar contributed to private pension plans on behalf of an employee, the employee will reduce his own savings by 60 to 68 cents.

In summary, the recent evidence contradicts the results of the earlier studies by Cagan and Katona.[20] The most useful hypothesis for policy purposes now appears to be that, at any given time, consumers reduce saving in other forms to compensate for the promise of pension benefits. To guess about the magnitude of this offsetting effect would be hazardous in light of the scant empirical evidence. Nevertheless, a reasonable conjecture might be that workers reduce saving by 65 cents for each dollar of saving through pension plans, resulting in a net increase in aggregate saving of 35 cents.

The Impact of Social Security on Saving

According to the life-cycle model, workers, aware that they will receive benefits in exchange for social security taxes, would be expected to save less on their own, thus substituting public for private saving. If social security were a funded retirement program, the reduction in individual saving would simply be offset by increased asset accumulation by the government. But social security is financed on a pay-as-you-go basis, and contributions are immediately paid out in benefits rather than accumulated in a fund. Thus in fact there is no public saving, and some economists have argued that the implied reduction in private saving leads to a corresponding reduction in the nation's total capital accumulation.

Theoretical Considerations

As more economists have studied the issue, the theoretical arguments surrounding the effect of social security on saving have become succes-

20. An exception is the study by Blinder, Gordon, and Wise, which failed to find any trade-off between private pension wealth and individual wealth accumulation. But the estimated impact of all variables in their study was very imprecise, since the life-cycle model was able to explain little of the variability in asset holdings, and the coefficients of almost all the key variables had large standard errors. See *An Empirical Study,* p. 4-36.

Table 4-1. Benefit–Tax Ratios for Hypothetical Workers Entering Covered Employment at Age Twenty-two in 1979

Worker or couple	Benefit–tax ratio [a]
Never married male, maximum earner	0.50
Married male with nonworking wife and two children, maximum earner	1.14
Never married female, maximum earner	0.66
Couple, two maximum earners	0.63[b]
Couple, male maximum earner, female median earner	0.82[b]
Never married male, average earner	0.76
Married male with dependents, average earner	1.74
Never married male, minimum wage earner	0.95
Married male with dependents, minimum wage earner	2.14

Source: *Report of the 1979 Advisory Council on Social Security,* Committee Print, House Committee on Ways and Means, 96 Cong. 1 sess. (GPO, 1980), p. 62.

a. The ratio is computed by using social security employee and employer contributions; the present value of taxes is calculated by using historic trust fund interest rates; and the present value of retirement benefits is calculated by using a nominal rate of return of 6.6 percent, assumed to be equivalent over the long run to a real return of 2.5 percent.

b. Ratio is for the couple, not the individuals.

sively more sophisticated. Unfortunately, the theoretical developments in this area have not yielded definitive conclusions.

THE BENEFIT EFFECT. The argument that social security reduces aggregate saving must be defined carefully. Consider a social security system in which workers contribute payroll taxes that in present-value terms are exactly equal to the benefits received in retirement. Since such a program would not change the lifetime resources of covered workers, the life-cycle model predicts that it would have no effect on individual consumption and saving.[21] While workers would reduce their private saving by the amount of their social security contributions, subsequent benefit payments would reduce the dissaving required to support retirement consumption.

Since for the average young working person today payroll tax contributions and social security benefits will be roughly equivalent in present-value terms (see table 4-1), social security will have little impact on the lifetime resources and saving of people in this generation. Rather, the argument for the negative effect on saving stems from the fact that since

21. Although individual saving would not be affected by an "actuarially fair" social security system, aggregate saving would decline in the face of rising incomes or population growth. With a growing population, savings would increase to the extent that savers outnumber dissavers. Similarly, with rising incomes the amount saved by workers would exceed that dissaved by retirees.

Table 4-2. Benefit–Tax Ratios for Hypothetical Workers Retiring at Age Sixty-five in 1979

Worker	Benefit–tax ratio[a]
Single male, maximum earner	2.49
Single male, average earner	2.76
Single male, low earner	3.54
Single female, maximum earner	3.11
Single female, average earner	3.44
Single female, low earner	4.41
Married male with dependent spouse, maximum earner	4.60
Married male with dependent spouse, average earner	5.09
Married male with dependent spouse, low earner	6.53

Source: *Report of the 1979 Advisory Council*, p. 65.
a. The ratio is computed by using social security employee and employer contributions.

the start of the social security system retirees have received benefits that in present-value terms far exceed the payroll tax contributions they have made (see table 4-2). This noncontributory component has increased the lifetime wealth of workers in the first generations of retirees, inducing them to consume more and save less.

A simplified example may clarify how the benefit effect could alter a worker's saving behavior.[22] Suppose a worker enters the labor force at twenty-five, earns $12,000 a year, plans to retire at seventy, and expects to live until eighty. Assume further that he plans no bequests and wants to have an annual income of $6,000 during retirement. At an interest rate of 5 percent, this worker would have to put aside $281, or 2.34 percent of earnings, each year to meet retirement income needs. If the worker were guaranteed annual retirement benefits of $3,000, he would cut private saving in half, to only 1.17 percent of income. This reduction in individual saving is the benefit effect. Whether the reduction in individual saving leads to a reduction in aggregate saving depends on whether benefits exceed contributions in present-value terms.

THE RETIREMENT EFFECT. In an extended life-cycle model, however, retirement as well as saving decisions may be affected by social security. Whereas, in the past, people could plan to work all their

22. This example is based on a presentation of the retirement and benefit effects by Selig D. Lesnoy and John C. Hambor, "Social Security, Saving, and Capital Formation," *Social Security Bulletin*, vol. 38 (July 1975), pp. 3–15.

lives, after the introduction of social security everyone was expected to withdraw from the labor force at sixty-five. This change in labor force participation induces a retirement effect that comes about in the following way. Suppose that in order to receive social security benefits the worker is forced to retire at sixty-five, five years earlier than planned. In the example of the typical worker described above, this reduction in working years and increase in retirement years requires a saving increase from 1.17 to 2.09 percent of earnings to attain the retirement income goal of $6,000 each year. The retirement effect thus increases the saving rate and acts to offset the decline in private saving brought about by the guarantee of benefits.

The individual retirement effect can be attributed to three factors. First, social security benefits raised the lifetime income of many people, creating the pure income effect that encouraged older workers to consume more leisure. Second, the earnings test made it impossible to receive full benefits without significantly cutting back on work effort.[23] Finally, social security may also have affected retirement patterns by conditioning both employers and employees to the idea that sixty-five is a normal retirement age. Thus by encouraging earlier retirement, the introduction of social security could have an offsetting positive effect on saving, since people increase saving over shorter working lives to provide for a longer retirement.

BEQUESTS. The retirement effect presents one source of ambiguity about the net impact of social security on personal saving; a further complication has been introduced by Robert Barro.[24] Barro notes that the private economy was characterized by a variety of intergenerational transfers before the introduction of social security and that insofar as social security simply replaced the existing intrafamily transfers the program should have no impact on saving. If the pay-as-you-go social security system exceeds the desired level of existing intrafamily transfers, people will undertake offsetting measures. For low-income families, this offsetting behavior may take the form of reduced support for elderly parents. For high-income families, the parents may increase

23. Until 1972 social security benefits were reduced $1 for each $1 of earnings in excess of some very low exemption. The earnings test was changed by the 1972 amendments so that the potential recipient loses only 50 cents for each $1 of earnings in excess of the limit. In 1981 the earnings limit was $5,500.

24. Robert Barro, "Are Government Bonds Net Wealth?" *Journal of Political Economy*, vol. 82 (November–December 1974), pp. 1095–117.

bequests to their children to offset the children's additional payroll tax burden. Therefore, to the extent that the social security program is nothing more than an orderly rearrangement of the transfer of funds across generations, the system will have no impact on saving.

MACROECONOMIC IMPLICATIONS. In a recent paper Robert Eisner has argued that when individuals' response to the increased wealth from the introduction of social security is considered in the context of a macroeconomic model, it appears that the program may actually have increased saving.[25] In an economy characterized by high levels of unemployment, a program that encourages people to save less and consume more will actually increase aggregate saving and capital formation. Even under conditions of full employment, Eisner argues, the introduction of social security need not decrease saving. Rather, in this situation, increased efforts to consume because of greater social security wealth will lead to higher prices. If the monetary authorities allow the money supply to increase proportionately, higher prices will simply lower the real value of government bonds and real consumption will remain unchanged. On the other hand, if the money supply is not permitted to increase proportionately, the rate of interest will rise and there will be a negative effect on real capital formation, stemming not from increased social security wealth per se but from the interaction of the wealth and the restrictive monetary policy.

Eisner also rejects the argument that the retirement effect may increase saving. Instead, he contends that earlier retirement implies that in the aggregate fewer people are working. So even if those working save a higher proportion of their income, the reduction in total income due to lower employment may mean that total saving may be reduced.

Empirical Evidence

Since the impact of social security on saving is ambiguous theoretically, the question must ultimately be resolved empirically. This section summarizes the available evidence, ranging from casual empiricism to detailed econometric studies.

CASUAL EMPIRICISM. Three factors would tend to undermine the

25. Robert Eisner, "Social Security and Capital Formation," working paper (Northwestern University, 1980).

**Figure 4-4. Personal Saving as a Percentage of Disposable Income,
with and without Social Security, 1929–80**

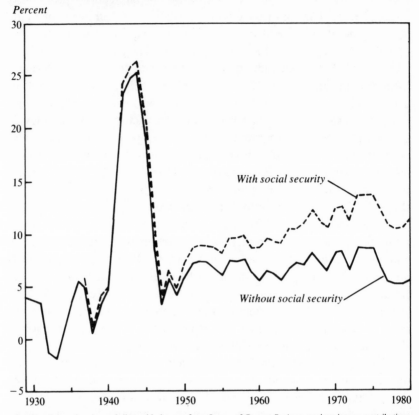

Sources: Personal saving and disposable income from *Survey of Current Business,* various issues; contributions to social security trust fund from *Social Security Bulletin,* various issues.

contention that social security has had a significantly negative effect on saving and capital accumulation. First, the saving rate has not declined since the introduction of social security (see figure 4-4). In fact, if social security contributions are assumed to displace personal savings dollar for dollar, the data indicate that a large secular increase in the saving rate will have occurred. Such an increase, however, is inconsistent with the life-cycle model; in theory, the increasing proportion of elderly dissavers in the United States between 1929 and 1981 should have contributed to a decline in the aggregate saving rate over time.[26]

26. In 1929 people aged sixty-five and over accounted for 5.3 percent of the population; by 1980 the ratio had increased to 11.3 percent. *Economic Report of the President, January 1982,* p. 265.

Second, if the promise of social security benefits significantly affected workers' incentive to save, resulting in a much smaller capital stock, then one would expect a secular rise in the rate of return on real assets. Several studies have examined this issue, but none has found any evidence of rising rates of return.[27] If anything, returns on real capital seem to have declined in recent decades.

Finally, information about the saving response of workers to social security can be gained from the surveys of OASI beneficiaries conducted periodically by the Social Security Administration between 1941 and 1975. Two pieces of evidence indicate that people retiring today have saved about the same proportion of their income as people who retired forty years ago, which suggests that social security has not led to a drastic reduction in saving. First, the income of elderly beneficiaries has increased since the introduction of social security. According to a 1975 social security survey, real median income of aged beneficiaries had nearly tripled since the early 1940s. Furthermore, a significantly smaller portion of income was derived from public assistance and contributions of relatives; the higher median income came from the retirees' own saving efforts.[28] Second, the real net worth of beneficiaries at retirement more than quadrupled over this period primarily because of the increase in homeownership, which represents the greater part of net worth. In early surveys slightly over 50 percent of married couples owned their own homes; by the 1975 survey this proportion had increased to 83 percent.

The impression one gains from such income and asset data is that saving for retirement by other means than social security has more than kept pace with increases in real income. This interpretation may tend to exaggerate somewhat the growth of wealth and income, since people retiring in the early 1940s had unusually low wealth and income because of the Depression. Nevertheless, the tripling of real retirement income,

27. See William D. Nordhaus, "The Falling Share of Profits," *Brookings Papers on Economic Activity, 1:1974*, p. 180; Daniel M. Holland and Stewart C. Myers, "Trends in Corporate Profitability and Capital Costs," in Robert Lindsay, ed., *The Nation's Capital Needs: Three Studies* (Committee for Economic Development, 1979), pp. 103–88; and Martin Feldstein and Lawrence Summers, "Is the Rate of Profit Falling?" *BPEA, 1:1977*, pp. 211–27.

28. See Edna C. Wentworth and Dena K. Motley, *Resources After Retirement,* Social Security Administration, Office of Research and Statistics, Research Report 34 (Government Printing Office, 1970), tables 2, 4; Lenore E. Bixby, "Income of People Aged 65 and Older: Overview from 1968 Survey of the Aged," *Social Security Bulletin,* vol. 33 (April 1970), pp. 12–14; and Joseph Friedman and Jane Sjogren, "The Assets of the Elderly as They Retire" (Cambridge, Mass: ABT Associates, 1980), p. 30.

the quadrupling of real net worth, and the increased reliance on personal resources rather than aid lend support to the hypothesis that, thus far, private saving for retirement has not been greatly reduced by social security.

U.S. TIME-SERIES STUDIES. The current debate over the impact of social security on private saving was initiated by two empirical studies of U.S. time-series data, one by Feldstein and the other by myself.[29] Each of these early studies estimated the effect of promised social security benefits on aggregate consumption and saving for the period 1929–71. Both studies used the same measure of expected benefits— namely, social security wealth calculated as the present discounted value of all future benefits to which the current working-age and retired population was entitled. Feldstein concluded that if there were no social security, personal saving might be double the actual levels. My study, which included an explicit measure of the labor force activity of the elderly, indicated that the retirement effect roughly offset the benefit effect, so that social security had no appreciable impact on aggregate saving. Two later studies, one by Barro and another by Darby, which also used the social security wealth variable, failed to provide conclusive evidence.[30]

Even these inconclusive results, however, are invalid in the wake of a recent study by Leimer and Lesnoy that revealed a substantial error in the construction of social security wealth.[31] This error, which arose from a programming mistake in the part of the program incorporating a 1957 change in benefits paid to surviving spouses, caused social security wealth to be overstated by 37 percent in 1974. Using a reconstructed and corrected social security wealth series, Leimer and Lesnoy reestimated Feldstein's equations for the periods 1930–74 and 1947–74. The results were dramatically different from Feldstein's original estimates. For the 1930–74 period the coefficient of social

29. Martin Feldstein, "Social Security, Induced Retirement, and Aggregate Capital Accumulation," *Journal of Political Economy*, vol. 82 (September–October 1974), pp. 905–26; and Alicia H. Munnell, *Effect of Social Security on Personal Saving*.

30. Robert J. Barro, *The Impact of Social Security on Private Saving: Evidence from the U.S. Time Series* (Washington, D.C.: American Enterprise Institute for Public Policy Research, 1978); and Michael R. Darby, *The Effects of Social Security on Income and the Capital Stock* (AEI, 1978).

31. Dean R. Leimer and Selig D. Lesnoy, "Social Security and Private Saving: A Reexamination of the Time Series Evidence Using Alternative Social Security Wealth Variables," Office of Research and Statistics, Working Paper (DHEW, 1980).

security wealth was statistically insignificant; in the postwar period the coefficient indicated that social security had a very significant positive effect on saving. Leimer and Lesnoy downplay these startling results for the latter period, since the size of the coefficient implies that saving would be negative in the absence of social security. Nevertheless, their replication of Feldstein's equation supports the contention that there is no current evidence that social security wealth decreases aggregate personal saving.

Leimer and Lesnoy then tested the effect of substituting alternative benefit and tax perception assumptions in the construction of the wealth variable. For a wide range of alternative social security wealth constructions, they were unable to find any significant negative effect of social security on saving.

In response to Leimer and Lesnoy's findings, Feldstein reconstructed his social security wealth variable, updated and reestimated his equations for the period 1929–76, and once again concluded that social security has reduced saving.[32] Very little weight, however, can be given to these latest results for two reasons. First, an ad hoc adjustment was made to the wealth series to reflect the 1972 benefit increases, although no similar adjustments were made for benefit increases in earlier years. Second, no equations were estimated for the years 1947–76, the period for which Leimer and Lesnoy found that social security had stimulated saving significantly. In short, time-series studies to date do not provide conclusive information about the impact of social security on personal saving.

Moreover, in a recent paper Auerbach and Kotlikoff argue that time-series analysis has little potential for settling the controversy about the impact of social security on personal saving.[33] To demonstrate their point, they run regressions on hypothetical data generated from a life-cycle growth model. Whereas in the model social security reduces the nation's capital stock by almost 20 percent, the time-series social security regression coefficients based on the hypothetical data vary enormously, depending on the time interval selected and other assumptions. The authors conclude that if the coefficients of such a controlled regression prove to be highly unstable, it is unrealistic to search for stable time-series coefficients in our complicated dynamic economy.

32. Martin S. Feldstein, "Social Security, Induced Retirement, and Aggregate Capital Accumulation: A Correction and Updating," working paper, 1980.

33. Alan J. Auerbach and Laurence J. Kotlikoff, "An Examination of Empirical Tests of Social Security and Savings," Working Paper 730 (National Bureau of Economic Research, 1981).

MICROECONOMIC EVIDENCE. Four studies have addressed the issue of the impact of social security on saving on a microeconomic level by examining the effect of individual social security wealth or expected annual benefits on private wealth accumulation. These studies attempt to verify the predictions of the life-cycle model—namely, that workers promised social security benefits in retirement will accumulate fewer assets on their own. Since the studies test the impact of social security only on individual saving, however, their results cannot be used to predict the impact of social security on saving in the aggregate. In an actuarially fair system workers would be expected to reduce their private saving in anticipation of social security benefits. But, assuming a stable population and no income growth, this reduction in private saving by the working population would be offset by the decline in dissaving among the retired population. The predicted negative effect of social security on saving is derived from the increment to lifetime wealth generated when benefits are paid in excess of contributions. Only the study by Kotlikoff examines whether this increment has reduced individual saving.

Generally the studies found considerable substitution between social security and private wealth accumulation. With data from the Federal Reserve Board's 1963 Survey of Financial Characteristics of Consumers, Feldstein and Pellechio related household net worth to various measures of income and each household's net social security wealth. For employed males between fifty-five and sixty-four, they found a strong substitution effect of social security wealth for private wealth.[34] A recent study by Diamond and Hausman indicated that for each dollar of social security benefits people reduced their saving in other forms by roughly 69 cents.[35] On the other hand, Blinder, Gordon, and Wise found somewhat less substitution of social security for private wealth among a sample of men from the Longitudinal Retirement History Survey.[36] Their estimates indicated that a dollar of social security wealth displaced approximately 39 cents of other assets.

34. Martin S. Feldstein and Anthony J. Pellechio, "Social Security and Household Wealth Accumulation: New Microeconometric Evidence," *Review of Economics and Statistics,* vol. 61 (August 1979), pp. 361–68.

35. Diamond and Hausman, "Individual Savings Behavior," found that for each $1 increase in annual social security benefits during retirement, a person would reduce his accumulation of private wealth by $6.93. This author's interpretation of their findings assumes an interest rate of 10 percent.

36. Blinder, Gordon, and Wise, *An Empirical Study.*

Kotlikoff examined the impact of two measures of social security wealth on household wealth accumulation for a 1966 sample of men selected from the National Longitudinal Survey of Men Aged 45–59.[37] The first social security variable, the accumulated value of employer and employee payroll tax contributions, had a statistically significant negative coefficient, indicating that workers reduce their saving by 67 cents for each dollar of payroll tax contribution. These results, together with those of the other studies, confirm the life-cycle model's prediction that people view their contribution to social security as a substitute for saving on their own and therefore reduce their saving in other forms.

To determine the effect of social security on aggregate saving, Kotlikoff tested the impact of a second social security variable. For each worker in the sample he constructed an "increment to lifetime wealth" variable, equal to the amount by which the present value of social security benefits exceeds the present value of a worker's payroll tax contributions. This net wealth increment variable did not have a significant effect on household asset accumulation before retirement. Kotlikoff concluded, therefore, that "since the argument for an historic aggregate reduction in savings involves the life cycle theory and the wealth increment effect, the findings lend little support to the notion that social security has reduced the capital stock."[38]

INTERNATIONAL EVIDENCE. International cross-sectional studies of social security and savings also provide mixed results. Feldstein examined both the retirement and benefit effects of social security on the saving rates in a cross-sectional sample of fifteen developed countries.[39] Estimates of saving functions and a model of retirement behavior were made, and the two results were combined to assess the net impact of intercountry differences in social security on private saving. The results indicate that a 25 percent increase in the ratio of benefits to income reduces the saving rate by about 2.7 percentage points, or about one-fifth of the sample average rate of saving (12.7 percent). At the same time, higher benefits induce a 6.2 percentage point decline in the labor force participation of the aged, causing a 1.5

37. Laurence J. Kotlikoff, "Testing the Theory of Social Security and Life Cycle Accumulation," *American Economic Review*, vol. 69 (June 1979), pp. 396–410.

38. Ibid., p. 408.

39. Martin Feldstein, "Social Security and Private Savings: International Evidence in an Extended Life Cycle Model," in Martin Feldstein and Robert Inman, eds., *The Economics of Public Services* (Macmillan, 1977).

percent increase in the saving rate, for a final reduction in the private saving rate of 1.2 percent. A later study, for which improved data permitted the inclusion of the benefit replacement rate rather than average benefits per recipient, confirmed the earlier results.[40]

Recent studies of international cross-sectional data by other economists contradict Feldstein's findings. In their 1979 study of sixteen industrial countries, Barro and MacDonald were unable to find any evidence that social security depressed private saving.[41] Similarly, in a recent study of the saving rates in twenty-one OECD countries over the period 1960–70, Modigliani and Sterling found that the social security benefit effect and the retirement effect roughly offset each other, indicating that the net impact of social security on saving is close to zero.[42] Moreover, a cross-country analysis by Kopits and Gotur found that social security had a net positive effect on household saving ratios in fourteen industrial countries.[43]

The conclusion that social security has had no adverse effect on personal saving appears to be confirmed by studies for individual countries. In a recent volume economists examined the impact of social security programs in Canada, Great Britain, West Germany, France, and Sweden.[44] In four of the five countries analyzed, no evidence was found to support the contention that social security has depressed personal saving. In the fifth country, Sweden, where the social security program is heavily funded, the reduction in personal saving was more than offset by the growth of fund assets. Thus the international evidence, like the time-series studies and the microeconomic analysis, provides no indication that social security has adversely affected private saving.

40. Martin Feldstein, "International Differences in Social Security and Saving," Working Paper 355 (National Bureau of Economic Research, May 1979).

41. Robert J. Barro and Glenn M. MacDonald, "Social Security and Consumer Spending in an International Cross Section," *Journal of Public Economics,* vol. 11 (June 1979), pp. 275–89.

42. Franco Modigliani and Arlie Sterling, "Determinants of Private Saving with Special Reference to the Role of Social Security—Cross Country Tests," Working Paper 1209-81 (Alfred P. Sloan School of Management, Massachusetts Institute of Technology, 1981).

43. George Kopits and Padma Gotur, "The Influence of Social Security on Household Savings: A Cross-Country Investigation," *International Monetary Fund Staff Paper,* vol. 27 (March 1980), p. 182.

44. George M. von Furstenberg, *Social Security versus Private Savings* (Ballinger, 1979), chaps. 4–8.

The Interaction of Social Security and Private Pensions

Regardless of its effect on aggregate saving, social security clearly has a unique relationship with saving done through private pension plans. The social security and private pension systems, which developed simultaneously, are alternative vehicles to achieve a targeted level of guaranteed retirement benefits. In fact, many private plans are explicitly integrated with social security and therefore reduce private pension benefits as social security benefits are increased.[45] If the average social security benefit had been established initially at current levels, the private pension system as we know it today might not exist. As discussed in chapter 2, an empirical analysis of the interaction of social security and private pensions reveals that a dollar of social security contributions tends to displace roughly 74 cents of private pension saving (see appendix A for model and regression results).

The key question is whether these results are inconsistent with the time-series evidence, which shows that the introduction of the social security system caused no reduction in aggregate saving. The apparent inconsistency can be eliminated by considering two states of the world—before 1935 and after 1935. During the nineteenth and early twentieth century, only a small minority provided for their old age by saving during their working years. Instead, the family farm, the predominant institution in the nineteenth century, allowed family members to reduce their work effort gradually as they grew older. When the elderly were no longer able to work, they were supported by their children. Even with the advent of industrialization, urban workers often would provide shelter and support for their elderly parents. Thus, before social security, a widespread pay-as-you-go pension system was already in operation. The social security program was a response to the devastating economic impact of the Depression, which shattered people's confidence in their tradition of self-reliance and created a psychological environment conducive to the establishment of organized saving programs. Through the passage of the Social Security Act, the federal government introduced a national pension scheme that relieved children of their traditional role of supporting their elderly parents. In effect, a public pay-as-you-go program was substituted for the existing system of private pay-as-you-go arrange-

45. See the section on integration in chapter 2.

ments. Thus social security would not be expected to affect aggregate saving.

Even though social security has not reduced the saving rate below pre-1935 levels, it has probably curbed the growth in saving that would have occurred had all organized saving been achieved through funded private pension plans. Since private plans accumulate funds in anticipation of future benefit payments, they would have added to saving, whereas social security, financed on a pay-as-you-go basis, had a neutral effect. As the empirical work indicated, a dollar increase in social security contributions implies that about a dollar less in benefits will be provided through private plans. To the extent that social security has checked the growth in private plans, the saving rate has not increased as much as it would have if all retirement saving were funded. In short, aggregate saving today is probably higher than it would have been without organized retirement programs, but lower than if all institutionalized saving had been accomplished through private pension plans.

Conclusion

The analysis of the effect of private pensions and social security on saving was undertaken to evaluate the potential effects on saving and capital formation of expanding social security or private plans at the margin.

Neither economic theory nor the scant empirical data provide a clearcut answer to the effect of private pension plans on saving. However, a reasonable conjecture might be that people reduce their own saving by 65 cents for each dollar of private pension saving, resulting in a net savings increase of 35 cents. It is impossible to determine whether this net increase is due to the favorable tax provisions or to such other features of private plans as uncertainty about future benefits, forced saving, and induced retirement. Nevertheless, if one were to assume that the entire increase is attributable to the tax treatment, would the net increment to saving justify the tax expenditure? In 1981 the tax expenditure amounted to $14.7 billion, and the net increase in private saving resulting from the $61.3 billion of contributions to private plans might have been (0.35 × $61.3) $21.5 billion.[46]

46. Treasury estimates (upon which the tax expenditure calculations are based) indicate that employers contributed $61.3 billion to private plans in 1981. Their actual contributions were probably higher, as indicated by the $64.8 billion estimate for 1980, shown in table 2-1.

Little evidence exists to support the contention that the pay-as-you-go social security program has depressed personal saving in the past. To a large extent social security probably replaced existing intergenerational transfers. Moreover, social security was introduced during the Depression and, insofar as social security exceeded existing intrafamily transfers, the wealth effect for the first generation of retirees may have led to higher consumption, income, and saving. Finally, social security is now very close to an actuarially fair system under which the present value of benefits will be roughly equal to the present value of taxes for the average young worker. Such a system will have no effect on the lifetime income or saving of covered persons and therefore would not be expected to have any impact on capital accumulation in the economy.

What, then, is the relative impact of private pensions and social security on saving? The answer is that at this stage expanding the funded private pension system would probably have a slightly more favorable impact on saving than increasing the pay-as-you-go social security program. It is important to note, however, that the positive impact of private pensions on saving can be expected to continue only until the system matures. At that time, contributions to private plans will equal benefit payments in each year, and private pensions, like social security, will exert no further influence on aggregate saving.

chapter five **Pension Plans as Financial Intermediaries**

By channeling money from savers to investors, private pension plans serve as major financial intermediaries. The enormous growth of these and other intermediaries during the postwar period has altered the financial structure of the United States and caused concern about the increased concentration of assets among institutional investors. This chapter examines the role of pensions as financial intermediaries, documents the investment patterns of pension funds, explores the performance of these funds, and summarizes the scant evidence available on the influence of pension funds on capital markets.

Assets of Private Pensions

Private pensions are employer promises of retirement income to employees who meet certain qualifying standards. The employer finances the retirement benefits with annual contributions throughout the employee's work life and accumulates the contributions in a fund that is invested to earn a return.[1] A pension plan is usually funded either through a group annuity contract offered by a life insurance company or through a trust established by the employer and administered by a bank or trust company.[2]

In the typical pension trust the employer engages the services of an

1. As noted earlier, some plans require contributions from the employee as well as the employer. But since employee contributions accounted for less than 6 percent of total contributions in 1980, private plans can be characterized as financed primarily by employers (see table 2-1).

2. Plans funded through an insurance company are sometimes referred to as insured plans; those funded through a bank or trust company are sometimes called trusteed or noninsured plans. In practice, many plans split their portfolios and provide financial arrangements through both a trust and an insurance company.

Table 5-1. Private Pension Assets Held in Trust or by Life Insurers, Selected Years, 1945–80

Amounts in billions of dollars

Year	Held in trust[a]		Held by life insurers[b]	
	Amount	Percent of total	Amount	Percent of total
1945	2.8	51.9	2.6	48.1
1950	6.5	53.7	5.6	46.3
1955	16.1	58.8	11.3	41.2
1960	33.1	63.8	18.8	36.2
1965	59.2	68.4	27.3	31.6
1970	97.0	70.8	40.1	29.2
1975	145.2	68.3	67.4	31.7
1980	256.9	62.8	151.0	37.0

Sources: Alfred M. Skolnik, "Private Pension Plans, 1950–74," *Social Security Bulletin,* vol. 39 (June 1976), p. 4; Martha Yohalem, "Employee Benefit Plans, 1975," *Social Security Bulletin,* vol. 40 (November 1977), p. 27; Securities and Exchange Commission, *Monthly Statistical Review,* vol. 40 (May 1981), p. 10; and American Council of Life Insurance, *Life Insurance Fact Book, 1972* (ACLI, 1972), p.40, *Life Insurance Fact Book, 1978* (ACLI, 1978), p. 54, and *Life Insurance Fact Book, 1981* (ACLI, 1981), p. 54.

a. These data may substantially understate the amount of pension assets held in trust. In a recent study of 5500 forms filed by pension funds for the 1977 plan year, the Department of Labor concluded that private pension assets held in trust are at least $100 billion more than the traditionally accepted figure provided by the Securities and Exchange Commission. The SEC estimate includes neither the assets of plans that invest part of their money through insurance companies and part through trusts nor the assets of plans formed after 1967, the benchmark for the survey. See Department of Labor, *Preliminary Estimates of Participant and Financial Characteristics of Private Pension Plans, 1977* (GPO, 1981). For consistency with earlier years, however, data for the pension assets held in trust are based on SEC estimates.

b. Does not include individual retirement accounts or tax-sheltered annuities, and includes only 40 percent of Keogh plans, which are assumed to be established by self-employed people for their employees. Since the data in table 5-4 include IRAs, tax-sheltered annuities, and 100 percent of Keogh plans, the pension assets in that table exceed the figures shown above.

actuary to determine annual contributions to the plan and employs a bank or trust company to serve as trustee. But the trustee does not necessarily have sole discretion over investment decisions, and in many cases advice may be purchased from an investment consultant, who becomes the effective manager of the assets. In some cases the employer may retain the authority to select investments or at least to approve a list of eligible securities recommended by the investment manager. Multiemployer plans are a subgroup of trust fund plans that, under the Taft-Hartley Act, are administered by a joint union-employer trusteeship.[3]

3. The Taft-Hartley Act, passed in 1947, states that all plans established after January 1, 1946, that require negotiated employer contributions to a fund be administered jointly by employers and employees. In contrast to these relatively new and numerous multiemployer plans that are jointly administered, a few large older union funds are administered solely by the union. See H. Robert Bartell, Jr., and Elizabeth T. Simpson, "Pension Funds of Multiemployer Industrial Groups, Unions and Nonprofit Organizations," Occasional Paper 105 (National Bureau of Economic Research, 1968), pp. 1–3.

Table 5-2. Distribution of Assets of Pension Trusts, Selected Years, 1946–80

Amounts in billions of dollars

Type of asset	1946 [a] Amount	Per-cent	1950 [a] Amount	Per-cent	1955 Amount	Per-cent	1960 Amount	Per-cent	1965 Amount	Per-cent	1970 Amount	Per-cent	1975 Amount	Per-cent	1980 Amount	Per-cent
Market value																
Cash and deposits	0.1	2.8	0.3	4.3	0.4	2.2	0.5	1.3	0.9	1.2	1.8	1.7	3.0	2.1	9.3	3.1
U.S. government securities	1.5	41.7	2.3	32.9	2.9	15.9	2.7	7.3	2.9	4.0	3.0	2.9	11.1	7.6	26.3	8.9
Corporate and other bonds	0.9	25.0	2.8	40.0	7.9	43.4	15.6	39.4	22.7	30.0	24.9	23.8	34.5	23.7	60.0	20.0
Stock	0.3	8.3	1.1	15.7	6.1	33.5	16.5	44.5	40.8	56.0	67.1	64.1	88.6	60.8	175.8	59.2
Mortgages	*	*	0.1	1.4	0.3	1.7	1.3	3.5	3.4	4.7	3.5	3.3	2.1	1.4	3.8	1.3
Other assets	0.8	22.2	0.4	5.7	0.6	3.3	1.4	3.8	3.0	4.1	4.4	4.2	6.3	4.3	22.0	7.4
Total	3.6	100.0	7.0	100.0	18.2	100.0	37.1	100.0	72.9	100.0	104.7	100.0	145.6	99.9	297.2	100.0
Book value																
Cash and deposits	...	...	...	...	0.4	2.5	0.5	1.5	0.9	1.5	1.8	1.9	3.0	2.1	9.3	3.6
U.S. government securities	...	...	...	...	3.0	18.5	2.7	8.2	3.0	5.1	3.0	3.1	10.8	7.4	28.3	11.0
Corporate and other bonds	...	...	...	...	7.9	48.8	15.7	47.4	23.1	39.0	29.7	30.6	37.8	26.0	63.9	24.8
Stock	...	...	...	...	4.0	24.7	11.5	34.7	25.9	43.8	53.5	55.1	84.8	58.4	129.8	50.5
Mortgages	...	...	...	...	0.3	1.8	1.3	3.9	3.4	5.7	4.2	4.3	2.4	1.7	4.1	1.6
Other assets	...	...	...	...	0.6	3.7	1.4	4.2	2.9	4.9	4.9	5.0	6.4	4.4	21.5	8.4
Total	...	...	...	...	16.2	100.0	33.1	100.0	59.2	100.0	97.0	100.0	145.2	100.0	256.9	100.0

Sources: Board of Governors of the Federal Reserve System, *Flow of Funds Accounts, 1946–1975: Annual Total Flows and Year-End Assets and Liabilities* (The Board, 1976). pp. 125–27; *Securities and Exchange Commission, Statistical Bulletin*, vol. 38 (July 1979), pp. 6, 10; and SEC, *Monthly Statistical Review*, vol. 40 (May 1981), p. 10. Figures are rounded.
* Less than $0.05 billion.
a. Market values of equities; book value of bonds.

As seen in table 5-1, the assets held in pension trusts have constituted a relatively stable proportion of total pension holdings—approximately 60 percent over the period 1945–80. In the beginning of the period pension trust assets grew faster than those held by life insurers, primarily because banks and trust companies could invest in common stocks, whereas the equity investments of life insurance companies were restricted by state insurance laws. As insurance laws were revised during the 1960s to allow life companies to hold pension assets in "separate accounts" that could be invested in common stocks, life insurers slowly began to recover their share of the market for pension assets. The relative importance of pension trusts therefore declined over the 1970s, and by 1980 only 63 percent of pension assets were held in trusts.

The portfolio distribution of pension trusts has changed markedly since the mid-1940s, as illustrated in table 5-2. In 1946 approximately two-thirds of the market value of total assets was invested in government securities and corporate bonds, while less than 10 percent was held in stock. By 1970 the proportions had changed dramatically, with stocks accounting for over 64 percent and bond holdings for only 27 percent of the total portfolio. Stocks declined somewhat in importance during the 1970s, amounting to 59 percent of total assets in 1980. If book values are assumed, the pattern of holdings is similar except that stocks account for a consistently lower proportion of total assets, peaking at 58 percent of the portfolio in 1975 and declining to 50 percent in 1980.

Pension assets held by life insurance companies are invested quite differently from those held in pension trusts. Because life insurance pension assets are combined with other assets managed by life insurance companies, their portfolio mix is similar to that of the overall holdings of the life insurance industry. The exception, of course, occurs when life insurers hold pension assets in separate accounts, which can be entirely invested in common stocks. In 1980, 20 percent of pension assets held by life companies—or $33.4 billion—were held in separate accounts; 47 percent of these funds were invested in common stocks.[4] As pensions have grown, pension fund assets have constituted an increasingly important component of the reserves of insurance companies. Whereas in 1946 pension fund assets accounted for less than 7 percent of total holdings, by 1980 they constituted 37.8 percent of total life insurance assets (see table 5-3).

4. American Council of Life Insurance, *Pension Facts, 1981* (Washington, D.C.: ACLI, 1981), p. 17.

Table 5-3. Distribution of Assets of Life Insurance Companies, Selected Years, 1946–80

| | Percent of total assets | | |
Year	Life insurance	Pension fund	Other
1946	86.0	6.9	7.1
1950	82.8	9.5	7.7
1955	77.1	13.8	9.2
1960	72.6	17.4	10.0
1965	69.7	19.3	11.1
1970	65.5	21.9	12.6
1975	59.4	27.0	13.3
1980	48.7	37.8	12.6

Sources: Board of Governors of the Federal Reserve System, *Flow of Funds Accounts, 1946–1975*, pp. 125–27, and *Flow of Funds Accounts: Assets and Liabilities Outstanding, 1957–80* (The Board, 1981), p. 27. Figures are rounded.

As shown in table 5-4, the portfolio of life insurance companies is surprisingly different from the asset profile of pension trusts. Since both intermediaries have sizable and predetermined inflows of funds and actuarially determinable liabilities, they might be expected to have similar asset structures. Yet pension trusts hold over half their assets in corporate equities, whereas insurance companies hold only one-tenth of their assets in that form. Likewise, insurance companies have invested one-third of their assets in mortgages, while pension trusts have traditionally allocated 1 to 4 percent of their portfolios to mortgages. The reasons for these dissimilar investment patterns seem to be institutional rather than economic.

Common Stock

Life insurance companies have historically been conservative investors on the presumption that their fundamental objective should be to match the maturity of assets to that of liabilities in order to achieve a secure cash flow. Their investment strategy is geared to minimize capital risk and interest rate risk simultaneously. Moreover, various statutory and institutional considerations have limited the investment alternatives for these companies' general accounts. Most life insurance company assets are held by companies licensed in New York, and originally New York state law prohibited any investment of life insurers' assets in corporate stock. Even with a relaxation of this restriction in 1951 that allowed investment of up to 3 percent of total assets in common stock, and subsequent amendments that gradually raised the limit to 10 percent, insurance companies' general accounts still face a severe constraint. Besides the limit on the amount of equity holdings, the New York law also prescribes the type of company whose stock is eligible for purchase.[5]

How much these statutory limitations have inhibited life insurance company investments in corporate equities is debatable. After the first liberalization of New York law in 1951, life insurance companies invested 40 percent less in stocks than in the previous year.[6] Moreover, a 1959 survey of the industry revealed that most insurance companies opposed substituting the "prudent man" rule for statutory limitations. But at the same time more than half the industry wanted the New York state law liberalized to allow 10 percent of a portfolio to be invested in stocks.[7] Nevertheless, most experts agree that state regulations have reinforced the life insurance companies' conservative investment policies.

These policies are further reinforced by the rules governing valuation of assets. According to standards set by the National Association of Insurance Commissioners, life companies should value bonds and preferred stocks at amortized cost and common stocks at market value.[8] For each of their investment classes they must then make annual contributions to a mandatory securities valuation reserve. The amount of a company's required contribution for bonds and preferred stocks is determined by the commissioners' annual classification of these securities. In the case of common stock, the company must contribute 1 percent of the market value of its common stock portfolio as of December 31 of each year. Net realized and unrealized gains are credited to the reserve until it reaches a certain amount; thereafter, they are added to surplus. Net realized and unrealized losses are charged to the reserve until it reaches zero, and thereafter are charged to surplus. Under these valuation procedures, investment in high-grade, long-term bonds requires minimal contributions to the valuation reserve and is unlikely to

5. A company must have paid a dividend in each of the previous ten years, and dividends must not have exceeded earnings in any year. See *Institutional Investor Study Report of the Securities and Exchange Commission Supplementary Vol. 1*, 92 Cong. 1 sess. (Government Printing Office, 1971), p. 219.

6. Andrew Brimmer, *Life Insurance Companies in the Capital Market* (East Lansing: Michigan State University Press, 1961), pp. 340–41.

7. Ibid., pp. 347–57.

8. According to New York insurance law, the superintendent of insurance can specify many of the valuation procedures for life company investments and may require compliance with the National Association of Insurance Commissioners' approved standards. See J. David Cummins, ed., *The Investment Activities of Life Insurance Companies* (Irwin, 1977), pp. 331–32.

Table 5-4. Distribution of Assets of Pension Plans Funded through Life Insurers, Selected Years, 1946–80
Amounts in billions of dollars

Type of asset	1946 Amount	1946 Per-cent	1950 Amount	1950 Per-cent	1955 Amount	1955 Per-cent	1960 Amount	1960 Per-cent	1965 Amount	1965 Per-cent	1970 Amount	1970 Per-cent	1975 Amount	1975 Per-cent	1980 Amount	1980 Per-cent
Cash and deposits	*	1.6	0.1	1.6	0.2	1.4	0.2	1.1	0.3	1.0	0.4	0.9	0.5	0.7	1.1	0.7
U.S. government securities	1.4	45.6	1.2	21.5	1.1	9.8	1.1	5.6	0.9	3.4	0.9	2.3	1.6	2.2	6.0	3.6
Corporate and other bonds	0.9	28.9	2.3	41.4	5.0	44.6	8.4	44.6	11.4	41.9	15.9	38.5	28.4	39.3	65.5	39.5
Stock	0.1	2.6	0.2	3.4	0.5	4.1	0.8	4.3	1.6[a]	5.9	3.2[a]	7.7	7.2[a]	10.0	18.6[a]	11.2
Mortgages	0.5	15.1	1.4	25.7	3.8	33.5	6.8	36.1	10.6	38.9	15.2	37.0	3.0	31.9	46.4	28.0
Other Assets	0.2	6.2	0.4	6.4	0.7	6.6	1.5	8.2	2.4	8.9	5.6	13.6	11.4	15.8	28.2	17.0
Total	3.1	100.0	5.6	100.0	11.3	100.0	18.8	100.0	27.3	100.0	41.2	100.0	72.2	100.0	165.8	100.0

Sources: Same as table 5-3. Figures are rounded.
* Less than $0.5 billion.
a. Includes stocks held in separate accounts.

have a great effect on surplus. Conversely, common stock investments, which are valued as of one day of the year, can exhaust the common stock component of the reserve and draw on surplus. This valuation system therefore tends to encourage investment in high-grade corporate bonds and to discourage investment in lower-grade debt issues and common stock.

In contrast to insurance companies, pension trusts are unconstrained by stringent state laws restricting investments in stocks, and they also pursue very different investment goals. In the decade after World War II, the managers of pension trusts quickly sold off the government securities they had accumulated during the war and converted primarily to investment in corporate stocks and bonds. Because interest rates on government long-term bonds were pegged at 2.5 percent and private bond rates were at similar levels, the higher return on common stocks provided a strong inducement to increase holdings of corporate equities. The largest companies with established records were the obvious investment vehicle. In the 1960s, as the management of pension assets moved somewhat from bank trust departments or self-management to private investment advisers, the increased competition for control of pension assets put emphasis on short-run gains available through investment in corporate equities. Although the market decline in 1973–74 slowed the growth of stocks as a component of pension trust portfolios, equities still accounted for more than half of total pension trust holdings in 1980.

Mortgages

Mortgages constitute the other main asset group in which the holdings of life insurance companies and pension trusts diverge. Mortgages, particularly residential mortgages, are certainly a logical investment for either intermediary, since the liabilities of life insurance and pensions both represent long-term, predictable commitments. Mortgages bear a fixed rate of return, regular payments of interest over the life of the loan, and scheduled repayment in a fixed number of dollars. Investment in such long-term obligations would provide a stable cash flow that matches the contractual obligations made by both life insurance companies and pension trusts. Yet in 1980 pension trusts held less than 2 percent of their total reserves in mortgages, whereas mortgages constituted 28 percent of the portfolios of life insurance companies.

Since the turn of the century, insurance companies have traditionally invested about 30 percent of their portfolio in mortgages.[9] Except for the years 1932–36 and 1942–45, periods marked by depression and war, mortgage holdings have increased every year.[10] After a low level of residential construction during the Depression and the war years, the need for more adequate housing in the postwar era substantially increased the demand for residential mortgage credit. In response to increased rates of return on home mortgages, life insurance companies reentered the home mortgage market and increased their mortgage lending. Home mortgages continued to play an important role in life company acquisitions through 1960, at which point life insurers began to shift out of home mortgage and into commercial mortgage lending (see table 5-5). This shift can be attributed, among other factors, to the attractive yields and the relatively short effective maturities of commercial mortgages (three to five years). Thus between 1960 and 1980 the importance of residential loans declined dramatically, and commercial mortgages increased from 24 to 62 percent of life insurers' total mortgage holdings (see table 5-6).

Pension trusts have allocated only a very small and declining portion of their portfolios to mortgages. Although unfavorable economic characteristics are often cited as reasons for the deficiency of mortgage lending, the lack of mortgage investment by pension trusts can be largely attributed to two institutional factors. First, the delegation of investment management authority to trustees outside the corporation tends to discourage investment in mortgages. About 65 percent of pension trust assets are managed by commercial bank and trust departments.[11] These

9. Life Insurance Association of America, *Life Insurance Companies as Financial Institutions,* prepared for the Commission on Money and Credit (Englewood Cliffs, N.J.: Prentice-Hall, 1962), p. 45.

10. The 1930s were years in which lenders, faced with serious delinquencies on mortgage loans in which the underlying security was depreciating rapidly, were forced to take title, either through foreclosure or voluntary conveyance, to protect policyholders, depositors, and stockholders. As a result, the decline in mortgage investments by life insurance companies was matched in part by a rise in their real-estate holdings. During the war years shortages of materials and manpower for nondefense construction sharply limited the demands for mortgage financing. Repayments of oustanding mortgages exceeded extensions of new mortgages, which reduced the holdings of these investments and made funds available for the acquisition of other assets—primarily U.S. government securities.

11. According to unpublished data from the Securities and Exchange Commission, in 1975, 15 percent of assets held by pension trusts were managed internally, 64 percent were managed by external banks and trusts, and 21 percent were managed by external investment advisers.

Table 5-5. Percent Distribution of Net Annual Purchases of Selected Externally Acquired Financial Assets of U.S. Life Insurance Companies, 1950–80

Year	Total purchases (billions of dollars)	Corporate shares	U.S. government securities	Corporate bonds	Mortgages Home	Commercial	Multi-family	Open market paper
1950	4.0	7.9	−45.3	45.5	59.6	7.6	8.0	...
1951	3.8	1.4	−64.5	71.4	53.3	12.2	10.9	...
1952	4.7	3.5	−16.6	66.0	24.4	7.6	5.5	...
1953	4.8	1.9	−8.8	56.3	30.0	7.9	1.6	...
1954	5.1	5.3	−14.9	41.2	38.4	9.7	0.8	...
1955	5.2	1.3	−9.5	32.7	48.2	11.3	2.8	...
1956	5.3	0.0	−19.3	41.5	46.6	15.2	1.2	...
1957	4.8	0.9	−11.0	56.3	27.3	18.7	−1.3	...
1958	5.1	1.5	4.0	47.1	18.3	16.0	−0.1	0.3
1959	5.1	3.8	−5.7	41.2	23.7	12.7	2.3	2.0
1960	5.1	6.9	−8.1	33.3	25.4	18.1	3.9	3.5
1961	5.7	8.2	−5.0	43.9	15.7	16.9	6.8	−1.8
1962	6.3	6.9	0.5	39.7	9.5	21.8	7.9	2.4
1963	6.6	3.7	−4.9	42.4	14.5	25.7	9.0	0.5
1964	7.4	7.4	−3.1	31.1	16.1	13.6	25.6	−1.8
1965	8.3	8.5	−5.3	33.7	12.8	20.5	19.0	0.5
1966	7.2	3.7	−1.8	33.3	8.9	28.6	20.5	1.2
1967	7.8	13.0	−3.1	48.7	−6.0	20.8	18.3	1.3
1968	8.2	16.5	−2.0	45.1	−8.9	23.4	12.6	0.6
1969	7.0	24.4	−3.4	24.3	−19.7	28.3	21.2	12.0
1970	7.7	25.8	0.8	19.5	−11.5	20.7	22.9	10.1
1971	11.7	31.1	−1.0	47.0	−18.1	21.7	6.4	5.4
1972	13.5	25.9	0.8	51.9	−17.3	23.0	4.4	1.6
1973	14.7	24.2	−1.6	40.1	−12.6	33.3	7.5	0.2
1974	13.9	16.5	0.8	28.8	−10.1	34.2	8.4	7.7
1975	19.0	10.1	9.0	47.9	−7.5	21.2	0.4	3.9
1976	26.8	11.1	5.7	63.0	−5.6	13.7	−1.7	1.5
1977	29.5	4.0	5.5	63.6	−4.6	18.7	−1.3	−1.1
1978	33.2	−0.3	6.2	52.1	−0.8	23.2	0.7	4.4
1979	33.1	0.0	9.0	35.0	5.0	27.0	1.0	5.0
1980	31.6	4.0	9.0	28.0	5.0	30.0	1.0	7.0

Sources: Robert A. Rennie, "Investment Strategy for the Life Insurance Company," in J. David Cummins, ed., *Investment Activities of Life Insurance Companies* (Irwin, 1977); and author's calculations based on data in Board of Governors of the Federal Reserve System, *Flow of Funds Accounts, 1949–1978* (The Board, 1979), pp. 39, 57, and *Flow of Funds Accounts, 3rd Quarter 1981* (November 1981), pp. 25, 37–39.

trustees generally lack knowledge about mortgages as investment possibilities and do not have the staff expertise needed to engage in extensive conventional mortgage lending. Second, responsibility for pension fund performance within the corporation usually rests with the corporate treasurer, a position that is traditionally a step in the career ladder of young executives. Because of the relatively short tenure of corporate

Table 5-6. Percent Distribution of Mortgages Held by Life Insurance Companies, Selected Years, 1946–80

Year	Total (billions of dollars)	Farm	Residential		Commercial
			1–4 families	Multifamily	
1946	7.2	11.1	35.6	20.5	32.8
1950	16.1	8.1	52.8	16.1	23.0
1955	29.4	7.8	59.8	12.2	20.3
1960	41.8	7.2	59.6	9.3	24.0
1965	60.0	8.0	49.3	14.7	28.0
1970	74.4	7.5	36.0	21.5	34.9
1975	89.4	7.6	19.7	22.0	50.7
1980	131.1	9.8	13.7	15.0	61.6

Sources: Board of Governors of the Federal Reserve System, *Flow of Funds Accounts, 1946–1975*, pp. 146–51, and *Flow of Funds Accounts: Assets and Liabilities Outstanding, 1957–80*, pp. 41–43. Figures are rounded.

treasurers, performance evaluation has usually been based on measures of short-term portfolio gains rather than on long-term risk-adjusted returns.[12] This focus on short-term performance encourages corporate managers to invest in stocks that are expected to appreciate significantly over a short period.

MORTGAGE CHARACTERISTICS. The importance of institutional considerations becomes apparent when the economic characteristics of mortgages are considered. Both the yield and risk associated with mortgages should make them a desirable investment for pension funds—especially in view of the recent innovations in the mortgage market. Mortgage rates compared favorably over the period 1960–80 with the rates on Moody's Aaa corporate bonds, which are roughly equivalent in terms of risk and capital loss characteristics (see table 5-7). The rate on mortgages insured by the Federal Housing Administration (FHA) in the secondary market exceeded the yield in Aaa bonds by more than 100 basis points during the 1960s and averaged more than 60 basis points higher during the 1970s.[13] The contract rate on conventional mortgages for new homes has also consistently exceeded the Aaa bond rate. During the 1960s the rate on FHA mortgages even exceeded the rate on Baa bonds—a rate that may be more typical of yields on those

12. Actually, over time, increasing attention has been focused on risk-adjusted returns as managers have become more aware of the trade-off between risk and yield.

13. Of course, once the servicing costs for mortgages are considered, the effective yield would be 0.38 to 0.50 percent lower on a single-family home and 0.10 percent lower on large multifamily projects.

Table 5-7. Yields on Mortgages and Corporate Bonds, 1960–80
Percent

	Mortgages		Corporate bonds	
Year	FHA insured[a]	Conventional[b]	Aaa	Baa
1960	6.24	6.08	4.41	5.19
1961	5.86	5.81	4.35	5.08
1962	5.75	5.71	4.33	5.02
1963	5.46	5.84	4.26	4.86
1964	5.45	5.78	4.40	4.83
1965	5.47	5.74	4.49	4.87
1966	6.38	6.14	5.13	5.67
1967	6.55	6.33	5.51	6.23
1968	7.21	6.83	6.18	6.94
1969	8.29	7.66	7.03	7.81
1970	9.05	8.27	8.04	9.11
1971	7.70	7.60	7.39	8.56
1972	7.53	7.45	7.21	8.16
1973	8.19	7.78	7.44	8.24
1974	9.55	8.71	8.57	9.50
1975	9.19	8.75	8.83	10.61
1976	8.82	8.76	8.43	9.75
1977	8.68	8.80	8.02	8.97
1978	9.70	9.30	8.73	9.49
1979	10.87	10.48	9.63	10.69
1980	13.42	12.25	11.94	13.67

Sources: *Federal Reserve Bulletin,* vol. 50 (December 1964), p. 1564; vol. 54 (December 1968), p. A51; vol. 58 (December 1972), p. A55; vol. 62 (December 1976), p. A45; vol. 65 (December 1979), p. A40; vol. 67 (May 1981), p. A38; and Moody's Investors Service, *Moody's Industrial Manual* (New York: MIS, 1980), vol. 1, pp. A34–A37.

a. Average gross yields on thirty-year, minimum downpayment, Federal Housing Administration–insured first mortgages for immediate delivery in the private secondary market.

b. Contract rate on conventional mortgages in the primary market.

bonds purchased by pension funds through private placement.[14] Although this relationship was reversed in the early seventies, the FHA rate once again rose above the Baa in 1978 and 1979, and then dropped slightly below in 1980.

The measure of an asset's risk as well as its yield plays a prominent role in portfolio choice. In the case of mortgages there are two classes of risks: capital loss and default. Capital loss risk arises from interest rate fluctuations that affect the market value of any fixed coupon debt instrument. One estimate of this type of risk is the standard deviation

14. "During the 1961–1977 period, the average yield on privately placed corporate bonds exceeded those on publicly issued corporate bonds—of roughly similar quality, duration and tax treatment—by about 50 basis points." Burton Zwick, "Yields on Privately Placed Corporate Bonds," *Journal of Finance,* vol. 35 (March 1980), p. 23.

of an asset's total rate of return, which basically measures the dispersion around the expected return. Table 5-8 shows the average total returns, including changes in asset values, and standard deviations of total returns for mortgages, stocks, bonds, and U.S. Treasury bills over the periods 1960–80 and 1970–80. Naturally, the standard deviations for both mortgages and bonds were significantly below those for common stocks over the period. But the risk associated with mortgages was below that for both long-term government and corporate bonds, even in the 1970s, a period of high inflation.

Default risk refers to the possibility that the borrower will not repay the principal or interest, or both, on his outstanding debt obligations. The default risk is greatest for privately insured mortgages; it is mitigated for FHA or VA (Veterans Administration) mortgages by the government insurance as well as by the borrower's credit and the value of the underlying property.[15] In short, although there is some risk associated with privately owned mortgages, the default risk associated with FHA- and VA-insured mortgages is minimal and probably comparable to that of the highest quality corporate bond.

Pension fund managers, however, have not taken into account these favorable economic characteristics of mortgages. In addition, they have been put off by the perceived illiquidity of mortgages—that is, the inability of investors to readily convert the asset into cash. Ironically, pension funds have very little need for liquidity, since they have fairly predictable cash outflow requirements and have generally experienced a net inflow of funds. But despite the lack of any fundamental need for liquidity, fund managers usually prefer liquid assets, which enable them to take advantage of market swings. In reality, the mortgage is not as

---

15. The risk of default under FHA insurance is small. After three months of delinquent payments, foreclosure begins, the mortgagee taking title to the property and subsequently assigning title to FHA. FHA then settles the mortgagees' insurance claim through a cash payment covering the outstanding unpaid balance of the mortgage and all the payments made by the mortgagee since default. FHA also pays two-thirds of all attorney fees and court costs, thereby limiting the loss to one-third of the legal costs and about one month's interest on the loan. The risk of default under the VA-insured loan is slightly larger. Although the foreclosure procedure is similar, the Veterans Administration has the option of limiting its guarantee payment to $17,500, thereby forcing the mortgagee to reduce the remaining loss through the sale of the property. The risk of loss is somewhat greater for private mortgage insurance, since the mortgagee is protected only from the first 20 to 25 percent of the loss and must rely on the value of the property to provide additional protection. See Kenneth T. Rosen, "The Role of Pension Funds in Housing Finance," Working Paper 35 (Joint Center for Urban Studies of the Massachusetts Institute of Technology and Harvard University, June 1975), p. 51.

Table 5-8. Total Rates of Return and Standard Deviation of Returns for FHA Mortgages and Other Assets, 1960–80 and 1970–80
Percent

	1960–80				1970–80			
	Total return				Total return			
Asset	Average	Mini-mum	Maxi-mum	Standard deviation	Average	Mini-mum	Maxi-mum	Standard deviation
FHA mortgages	5.1	−6.7	16.1	5.2	5.9	−6.7	16.1	6.6
Common stocks	8.0	−26.5	37.2	17.0	8.0	−26.5	37.2	20.0
Long-term corporate bonds	3.6	−8.1	18.4	7.0	5.4	−3.1	18.4	9.0
Long-term government bonds	3.1	−9.2	16.8	7.0	4.6	−1.2	16.8	7.0
U.S. Treasury bills	5.4	2.1	11.2	2.0	6.8	3.8	11.2	2.0

Sources: Roger G. Ibbotson and Rex A. Sinquefield, "Stocks, Bonds, Bills and Inflation: Year-by-Year Historical Returns (1926–1974)," *The Journal of Business,* vol. 49 (January 1976), pp. 20–31, and updates from Ibbotson and Sinquefield. Standard deviations and total returns for FHA mortgages are author's calculations.

illiquid as it is often assumed to be, since the prepayment system provides a high degree of liquidity. In fact, these prepayments reduce the actual average life of a mortgage from the nominal term of twenty-five to thirty years specified in most contracts to ten to twelve years. Moreover, the growing importance of the secondary mortgage market through the presence of the Federal National Mortgage Association and the Federal Home Loan Mortgage Corporation has increased liquidity considerably.[16]

Insured and guaranteed mortgages may be unattractive to fund managers because after three years they frequently can be paid off without penalty at the discretion of the borrower.[17] The possibility of prepayment is detrimental to the lender because, rather than being guaranteed a high-yielding investment, he may be forced to accept prepayment and therefore to reinvest his capital at lower rates of interest. But since many corporate bonds have call features or sinking funds, they too sometimes suffer from the unpredictability of prepayments.[18]

One final factor influencing portfolio choice is information and transaction costs. Mortgages have traditionally been viewed as involving high

16. These two agencies do not provide a true secondary market, since they will not accept mortgages originated more than one year before their purchase.

17. Under many state laws prepayment penalties cannot be applied to insured and guaranteed home mortgages for more than three years after the origination date of the mortgage. Conventional mortgages—namely, mortgages that are not insured or guaranteed—may have any built-in prepayment penalties that the lender desires.

18. Callability refers to the right, often retained by the borrower, to repay the issue, usually because interest rates have fallen and it becomes advantageous to refinance at a lower rate. In addition, indentures on corporate issues often require that the issuer make annual payments to a sinking fund.

costs for the initial transaction and for servicing the loan. For example, mortgage lending requires a higher degree of staff expertise and legal talent than investments in publicly offered bonds or perhaps even private placements. But while mortgages do involve greater transaction costs, many of the difficulties of originating and servicing mortgages are eliminated by the mortgage banker. Moreover, despite high service costs (0.38 to 0.50 percent on a single family home; 0.10 percent on large multifamily projects), the net yield on mortgages is still substantial.[19] Finally, FHA and VA insurance eliminates some of the variability in yields, liquidity, and risk.

In short, though the stable flow of savings into pension funds could be used to provide a large and stable source of funds to the mortgage market, such has not been the case. The major obstacles appear to be institutional—namely, the management trustee system that delegates authority for pension trust investment decisions to commercial bank trust departments, which lack the necessary expertise for conventional mortgage lending, and the corporate structure whereby the treasurer's career potential depends in part on the short-run performance of the pension fund.

MORTGAGE-BACKED SECURITIES. Institutional factors also partially explain why pension funds have not been actively acquiring the new mortgage-backed securities issued by the Government National Mortgage Association (GNMA) and the Federal Home Loan Mortgage Corporation. Whereas until recently most mortgage investment involved direct holdings, the development of mortgage-backed securities has led to a proliferation of mortgage investment alternatives.

Mortgage-backed securities were originated by the GNMA, a federal agency created in 1968 primarily to provide subsidies for low-income housing. In 1970, however, the agency established a program whereby the government guarantees the timely payment of principal and interest on privately issued securities that are backed by pools of government-insured or government-guaranteed mortgages. GNMA pass-through securities pay monthly interest plus amortization of principal, whether or not collected by the servicer, together with any principal prepayment. The GNMA certificate rate is 50 basis points below the contract rate of the underlying mortgages: 44 basis points go to the originator for servicing and 6 to GNMA for providing the guarantees.[20] These pass-

19. Rosen, "Role of Pension Funds," p. 56.

20. Charles M. Sivesind, "Mortgage-Backed Securities: The Revolution in Real Estate Finance," *Quarterly Review*, vol. 4 (Federal Reserve Bank of New York, Autumn 1979), p. 4.

through securities were designed to appeal to pension funds and other institutional investors not wishing to originate and service their own mortgages. However, at the end of 1980 pension funds held only 9 percent of the $93.9 billion of outstanding GNMA certificates. Moreover, the bulk of this 9 percent was probably held by state-local pension plans rather than by private pension trusts.[21]

The other major mortgage-backed security was originated by the Federal Home Loan Mortgage Corporation, an agency created by Congress in 1970 that is wholly owned by the Federal Home Loan Banks. The agency's original goal was the development of a secondary market in conventional mortgages. Initially, the agency purchased conventional loans from thrift institutions for its own portfolio and financed these purchases by borrowing from the Treasury and the Federal Home Loan Banks and by issuing its own mortgage-backed bonds. In 1974, however, it started issuing mortgage participation certificates and guaranteed mortgage certificates.[22] Participation certificates are similar to GNMA certificates in that they represent ownership in pools of mortgages with a guaranteed pass-through of interest, scheduled amortization, and ultimate repayment of principal. But they are issued by the Federal Home Loan Mortgage Corporation rather than individual mortgage lenders and are insured by that agency rather than by the federal government. The originator services the loans for a fee of 0.375 percent, and the spread between the prices paid and received by the agency (usually 30 to 50 basis points) covers its insurance and administrative costs.

The guaranteed mortgage certificate provides a mortgage instrument that has much of the convenience of a bond. Like a GNMA pass-through security, it represents ownership interests in a pool of mortgages. But interest on the certificate is paid semiannually and principal repayments are made annually, like some bonds with sinking provisions. The agency guarantees timely payments of interest, full payment of principal, and repurchase of any principal that remains unretired after fifteen years.[23]

The proliferation of these indirect mortgage securities sharply reduces the risk, liquidity, and valuation problems associated with

21. Board of Governors of the Federal Reserve System, *Capital Market Developments* (The Board, 1980), p. 23; and 1980 data from the Government National Mortgage Association.

22. Sivesind, "Mortgage-Backed Securities," p. 5.

23. Ibid.

direct mortgage investments.[24] Whether private pension funds will avail themselves of these opportunities to invest in mortgages remains to be seen.

Pension Fund Performance

Until recently the investment performance of pension funds could be measured simply by the total rate of return earned on fund assets. In recent years, however, critics have charged that many pension investments are inconsistent with workers' interests. Since socially desirable investment and maximization of returns may conflict in many cases, both facets of investment performance are discussed below.

Rate of Return

The rates of return for pension trusts and life insurance companies during the period 1960–80 are presented in table 5-9. The large swings in the earnings of the pension trusts contrast sharply with the more modest, consistently positive returns of the life insurance industry. The data for pension trusts include realized and unrealized capital gains and losses; the life insurance information is limited to investment earnings. Nevertheless, the data provide a fairly accurate picture of the relative performance of the two institutions, since gains and losses are minimal for insurance companies, which have only about 10 percent of their assets invested in equities. The great volatility of pension trust returns caused by swings in the stock market raises the question whether common stocks are appropriate investments for pensions. On the one hand, pension plans seem suited for this type of investment. Because contributions considerably exceed benefits, pensions experience a net inflow of funds every year that provides a cushion to weather swings in security prices. Pension funds, therefore, have the unique opportunity to profit from the higher return on equities.

On the other hand, ERISA has introduced an institutional constraint that makes large capital losses undesirable. The new law requires

24. One expert suggests that pension funds would be more likely to buy pass-through securities if they paid quarterly or semiannually rather than monthly like GNMAs and if they had longer effective maturities. See Roy A. Schotland, "The Opponent's Arguments: A Review and Comment," in Dallas L. Salisbury, ed., *Should Pension Assets Be Managed for Social/Political Purposes?* (Washington, D.C.: Employee Benefit Research Institute, 1980), p. 168.

Table 5-9. Rates of Return for Pension Trusts and Life Insurance Companies, 1960–80

Percent

Year or period	Pension trusts[a]	Insurance companies[b]
1960	6.3	4.1
1961	15.0	4.2
1962	−2.6	4.3
1963	11.1	4.4
1964	11.3	4.5
1965	8.6	4.6
1966	−5.1	4.7
1967	11.9	4.8
1968	7.6	5.0
1969	−5.8	5.1
1970	5.6	5.3
1971	16.1	5.4
1972	17.2	5.6
1973	−18.4	5.9
1974	−21.3	6.2
1975	22.2	6.4
1976	12.1	6.6
1977	−2.2	6.9
1978	4.1	7.3
1979	4.2	7.7
1980	24.4	8.0
	Average annual rate of return[c]	
1960–80	5.2	5.6
1960–70	5.5	4.6
1970–80	4.9	6.5

Sources: Skolnik, "Private Pension Plans, 1950–74," p. 4; Martha Yohalem, "Employee Benefit Plans, 1975," *Social Security Bulletin,* vol. 40 (November 1977), p. 27; Securities and Exchange Commission, *Statistical Bulletin,* vol. 36 (May 1978), and *Statistical Bulletin,* vol. 38 (July 1980); American Council of Life Insurance, *Life Insurance Fact Book, 1981* (ACLI, 1981), p. 61.

a. Author's calculations. Rate of return = $[(\text{assets}_t - \text{assets}_{t-1}) - (\text{contributions}_t - \text{benefits}_t)]/\text{assets}_{t-1}$, where assets are valued at market value. Data for "contributions" and "benefits" 1976–80 are derived from table 2-1.

b. The rate of return includes investment income for separate accounts but not their capital gains and losses. Hence the figures are not strictly comparable to those for pension trusts. But the gains and losses on the separate accounts are relatively small compared with total investment income.

c. Average annual growth rate over n years is calculated as follows:

$$\left\{ \left[\prod_{t=1}^{n} \left(1 + \frac{\text{rate of return}_t}{100} \right) \right]^{1/n} - 1 \right\} 100.$$

This average annual growth rate obviously differs from the average of the annual growth rates.

companies to reassess their actuarial assumptions in light of investment gains and losses every three years. When a plan's actual results deviate significantly from those projected under its actuarial assumptions, the administrators of the plan must adjust contributions according to the "experience" gains or losses. Any required increase in contributions will increase the employer's annual pension costs and in turn reduce corporate profits. Although investment gains and losses, which are amortized over fifteen years, do not affect pension costs as much as benefit or salary increases do, the possibility of increased fluctuations in annual profits does lessen the attractiveness of stocks as investments.

ERISA regulations and the disastrous performance of the stock market in 1973–74 encouraged pension trust managers to reduce their stock holdings somewhat. Between 1972 and 1980 corporate equities declined from 65 percent to 50 percent of the book value of trust fund assets. This response seems due in part to a heightened awareness of the long-run trade-off between risk and return and the greater acceptance of modern portfolio theory.

Social Considerations

In recent years another criterion has emerged on which to evaluate the performance of pension funds—namely, the social and economic implications of pension fund investments. This controverisal issue received considerable publicity after the 1978 publication of *The North Will Rise Again,* in which the authors, Jeremy Rifkin and Randy Barber, argue that pension investments should be consistent with the goals of plan participants.[25] They contend that union pension fund money from the North and Midwest is often used to support corporations located where labor costs are lower, either abroad or in the nonunion sunbelt.

The controversy was heightened in the summer of 1979, when Corporate Data Exchange released a study showing that many pension assets were invested in companies that were predominantly nonunion, "OSHA [Occupational Safety and Health Administration] violators," "EEO [equal employment opportunity] violators," and/or doing business with South Africa.[26] Although the study was subsequently criticized for alleged inaccuracies and technical flaws, it attracted widespread attention throughout the pension industry.[27]

25. Jeremy Rifkin and Randy Barber, *The North Will Rise Again: Pensions, Politics and Power in the 1980s* (Beacon Press, 1978).

26. Corporate Data Exchange, *CDE Handbook—Pension Investments: A Social Audit* (New York: CDE, 1979).

27. For a criticism of the Corporate Data Exchange report, see Roy A. Schotland, "Flaws in CDE Audit Criticized," *Pensions and Investments* (December 17, 1979), pp. 29, 50. For the response to Schotland, see Christopher S. Taylor and Michael Locker, "CDE Directors Rebut Schotland," *Pensions and Investments* (February 4, 1980), p. 24. A more detailed version of Schotland's remarks appears in "The Opponent's Arguments," pp. 148–56.

Shortly after the release of the study, Drexel Burnham Lambert announced that it would begin to use social criteria to screen investments of union pension fund money. The objective of that corporation's program was to guard against investments that are counterproductive to unions. Later in 1979 Control Data Corporation instructed its pension managers to use socially responsible criteria in making investment decisions. Consideration was to be given to such factors as equal employment opportunities, urban development, and employee health and safety.[28]

Opinions differ widely about what constitutes social investment and about whether social considerations are appropriate in pension fund investment decisions. Advocates of social investment encompass both those who argue for greater diversification of pension investments through the inclusion of what they consider to be socially desirable assets, such as home mortgages and low-cost housing for the poor and elderly, and those who call for the exclusion of investments in companies with socially undesirable characteristics, such as business activity in South Africa, a nonunion work force, or safety and health or equal opportunity violations.[29] Some advocates take the extreme position that economic return should be secondary to social considerations; others take the moderate position that nonfinancial criteria should be permitted when investments have equal risk and return. Opponents argue that opportunities with equal risk and return but alternative social implications are so rare that devising a social investment policy to distinguish among these investments is meaningless.[30]

While the debate still rages, the area of disagreement seems to have become more clearly defined. All agree that the primary purpose of pension plans is to provide retirement income for participants, and most agree that when comparable investments are available social implications may be considered in the final investment decision. The area of disagreement is whether nonfinancial criteria should be permitted in invest-

28. Maria Crawford Scott, "Social Investing Debate Continues," *Pensions and Investments* (December 17, 1979), pp. 12, 47.

29. The 1979 agreement by Chrysler to include social considerations when investing its part of the $850 million United Automobile Workers Pension Fund involved both approaches. Under the agreement 10 percent of new net contributions were to be used to expand the portfolio to "include" investments in mortgages, nursing homes, health maintenance organizations, and day-care centers in cities where union members live. On the other hand, the union submitted a list of companies doing business in South Africa that it wanted to "exclude" from the pension portfolio. "UAW Granted 'Social' Investment Voice," *Pensions and Investments* (November 4, 1979), p. 2.

30. Schotland, "Opponent's Arguments," pp. 112–13.

ment selection if they increase the investment risk or diminish the return potential.

Advocates of sacrificing return for social considerations argue that since pension plan assets are deferred wages, employees should be able to determine fund investments. Thus if plan participants desire to accept greater risk or lower returns to support an investment that directly benefits them, they should be permitted to do so. Lower immediate returns on the pension fund might result in greater long-run economic benefit to plan participants. Therefore, advocates would support Taft-Hartley plans investing in companies that encourage unionization or in housing construction for areas where plan participants live.

Opponents of social investing at the expense of financial return point to a host of practical problems, such as decisions about which goals should be pursued, who should establish the goals, and how the performance of a socially oriented investment fund should be measured. Moreover, while some argue that plan assets are deferred compensation and should therefore be managed by plan participants, the fact is that corporations which offer defined benefit plans must bear the burden of any shortfall in plan returns.[31] As long as the ultimate risk rests with the company, it is difficult to justify the participants' decisions to sacrifice returns for social considerations.

Legal constraints also limit the extent to which plan assets can be managed for other than maximum financial return.[32] The central ERISA provision regulating investment activities requires that the fiduciary discharge his duty "solely in the interest of the participants and beneficiaries and . . . (A) for the exclusive purpose of: (i) providing benefits to participants and their beneficiaries; and (ii) defraying reasonable expenses of administering the plan; (B) with the care, skill, prudence, and diligence under the circumstances then prevailing that a prudent man acting in a like capacity . . . would use . . .; (C) by diversifying the

31. Some analysts claim that employees also bear significant investment risk. They argue that poor pension fund investment performance will increase the amount of employer contributions needed to finance a given level of benefits, and thereby reduce the employer's willingness to increase benefit levels or to provide cost-of-living increases. If benefit levels are not increased periodically and inflation persists at current levels, the real purchasing power of plan participants' benefits will decline rapidly.

32. For an interesting discussion of the legal implications, see James D. Hutchinson and Charles G. Cole, "Legal Standards Governing the Investment of Private Pension Capital," in Salisbury, ed., *Should Pension Assets Be Managed for Social/Political Purposes?* pp. 27–92.

investments . . . to minimize the risk of large losses . . .; (D) in accordance with the documents and instruments governing the plan.''[33]

The prudence and diversification requirements of the statute require that investments meet reasonable standards of safety, return, and marketability, and therefore neither absolutely preclude nor specifically authorize the selection of investments on the basis of nonfinancial considerations. Careful analysis may produce a range of investment alternatives that can equally serve the plan's financial objectives, thereby permitting some consideration of the nonfinancial characteristics of those alternatives. But other provisions of ERISA's fiduciary standards may further constrain investment options.

An investment that meets ERISA's financial requirements must also be undertaken ''solely in the interest of'' and ''for the exclusive purpose of providing benefits to participants and their beneficiaries.'' These provisions raise questions about the legality of investments to support a particular company or union rather than to support plan participants directly. The most ambiguous issue is whether an investment policy that confers benefits on plan participants as part of a much larger group, such as local residents or workers generally, is consistent with the ''solely in the interest'' standard. In addition, the ''exclusive purpose'' language may be interpreted as a further restriction, suggesting that pension trusts covered by ERISA are to be invested for the limited purpose of providing retirement benefits and not for other socially desirable purposes that might provide peripheral or speculative benefits to plan participants.

Regulators have tended not to emphasize these restrictions and have taken the position that when two investments are equally desirable from an economic standpoint, social factors may be considered in determining which investment to select.[34] Because of the ambiguity of the ERISA statutes, one legal expert has cautioned plan fiduciaries to limit their social investments to those that benefit participants as participants, not as members of some larger community.[35] Actually, the issue is complicated by the fact that in some instances social investments may benefit some plan members at the expense of others. For example, if a pension

33. Employee Retirement Income Security Act of 1974, 88 Stat. 877.

34. Statement of Ian Lanoff, administrator of pension and welfare benefit programs of the Department of Labor, in *Beneficiary Participation in Private Pension Plans,* Staff Report of the Subcommittee on Antitrust, Monopoly, and Business Rights, Senate Committee on the Judiciary, 96 Cong. 1 sess. (GPO, 1979), p. 13.

35. Hutchinson and Cole, ''Legal Standards Governing the Investment of Private Pension Capital,'' p. 88.

fund decides to provide home mortgage funds to participants at favorable
rates, plan members who do not wish to borrow mortgage funds may feel
that they are being forced to subsidize loans to other participants. The
degree to which social considerations influence plan investments will be
determined in part by future interpretations of ERISA provisions. Social
investment is a relatively recent concern, and the extent of its influence
on pension investment policy will be seen in coming decades.

The Effect of Pension Funds on Capital Markets

Between 1940 and 1980 private pension funds mushroomed from $2.4
billion to over $400 billion. Their growth has been accompanied by the
expansion of other institutional investors. Institutions now own approximately one-third of the value of stocks on the New York Stock
Exchange, and private pension trusts are by far the largest investors in
the stock market. Moreover, the three major institutions—insurance
companies, mutual funds, and the pension industry—account for half
the New York Stock Exchange volume.[36] An important question, then,
is whether the growth of institutional investors has influenced stock
prices or the relative yields of various securities. Since pension funds,
insurance companies, and mutual funds are no more than intermediaries,
the assets held by them are ultimately still owned by the public. Financial
intermediaries affect yields or stock prices only insofar as they alter the
portfolio mix of these assets or adopt trading behavior different from
that of individuals.

Bond Yields

A recent study by Benjamin Friedman investigates the impact of
pension fund growth both on the portfolio mix of total household assets
and on asset yields.[37] Friedman notes that to prevent the institutional
arrangements under which wealth is held from affecting the portfolio
mix, one of two types of ultrarational responses would be required: (1)
pension managers could invest the funds entrusted to them so as to

36. New York Stock Exchange, *1979 Fact Book* (NYSE, 1979), pp. 50–51.
37. Benjamin M. Friedman, "The Effect of Shifting Wealth Ownership on the Term
Structure of Interest Rates: The Case of Pensions," Working Paper 239 (National Bureau
of Economic Research, February 1978).

reproduce the composition of the aggregate portfolio directly held by the public, or (2) the public could rearrange its directly held portfolio to offset any movements in the portfolio held by its pension funds. For instance, if pension plans accumulated more long-term bonds than individuals wanted to hold, individuals could sell bonds from their private portfolios to maintain their same combined investment position.

Friedman argues that pension managers will not try to reproduce the portfolio of individuals, since pension plans have characteristics that differ fundamentally from those of the participants. First, pension plans are bound by a variety of regulatory restrictions not imposed on individuals. Second, the tax-exempt status of pension funds will shift preferences away from fully or partially tax-exempt investments, such as municipal bonds or equities that yield capital gains, toward assets with fully taxable yields, such as corporate bonds or stocks with high dividends. Third, by pooling their assets, pension funds can reduce their unit cost of acquiring information and engaging in transactions. Finally, since pension funds have contractually established liabilities, they are assured a more stable and predictable cash outflow than individuals.

Friedman goes on to say that not only is it likely that the portfolio preference of pension funds will differ from that of individuals, but individuals are not always able to fully offset the portfolio allocations made by pension funds. For instance, while in principle individuals can sell bonds to offset the purchases of bonds on their behalf by pension funds, in fact few individuals hold bonds, and market arrangements make such sales difficult if not impossible in small amounts.

The great difference between the asset holdings of households and those of pension funds is documented in table 5-10. Individuals hold almost 50 percent of their financial assets in short-term instruments, but short-term assets account for only 7 percent of the portfolio of private pensions. Average net financial flows for households and pension trusts over the period 1960–80 reveal even greater divergence (see table 5-11). Whereas households invested only about one-sixth of their direct financial assets in long-term credit market instruments over this period, pension funds invested in virtually nothing else.

Friedman concludes that since pension plans tend to focus on longer-term assets than individuals, the demand for those assets has probably increased relative to that for short-term ones. He then calculates the change in the slope of the yield curve that is attributable to the increased demand for long-term assets resulting from a rechanneling of saving from

Table 5-10. Household and Pension Fund Holdings of Financial Assets, End of 1980
Amounts in billions of dollars

Asset	Households		Private pension funds	
	Amount	Percent	Amount	Percent
Short term				
Currency and deposits[a]	1,616.0	43.5	13.2	4.6
U.S. government securities	83.8	2.3	8.1	2.8
Open market paper	30.8	0.8	. . .	. . .
Long term				
Stocks	1,414.4	38.0	171.1	59.8
Corporate bonds	82.5	2.2	60.1	21.0
State-local bonds	62.9	1.7	. . .	. . .
Mortgages	127.5	3.4	4.0	1.4
U.S. government securities	205.0	2.5	23.5	8.2
Other	92.2	2.7	6.2	2.2
Total	3,715.1	100.0	286.1	100.0

Source: Board of Governors of the Federal Reserve System, *Flow of Funds Accounts: Assets and Liabilities Outstanding, 1957–1980*, pp. 9, 35. Figures are rounded.
a. Includes money market fund shares.

individuals to pension funds. He estimates that this redistribution of saving toward investors with preferences for long-term assets sharply reduced long-term yields relative to short-term yields. According to his model, if $10 billion had been shifted from private savings to pension funds annually during the period 1967–73, the average slope of the yield curve would have been reduced from the historical 1.12 percent to 0.75 percent; if $25 billion had been shifted, it would have been reduced to 0.20 percent. Such shifts in the term structure are much larger than those discussed under the "Operation Twist" surrogate debt management plan of the early 1960s.[38]

Friedman's conclusion that pensions have increased the demand for long-term assets is based on the implicit assumption that if individuals saved $10 billion directly rather than through pension or insurance funds, they would allocate this sum in the same way as their current direct financial investments. This assumption ignores the possibility that households' strong preference for short-term assets may be largely due to the increase in their holdings of pension and insurance claims. These claims

38. Operation Twist was an effort by the Treasury to raise short-term interest rates to attract foreign capital while holding long-term rates low to stimulate domestic investment. Franco Modigliani and Richard Sutch, "Innovations in Interest Rate Policy," *American Economic Review*, vol. 56 (May 1966, *Papers and Proceedings, 1965*), pp. 178–97.

Table 5-11. Average Annual Net Financial Asset Accumulations, 1960–80
Amounts in billions of dollars

	Households		Private pension funds	
Asset	Amount	Percent	Amount	Percent
Short term				
Currency and deposits[a]	62.9	75.2	0.7	7.3
U.S. government securities	2.8	3.3	0.4	4.2
Open market paper	0.8	1.0	. . .	. . .
Long term				
Stocks	−3.8	−4.5	5.2	54.2
Corporate bonds	3.4	4.1	2.1	21.9
State-local bonds	2.1	2.5	. . .	. . .
Mortgages	5.0	6.0	0.2	2.1
U.S. government securities	6.8	8.1	1.0	10.4
Other	3.6	4.3	. . .	. . .
Total	83.6	100.0	9.6	100.0

Sources: Board of Governors of the Federal Reserve System, *Flow of Funds Accounts, 1946–1975*, pp. 11–12, and *Flow of Funds Accounts, 4th Quarter, 1980* (February 1981), pp. 6–7, 24–25. Figures are rounded.
a. Includes money market fund shares.

may have satisfied individual demand for long-term financial assets, causing households to reduce their holdings of other long-term credit instruments and to accumulate liquid assets.[39]

When pension and insurance assets are included, individual holdings and net acquisition of financial assets over the period 1960–80 appear much more balanced between long-term and short-term credit instruments (see tables 5-12 and 5-13). This suggests that the growth of pensions has probably led to a substitution of pension and insurance reserves for other long-term assets formerly held directly by households rather than to a net increase in the demand for long-term securities. Thus it seems unlikely that pension plans have affected the relative yields of long-term and short-term securities.

This view of pension rights as long-term assets would apply regardless of the portfolio composition of pension funds, and therefore is quite different from the argument that individuals regard their claims as indirect ownership of pension assets. Since most pension plans are defined benefit plans, the risks associated with returns on plan assets are usually borne by the plan sponsor. For example, if a pension fund held only corporate equities, individuals covered by the plans would not view

39. Actually the pension assets understate future income claims, since most pensions are not fully funded.

Table 5-12. **Total Financial Assets of Households, Including Pension and Insurance Reserves, Selected Years, 1960–80**
Amounts in billions of dollars

Asset	1960		1965		1970		1975		1980	
	Amount	Percent	Amount	Percent	Amount	Percent	Amount	Percent	Amount	Percent
Short term										
Currency and deposits[a]	238.0	24.5	373.2	25.4	544.5	28.3	943.2	37.0	1,616.0	36.8
U.S. government securities	10.6	1.1	18.0	1.2	21.0	1.1	41.0	1.6	83.8	1.9
Open market paper	...	...	...	...	11.7	0.6	15.1	0.6	30.8	0.7
Long term										
Stocks	395.4	40.7	635.5	43.4	729.4	37.9	659.7	25.9	1,141.4	26.0
Corporate bonds	10.0	1.0	10.8	0.7	34.3	1.8	63.5	2.5	82.5	1.9
State-local bonds	30.8	3.2	36.4	2.5	46.0	2.4	68.1	2.7	62.9	1.4
Mortgages	33.4	3.4	42.2	2.9	52.9	2.7	71.9	2.8	127.5	2.9
U.S. government securities	63.4	6.5	69.0	4.7	86.2	4.5	111.8	4.4	205.0	4.7
Pension and insurance reserves	176.0	18.1	260.7	17.8	369.9	19.2	532.3	20.9	953.0	21.7
Other	14.4	1.5	19.5	1.3	30.7	1.6	45.1	1.8	92.2	2.1
Total	972.1	100.0	1,465.3	100.0	1,926.6	100.0	2,551.7	100.0	4,395.1	100.0

Sources: Board of Governors of the Federal Reserve System, *Flow of Funds Accounts, 1946–1975*, pp. 99, 138, and *Flow of Funds Accounts: Assets and Liabilities Outstanding, 1957–1980*, pp. 9, 35. Figures are rounded.

a. Includes money market fund shares.

Table 5-13. Household Average Annual Net Financial Asset Accumulation, Including Pension and Insurance Reserves, 1960–80
Amounts in billions of dollars

Asset	Net accumulation	
	Amount	Percent
Short term		
Currency and deposits[a]	62.9	53.5
U.S. government securities	2.8	2.4
Open market paper	0.8	0.7
Long term		
Stocks	− 3.8	− 3.2
Corporate bonds	3.4	2.9
State-local bonds	2.1	1.8
Mortgages	5.0	4.3
U.S. government securities	6.8	5.8
Pension and insurance reserves	33.9	28.9
Other	3.6	3.1
Total	117.50	100.0

Sources: Board of Governors of the Federal Reserve System, *Flow of Funds Accounts, 1946–1975*, pp. 11–12, and *Flow of Funds Accounts, 4th Quarter 1980*, pp. 6–7.

a. Includes money market fund shares.

these investments in the same way as they would if they held the stocks directly. For a plan participant, the pension right would transform the assets from high-risk, high-return corporate equities to a guaranteed retirement income, the level of which is determined by years of service and salary rather than by the performance of the stock market. Likewise, if pension plans held all their assets in Treasury bills, individuals would probably not perceive this as an increase in their holdings of short-term credit instruments. The commitment of the defined benefit pension plan would be considered a long-term asset regardless of the investment holdings of the pension fund.

Because of the long-term characteristics of pension and insurance assets, neither the current portfolio of household financial assets nor current patterns of household direct net investment can be used to support the argument that pensions have increased the demand for long-term credit instruments. Rather, the analysis must take account of the impact of the growth in pension and insurance reserves on household portfolio selection. Thus further research is required to determine whether pensions have affected relative yields of short- and long-term assets.

Stock Market Performance

Critics have charged that "large institutional investors are destroying the nation's securities system by drying up the liquidity of the marketplace with huge block trades, driving prices of individual stocks up or down in sudden irrational spurts and scaring the small individual investor out of the market altogether."[40] Some argue that since the portfolios of large institutional investors tend to be concentrated disproportionately in high-priced stocks, financial institutions have created a two-tier market. But while such charges permeate the financial press and congressional hearings, relatively little research has been developed either to substantiate or repudiate these claims.[41] This section explores the impact that large institutions are alleged to have on the stock market, summarizing the available data.

BANKS AND THE TWO-TIER MARKET. Although the ownership of pension trusts is diverse, most of them are managed by a small number of financial institutions. As shown in table 5-14, the trust departments of the largest commercial banks in 1980 managed over $120 billion of pension assets, an amount equal to almost half the assets held in pension trusts.

Morgan Guaranty has the largest trust department, managing $36 billion in assets, with employee benefit accounts amounting to $22 billion. In 1980 Morgan had more than $16 billion of common stocks invested primarily in a few very large companies. Such a concentration of assets is conventionally believed to be dictated by the mere size of the institution's holdings.[42] Morgan's managers argue that they are investors, not traders, and that they buy assets with the intention of holding them rather than of "selling high and buying back low."[43] Actually the bank has no alternative, since it would be difficult to turn over $36 billion, or even a significant part of it, very frequently. Therefore, Morgan is forced to invest most of its holdings either in

40. Dan Rottenberg, "The Money Weight Champion," *New York Times*, February 22, 1976.

41. See *The Impact of Institutional Investors in the Stock Market*, Hearings before the Subcommittee on Financial Markets of the Senate Committee on Finance, 93 Cong. 1 sess. (GPO, 1973).

42. Computor Directions Advisors, Inc., *Spectrum 4:13(f) Institutional Portfolios* (Silver Spring, Md.: CDA, December 1980), pp. 647–59.

43. Carol J. Loomis, "How the Terrible Two-Tier Market Came to Wall Street," *Fortune* (July 1973), p. 188.

Table 5-14. Total Assets and Assets of Employee Benefit Plans Managed by Large Commercial Banks, December 31, 1980
Billions of dollars

Bank	Total trust assets	Assets of employee benefit plans
Morgan Guaranty Trust Company	36.1	21.8
Bankers Trust Company	17.7	13.3
Citibank, N.A.	26.3	9.6
Mellon Bank, N.A.	12.6	8.2
Harris Trust and Savings Bank	12.4	6.9
Manufacturers Hanover Trust Company	10.5	6.1
First National Bank of Boston	7.8	5.3
Chemical Bank	9.1	5.0
Wilmington Trust Company	8.4	5.0
Wells Fargo Bank	9.2	4.9
Bank of America	9.3	4.3
National Bank of Detroit	6.6	4.3
First National Bank of Chicago	9.6	4.1
Chase Manhattan Bank	8.7	3.9
Continental Illinois National Bank	10.1	3.8
American National Bank and Trust Company/ Chicago	4.1	3.6
Northern Trust Company	9.1	3.0
AmeriTrust Company	6.1	2.9
Crocker National Bank	5.4	2.7
First National Bank of Dallas	3.9	2.4
Total	223.0	121.1

Source: Federal Deposit Insurance Corporation, *Trust Assets of Banks and Trust Companies—1980* (Washington, D.C.: Federal Financial Institutions Examination Council, 1981), pp. 76–77.

stocks that can be purchased and put away with the expectation of continued earnings over the long run or in stocks in which trading volume is large enough to assure liquidity.

Other large banks usually follow investment patterns like Morgan's, and the somewhat smaller banks seem to follow the lead of the larger institutions. As a result, bank portfolios tend to look alike.[44] For example, nine of the twenty commercial banks with over $3 billion of common stocks in 1980 had International Business Machines Corporation as their largest holding; for four IBM was second; and for the

44. The following discussion is based on data from Computer Directions Advisors, *Spectrum 4:13(f) Institutional Portfolios*.

remaining banks it was in the top seven holdings. Exxon stock was held by all twenty of these banks and ranked in the top three holdings of twelve of them. Similarly, American Telephone and Telegraph was held by all but four of the twenty largest banks. In the aggregate the value of these banks' twenty largest holdings accounted for almost half (46 percent) their total equity portfolio. In terms of the total value of the companies' stock outstanding, the twenty trust departments held over 16 percent of IBM and about 13 percent of Exxon, General Electric, and Eastman Kodak. Thus an examination of the portfolios of large commercial banks lends support to the contention that financial intermediaries have created a two-tier market by concentrating their holdings in the stock of the large companies.

Those who believe in the existence of a two-tier market claim it has caused three major problems: (1) the individual investor has been driven out of the market because of the "unfair advantages and access by institutions";[45] (2) companies in the lower tier and venture capital firms have been precluded from raising investment funds; and (3) the large institutions have dramatically increased the volatility in stock prices.

THE INDIVIDUAL INVESTOR. Individuals have been net sellers of stock since the early sixties, divesting themselves of $4 billion a year between 1960 and 1980 (see table 5-11). As a result, the share of the market value of stocks held directly by individuals declined from 72 percent in 1960 to 60 percent in 1980 (see table 5-15). Moreover, the growth in the number of individuals owning stock slowed in the sixties, and the number of individual shareholders actually declined in the seventies from 30.8 million in 1970 to 25.3 million in 1975.[46] This decline in stock ownership has been reflected in individual activity on the New York Stock Exchange. Whereas in 1960 individual trading accounted for 53 percent of the total volume of stocks traded per day, by 1976 it had declined to 33 percent. In terms of the value of stock traded by the public, individual trading declined in the same period from 60 to 30 percent of

45. "The Role of Institutional Investors in the Stock Market," in *Financial Markets*, Hearings before the Subcommittee on Financial Markets of the Senate Committee on Finance, 93 Cong. 1 sess. (GPO, 1973), p. 277.

46. New York Stock Exchange, *Share Ownership in America: 1959* (NYSE, 1959), p. 10; *Shareownership USA: 1965 Census of Shareholders* (NYSE, 1965), p. 7; *Shareownership—1970: Census of Shareowners* (NYSE, 1970), p. 1; and *Shareownership 1975* (NYSE, 1976), p. 1.

Table 5-15. Ownership of Corporate Equities by Sector, Selected Years, 1946–80
Percent

Sector	1946	1950	1955	1960	1965	1970	1975	1980
Households [a]	93.2	91.4	88.6	86.2	83.5	78.9	72.3	69.6
Direct	n.a.	n.a.	74.3	72.0	69.6	65.9	58.4	60.8
Personal trust [b]	n.a.	n.a.	9.7	10.2	10.2	9.6	10.2	8.8
Foundations [c]	...	...	4.6	4.0	3.7	3.4	3.7	3.4
Investment companies [d,e]	0.9	2.0	3.8	4.6	5.3	5.3	4.6	2.9
Insurance companies								
Life	1.1	1.5	1.2	1.1	1.3	1.8	3.3	3.4
Other	1.6	1.8	1.7	1.7	1.7	1.5	1.7	2.3
Pension funds								
Private	0.3	0.8	1.9	3.8	5.7	7.8	10.4	11.3
State and local								
government	0.0	0.0	0.1	0.1	0.2	0.9	2.7	3.6
Foreign [f]	2.5	2.0	2.1	2.1	2.0	3.1	4.1	4.1
Other [g]	0.5	0.5	0.6	0.4	0.4	0.6	1.0	0.5
Addendum								
Total market value [h]								
(billions of dollars)	109.7	142.6	309.1	434.0	713.7	859.4	812.5	1.518.2

Sources: Board of Governors of the Federal Reserve System, *Flow of Funds Accounts, 1946–1975*, pp. 143–45, and *Flow of Funds Accounts: Assets and Liabilities Outstanding, 1957–1980*, p. 39; Securities and Exchange Commission, *Statistical Bulletin*, vol. 38 (July 1979), pp. 16–18; SEC, *Monthly Statistical Review*, vol. 40 (August 1981), p. 8. Figures are rounded.

n.a. Not available.

a. Computed as a residual; includes both individuals and institutions not elsewhere classified.

b. Includes common trust funds.

c. Because foundations (which include educational endowments) hold some mutual funds, a degree of double counting exists here.

d. Includes only open-end investment companies in 1946 and 1950; from 1955 to 1978 includes open-end and other investment companies.

e. Because households also hold most investment company shares, the estimates of household holdings of corporate equities are somewhat understated.

f. Because of a change in method of reporting, this figure appears substantially larger after 1966.

g. Includes commercial banks, mutual savings banks, brokers, and dealers.

h. Excludes household holdings of open-end investment company shares.

the value of daily stock transactions performed by other than stock exchange members, while institutional selling increased from 40 to 70 percent.[47]

The rout of the individual from the stock market has often been attributed to the advance of institutional investors. A 1973 study by Arthur D. Little concluded that people lost confidence in the stock market because of their concern that the large financial institutions were manipulating it. Both investors and noninvestors also felt that institutions benefited from unfair advantages and access to informa-

47. New York Stock Exchange, *Public Transaction Study: 1976 (NYSE, 1977)*, pp. 6, 8.

tion.[48] Except for this survey and for anecdotal information, however, little evidence exists to support the contention that individuals have been driven from the stock market by large institutional investors. Nevertheless, the portfolio behavior of individuals during the 1960–80 period is somewhat puzzling. They continually divested themselves of stocks, which proved to be the highest-yielding financial asset, and acquired money market shares and savings deposits, which frequently yielded negative real rates of return. A recent study concluded that the most likely explanation lay in the role of liquid savings deposits as a hedge against the uncertainty of an inflationary environment.[49]

Another explanation for the movement of individuals away from corporate equities might be that they wanted to maintain the balance of short-term and long-term credit instruments in their portfolios in light of the tremendous growth in pensions and insurance reserves. This argument is quite different from the contention that individuals divested themselves of stock in response to an increase in their indirect holdings of equities through pension funds. The fact that liquidation of common stocks accounted for most of this adjustment was virtually dictated by the initial portfolio of individuals in 1960. At that time, common stocks accounted for 41 percent of their total financial assets, 50 percent of direct holdings (excluding pension and insurance reserves), and, more important, 75 percent of direct holdings of long-term assets. Individuals simply did not hold enough other long-term financial assets, such as corporate or government bonds and mortgages, to make the required adjustments in these assets. Moreover, if individuals were holding stocks for long-term capital appreciation to finance retirement, the guaranteed income provided by pensions would be a reasonable substitute. Thus, while the growth of financial intermediaries has been accompanied by the retreat of individuals from the stock market, this coincidence may reflect a rational portfolio adjustment rather than a response to perceived unfair competitive advantages of institutional traders.

SMALL COMPANIES. The seriousness of the second allegation—that investment funds are lacking for small companies—must be evaluated in light of the fact that individuals still directly own 60 percent of the

48. See discussion of the Arthur D. Little survey in *Financial Markets*, Hearings, p. 277.
49. Philip Cagan and Robert E. Lipsey, *The Financial Effects of Inflation* (Ballinger for the National Bureau of Economic Research, 1978).

market value of corporate equities (see table 5-15). Although it does appear that financial institutions tend to invest in the same large companies (with an increasing trend toward conservatism in the wake of ERISA), individuals are and will probably continue to be the largest group of investors in stocks. Even if a two-tier market exists, the second tier is large and capable of providing a substantial source of funds to smaller firms. Moreover, venture capital was never derived from stock market transactions, so that the growth of institutional investors probably has not affected that source of financing adversely.

VOLATILITY OF STOCK PRICES. The final question, then, is whether the growth of the institutional investor has increased the volatility of stock prices. Certainly it seems that stock prices have become more volatile since institutional investors have come to dominate the market in trading volume. Indeed, many articles have appeared in the press attributing swings in the market or dramatic changes in specific stocks to "herdlike trading" and "institutional dumping."

In a 1977 study Neil Berkman examined the impact of institutional investors on the stock market.[50] He derived a measure of stock market volatility based on the magnitude and frequency of cyclical swings in Standard and Poor's composite index. Since the index constantly fluctuates, various filters were applied to monthly data to eliminate minor swings. Calculations were made for those cycles whose fluctuations exceeded 10, 15, and 20 percent of Standard and Poor's index; these results are summarized in table 5-16. Although the 10 percent filter failed to provide any evidence of an increase in the frequency or magnitude of cyclical swings, the larger filters revealed some increase in the duration and magnitude of upswings. Berkman found that most of the cyclical swings could be explained by fluctuations in corporate profits, and he therefore rejected the notion of a permanent, secular increase in stock price volatility.[51]

Even in the absence of a demonstrated effect on volatility, many claim that institutional investors behave differently from individual investors and that as a result they have altered price behavior in the stock market. One obvious difference between the two groups is the

50. Neil Berkman, "Institutional Investors and the Stock Market," *New England Economic Review* (November–December 1977).
51. A later study by McClay also found little evidence of increased volatility. See Marvin McClay, "Is the Equity Market Becoming More Volatile?" *The Journal of Portfolio Management,* vol. 7 (Spring 1981), pp. 51–54.

Table 5-16. Major Swings in Standard and Poor's Composite Index, 1950–76

Upward swing	Dura- tion in months	Level of index (low to high)	Percent up from previous low	Downward swing	Dura- tion in months	Level of index (high to low)	Percent down from previous high
			10 percent filter				
January 1950–		16.88–		January 1953–		26.18–	
January 1953	36	26.18	55	September 1953	8	23.27	11
September 1953–		23.27–		July 1956–		48.78–	
July 1956	34	48.78	110	February 1957	7	43.47	11
February 1957–		43.47–		July 1957–		48.51–	
July 1957	5	48.51	12	December 1957	5	40.33	17
December 1957–		40.33–		July 1959–		59.74–	
July 1959	19	59.74	49	October 1960	15	53.73	10
October 1960–		53.73–		December 1961–		71.74–	
December 1961	14	71.74	34	June 1962	6	55.63	22
June 1962–		55.63–		January 1966–		93.32–	
January 1966	43	93.32	68	October 1966	9	77.13	17
October 1966–		77.13–		December 1968–		106.50–	
December 1968	27	106.50	38	June 1970	18	75.59	29
June 1970–		75.59–		April 1971–		103.00–	
April 1971	10	103.00	36	November 1971	7	92.78	10
November 1971–		92.78–		January 1973–		118.40–	
January 1973	14	118.40	28	December 1974	23	67.07	43
December 1974–		67.07–					
December 1976	24	104.66	56	. . .	. . .	. . .	. . .
Average	**22.6**	. . .	**48.6**	**Average**	**10.9**	. . .	**18.9**
			15 percent filter				
January 1950–		16.88–		July 1957–		48.51–	
July 1957	90	48.51	261	December 1957	5	40.33	17
December 1957–		40.33–		December 1961–		71.74–	
December 1961	48	71.74	78	June 1962	6	55.63	22
June 1962–		43.32–		January 1966–		93.32–	
January 1966	43	55.63	68	October 1966	9	77.13	17
October 1966–		77.13–		December 1968–		106.50–	
December 1968	26	106.50	38	June 1970	18	75.59	29
June 1970–		75.59–		January 1973–		118.40–	
January 1973	31	118.40	57	December 1974	24	67.07	43
December 1974–		67.07–					
December 1976	24	104.66	56	. . .	. . .	. . .	. . .
Average	**43.7**	. . .	**93.0**	**Average**	**12.4**	. . .	**25.6**
			20 percent filter				
January 1950–		16.88–		December 1961–		71.74–	
December 1961	143	71.74	325	June 1962	6	55.63	22
June 1962–		55.63–		December 1968–		106.50–	
December 1968	78	106.50	91	June 1970	18	75.59	29
December 1974–		67.07–					
December 1976	24	104.66	56	. . .	. . .	. . .	. . .
Average	**69.0**	. . .	**132.3**	**Average**	**16.0**	. . .	**31.3**

Source: Neil Berkman, "Institutional Investors and the Stock Market," *New England Economic Review* (November–December 1977), pp. 63–65.

average size of their trade. Whereas orders by individuals generally involve a single round lot (100 shares) or less, institutional trades usually involve several round lots and can exceed 10,000 shares.[52] Both the tendency of institutions to trade in large lots and their growing share of daily trading volume have clearly changed the structure of the stock market. But whether this change has led to an increase in price volatility is doubtful.

Several studies have attempted to determine the relation between large block trends and price changes. Generally, the results indicate that block trades executed through the regular auction market on the exchange floor have only a marginal, transitory effect of about 1 to 3 percent on prices.[53] The size of this effect may be partly explained by the special mechanisms designed to prevent large block trades from strongly affecting prices.[54]

In his study Berkman also examined one major institutional investor—mutual funds—and found little speculative behavior that would contribute to large price movements. He found no evidence of an increase in "herdlike" trading—a concentration of sales in one stock— or "short-swing trading"—a tendency toward repeated trades into and out of a specific stock.

In short, though it is popularly believed that the growth of institutional investors has increased price volatility, there is little evidence to support this contention. Price volatility does not appear in any measurable sense to be higher today than earlier in the postwar period,

52. Securities and Exchange Commission, *Institutional Investor Study Report,* vol. 4 (GPO, 1971), p. 2262.

53. See, for example, Irwin Friend, Marshall Blume, and Jean Crockett, *Mutual Funds and Other Institutional Investors* (McGraw-Hill, 1970); H. G. Guthmann and A. J. Bakay, "The Market Impact of the Sale of Large Blocks of Stock," *Journal of Finance,* vol. 20 (December 1965), pp. 617–31; Securities and Exchange Commission, *Institutional Investor Study Report,* vol. 4, pp. 87–95; and Wharton School of Finance and Commerce, *A Study of Mutual Funds: Report of the Committee on Interstate and Foreign Commerce* (GPO, 1962).

54. These mechanisms include (1) exchange distributions, whereby, through a prearranged transaction by a broker acting for any number of institutions, the orders are passed on the floor at prices between the current bid-and-asked quotations; (2) special offerings, whereby a block is offered for sale or purchase at a price equal to the lower of the last sale or current offer price, transactions being made on the exchange floor but not as part of the auction market; and (3) secondary distributions, which are used for extremely large sell orders and involve the formation of a syndicate to purchase the block at a price no greater than the day's closing price (these usually take place after hours). However, in 1978 only 11.3 million of the 7,205.1 million shares traded were offered by these special methods, with 11.1 million of the 11.3 million in secondary distributions. See New York Stock Exchange, *1979 Fact Book,* p. 14.

and except for the high turnover rates of some institutional investors, it is difficult to document speculative trading. Therefore, although the growth of institutional investors has certainly affected the structure of stock market trading, this change in structure does not appear to have affected price volatility.

Conclusion

Private pension plans have become important financial intermediaries, funneling the deferred wages of workers into investments. The pattern of these investments, however, depends on whether plan assets are held by life insurers or in a trust fund. The assets of pension trusts tend to be concentrated in common stock, whereas the assets of plans funded through insurance companies are invested primarily in bonds and mortgages. These diverse portfolios yield very different investment results. During the 1960–80 period pension trusts realized total returns as low as − 21.3 percent and as high as 24.4 percent, while life insurance companies realized consistently positive returns, with capital gains and losses playing a minor role.

The investment patterns of pension trusts have been criticized not only for their mediocre performance in recent years but also for their lack of attention to social considerations. Pension managers are alleged to have supported companies with interests antithetical to those of employees. Even though the fiduciaries of private plans are restricted by ERISA from sacrificing returns for nonfinancial considerations, increased investment in mortgages might both balance the portfolios of pension trusts and satisfy the increasing demand for socially oriented investments. Moreover, the yield on mortgages relative to other investments will most likely increase in the future as the traditional suppliers of mortgage funds, namely, the thrift institutions, come under increasing pressure. Insured mortgages, and particularly the new mortgage pass-through securities issued by the Government National Mortgage Association and the Federal Home Loan Mortgage Corporation, are in many ways comparable to high-grade bonds, so that neither increased risk would be incurred nor returns forfeited by investing in those securities.

The growth of pension plans and other financial intermediaries is alleged to have had significant effects on relative yields and stock market performance. While considerably more work is required in this area, the available evidence does not seem to support the allegation. Although pension assets are more concentrated in long-term investments than are the direct financial holdings of householders, individuals have reduced their direct holdings of long-term assets as pension and life insurance reserves have grown in importance. Thus the increased demand by pensions for long-term assets has probably been offset by a reduced demand by individuals. In terms of the stock market, there is little evidence to support the contention that price volatility increased because of speculative trading by institutions.

In short, while private plans play an enormously important role as financial intermediaries, their development appears to have had only a minor impact on the performance of financial markets.

chapter six **Pensions and Corporate Finance**

In recent years pension plans have been recognized as a major component of the financial structure of corporations. This recognition can be attributed to two developments—the rapid growth of pension plans in the postwar period and the change in the legal status of pension liabilities under the Employee Retirement Income Security Act of 1974.

The importance of private pension plans in corporate activity was confirmed by a recent survey of 470 of the Fortune 500 companies, which showed that in 1980 these companies incurred $21.5 billion in pension costs, an amount equal to 8.1 percent of wages and salaries, or approximately 12.6 percent of pretax profits.[1] Pension assets for the companies amounted to about 31 percent of net worth, which, assuming a typical debt to net worth ratio, implies that they constituted roughly 13 percent of total corporate assets.[2] On the liability side, the companies had accumulated nearly $151 billion of vested pension liabilities, an amount equal to approximately 24 percent of outstanding corporate liabilities.

The nature of pension liabilities changed radically with the passage of ERISA. Before 1974 the legal claim of pension beneficiaries was limited to pension assets, but ERISA extended this claim for terminated plans to include other corporate assets up to 30 percent of a firm's net worth. By doing so, ERISA placed ultimate responsibility for pension obligations with the stockholders, thereby forcing corporate managers to consolidaɩe pension investment policy with other corporate financial policies.

1. Johnson and Higgins, *Funding Costs and Liabilities of Large Corporate Pension Plans: 1981 Executive Report* (New York: Johnson and Higgins,1981), pp. 4–5.
2. The debt–net worth ratio for all corporations was 1.26 in 1980, when assets were valued on a historical cost basis. Board of Governors of the Federal Reserve System, "Balance Sheets for the U.S. Economy" (April 1981).

This chapter explores the relation between pension plans and the corporation, highlighting the implications of ERISA for employers, plan participants, and investors.

The Advent of ERISA

The private pension system was in existence for nearly a century before ERISA was enacted. Private plans continued to grow throughout the period, but never more rapidly than after World War II. Between 1950 and 1973 the number of covered workers rose threefold to almost 30 million, the number of retirees collecting benefits increased thirteenfold to 6 million, pension assets grew fifteenfold to $180 billion, and benefits increased thirtyfold to over $11 billion annually.[3]

Even though the private pension system was well established by the 1970s, the potential weaknesses of private plans were becoming evident. A 1972 study indicated that only one-half of full-time workers in private industry were covered by private pension plans and that of those covered only one-third had vested benefits. Even among employees over fifty with ten or more years of service, only one-half were fully vested.[4]

Some employers imposed such stringent vesting and participation standards that many of their workers reached retirement age only to discover that because of some layoff, merger, or other event causing a break in service, they were not eligible for a pension. Endless stories of workers denied pension benefits were publicized in feature articles of major newspapers, in a controversial NBC television documentary, and during several years of congressional hearings. Ralph Nader and Kate Blackwell published a study documenting many instances in which people who had worked twenty years or more for one employer were denied pension benefits.[5] They interviewed one man who had worked twenty-four years for a Colorado manufacturing company when the factory shut down. Since he believed that his more than twenty years of

3. Alfred M. Skolnik, "Private Pension Plans, 1950–74," *Social Security Bulletin*, vol. 39 (June 1976), p. 4.

4. Walter W. Kolodrubetz and Donald M. Landay, "Coverage and Vesting of Full-Time Employees under Private Retirement Plans," *Social Security Bulletin*, vol. 36 (November 1973), pp. 28–31.

5. Ralph Nader and Kate Blackwell, *You and Your Pension* (Grossman Publishers, 1973).

continuous service entitled him to a pension, he declined a job in one of the company's other facilities. But when he applied for a pension at age sixty-five, he found he was ineligible because he had left company employment before retirement.[6] In another case, a coal miner laid off after twenty-three years was forced to find a job outside the coal industry. Thirteen years later, when he applied for a pension based on his twenty-three years of continuous service, he found he was ineligible for benefits because of a rule requiring twenty years of service within the thirty years preceding application for benefits.[7] A woman employed by an electronics company for thirty years was laid off periodically for months at a time, the longest period being from May 1966 to May 1968. When she applied for a pension she found that none of her service from 1941 to 1968 counted toward her retirement benefits because she had been laid off for more than eighteen months during that period.[8]

Even the workers who satisfied their plans' participation and vesting requirements had no assurance that accumulated pension fund assets would be adequate to finance benefits. Although employers were expected to fund their pension plans over periods of ten to forty years, they were not legally required to do so. The only regulatory provisions governing pension funding were contained in the Internal Revenue Code, and its regulations were designed to prevent tax evasion rather than to ensure pension plans' financial soundness.[9] Workers covered by inadequately funded plans risked losing pension benefits if their plan was terminated, as happened to workers in the South Bend, Indiana, automobile plant closed by Studebaker in 1964. Inadequate funding left most of the 8,500 Studebaker employees with either reduced pensions or with no pensions at all. Only those sixty or older with at least ten years of service received full benefits. Workers between fifty and fifty-nine with ten years of service received only 15 percent of their promised benefits, and the remaining plant employees received nothing.[10]

Not only were many pension plans funded inadequately, but also a few were administered in a dishonest, incompetent, or irresponsible

6. Ibid., p. 30.
7. Ibid., p. 4.
8. Ibid., p. 34.
9. In fact, the IRS code placed primary emphasis on ensuring that employers' deductions for pension contributions did not exceed the sum of the normal cost of their plans plus 10 percent of their accrued unfunded liability. See C. L. Trowbridge and C. E. Farr, *The Theory and Practice of Pension Funding* (Irwin, 1976), pp. 124–28.
10. Nader and Blackwell, *You and Your Pension*, p. 9.

way. For example, a large portion of the Teamsters Union Central States, Southeast and Southwest Area Pension Fund was used for the financial benefit of plan trustees and their associates.[11] Substantial misuse of funds was also uncovered in the case of the United Mine Workers Welfare and Retirement Fund. The U.S. District Court for the District of Columbia found that the trustees had deposited $75 million, or 44 percent of the fund's assets, in the National Bank of Washington, where the money drew no interest whatsoever.[12] Since the union held 74 percent of the bank's stock, it was able to use the retirement fund's money on an interest-free basis. Furthermore, the court found that the trustees were using pension fund monies to purchase large blocks of electric utility stocks in an effort to pressure the management of these utilities to buy only union-mined coal.

Other forms of financial manipulation, while not illegal, also jeopardized the welfare of plan participants. Pension assets were often concentrated in the stock of the plan-sponsoring company or were used to make large loans to the company. This disregard for the need for diversification often left workers' benefits dependent on the vagaries of the local economy or the financial condition of the firm.

The outstanding characteristic of the pre-ERISA era was that pension plan participants were generally at the mercy of plan sponsors. If the pension fund were insufficiently funded or suffered investment losses and the company was either unwilling or unable to increase contributions to the fund, the claimants could conceivably forfeit part or all of their benefits.[13] This risk was not consistent with the economic reality that pension benefits were often negotiated as forms of deferred compensation to which workers were legally entitled. Pension reform legislation was needed to redefine the rights of workers and to secure their benefit claims.

After ten years of hearings and prolonged debate, Congress adopted ERISA in 1974, thereby regulating five areas of pensions: reporting and disclosure of plan administration; employee participation and vesting standards; funding schedules and fiduciary integrity; retirement plans

11. Ibid., pp. 68–69.
12. Ibid., pp. 70–71.
13. On the other hand, participants rarely gained from successful risk-taking, since their benefits were usually defined independently of the condition of the pension fund. The exceptions, of course, were situations in which plan assets would have been insufficient to fulfill defined benefit commitments if the risky, high-return investment had not been undertaken.

for the self-employed; and the delivery of vested pension benefits.[14] To satisfy divergent interest groups, Congress gave the Department of Labor jurisdiction over reporting, disclosure, and fiduciary matters, while authorizing the Internal Revenue Service to regulate participation, vesting, and funding of private plans. The legislation's principal objective was to secure the rights of plan participants so that a greater number of covered workers would receive their promised benefits. Thus ERISA's vesting and participation standards enable workers to establish a legal claim to benefits. The implementation of funding and fiduciary standards and the establishment of the Pension Benefit Guaranty Corporation ensure that money will be available to pay the legal benefit claims.

Participation and Vesting

Before ERISA many companies severely restricted participation in their pension plans. It was common practice to exclude younger workers, especially those under thirty, workers with less than five or ten years of service, and workers hired late in life. ERISA broadened participation substantially by requiring that all employees who are at least twenty-five and have completed one year of service be covered by their company's pension plan.

Once workers begin to participate in a pension plan they must usually complete some period of service specified under the plan in order to have their benefits become "vested"; that is, to ensure that they will receive a pension benefit at retirement regardless of whether they remain with the firm. Before ERISA many companies had very stringent vesting standards, which led to the tragic loss of benefits discussed earlier. To ensure that long-service employees do not forfeit their accrued benefits, ERISA now requires employers to adopt one of three vesting methods as a minimum standard. Under all three methods a participant's benefits must be at least 50 percent vested after ten years and fully vested after fifteen years.[15]

14. For a discussion of ERISA's provisions, see Alfred M. Skolnik, "Pension Reform Legislation of 1974," *Social Security Bulletin,* vol. 37 (December 1974), pp. 35–42.

15. The vesting objectives may be achieved in one of three ways: (1) 100 percent vesting after ten years of credited service; (2) 25 percent vesting after five years of service, 5 percent additional vesting for each of the next five years, and 10 percent additional vesting for the following five years; or (3) the "rule of 45," whereby there is 50 percent vesting when the employee's combination of age and service (a minimum of five years) equals forty-five and 10 percent vesting for the next five years. For further details see Dan M.

To ensure that the spirit of earlier vesting was not violated by employers' "backloading" the benefit formulas, ERISA introduced rules designed to prevent the disproportionate accrual of benefits until late in the worker's employment. Under a backloaded plan, in which an employee might accrue $5 for every year of service up to age sixty and $20 for each year between sixty and sixty-five, even a fully vested worker who was fired in his late fifties would receive only a minuscule benefit. This practice would thwart the goals of vesting, since workers would be prevented from qualifying for any substantial benefit unless they remained with the firm until retirement. To avoid this problem, ERISA mandated that plan sponsors follow one of three rules that limit differences in the benefit accrual rate between earlier and later years of the worker's employment.[16]

ERISA also established specific guidelines for defining a "break in service." Until the passage of ERISA, most plans required that employees complete a certain period of strictly continuous service before their benefits became vested. Blue-collar workers subject to layoffs and women, who frequently quit temporarily or switched to part-time work during their childbearing years, often failed to qualify for vested benefits because of so-called breaks in service. ERISA eliminated this possibility for employees who switch to a part-time schedule; a break in service now occurs only if an employee works fewer than 500 hours a year. Moreover, under ERISA's guidelines an employee who does experience a break in service before vesting can return to the company and after one year combine his pre-break and post-break service to satisfy the plan's vesting requirements, so long as his absence was shorter than the length of his earlier service.[17]

McGill, *Fundamentals of Private Pension Plans,* 4th ed. (Irwin, 1979), pp. 139–43. Most U.S. corporations have adopted the first option and provide 100 percent vesting after ten years of service. See William J. Mischo, Sook-Kuen Chang, and Eugene P. Kaston, *Corporate Pension Plan Study: A Guide for the 1980's,* Bankers Trust Company, Employee Benefits Division (New York: Bankers Trust, 1980), pp. 338–40.

16. The "3 percent rule" requires that the participant's total accrued benefit at least equal the product of his years of participation times 3 percent of the benefit payable to a career employee. Under the "133⅓ percent rule" the benefit accrual rate for any participant for any future year of service may not be more than one-third higher than the accrual rate for the current year. Finally, the minimum required benefit accrual under the "fractional rule" equals the participant's projected benefit based on current salary multiplied by the ratio of the years of participation in the plan to the years of participation if the employee continued working until retirement.

17. For instance, if an employee worked for a firm for four years, was separated for

In short, ERISA's participation, vesting, backloading, and break-in-service rules have enhanced workers' chances of securing pension rights. To ensure that vested benefits are paid, ERISA established funding schedules, mandated fiduciary standards, and created the Pension Benefit Guaranty Corporation.

Funding Requirements

Before ERISA companies were required to make annual pension fund contributions equal to their plans' normal cost (the cost attributable to benefit accruals for the current year's service) plus the interest on their unfunded prior service cost (the cost of benefit accruals from prior years of service for which no assets have been accumulated). Many companies voluntarily went beyond these minimum funding standards and amortized their unfunded liabilities over a period of thirty to forty years.[18] ERISA formalized this traditional practice by requiring that normal costs be fully funded each year, that liabilities from employees' prior service be amortized over not more than forty years, and that liabilities due either to the formation of new plans or to benefit liberalizations in old plans be amortized over a thirty-year period.

ERISA also introduced some requirements that departed significantly from employers' traditional practices. For example, before the passage of the act most companies could value pension assets at cost or adjusted cost when calculating their unfunded pension liabilities.[19] Employers' freedom to recognize or not recognize unrealized gains allowed companies considerable latitude in calculating their annual pension contributions. Under ERISA companies now must determine their experience gains and losses at least once every three years and amortize them over a fifteen-year period.[20] For this calculation bonds are valued at cost, but all other assets must be valued on a basis that reflects market value.

three years, and then returned, after one year of service the four years of pre-break service would be restored for determining the worker's place on the vesting schedule. But if the employee was separated for four years or more, he would not be able to recover credit for his pre-break service if he later reentered the plan. See McGill, *Fundamentals of Private Pension Plans,* p. 147.

18. Jack L. Treynor, Patrick J. Regan, and William W. Priest, Jr., *The Financial Reality of Pension Funding under ERISA* (Dow Jones-Irwin, 1976), p. 10.

19. The Conference Board, *Financial Management of Company Pension Plans* (New York: The Board, 1973), p. 27.

20. Treynor and others, *Financial Reality of Pension Funding,* p. 10.

ERISA has thus limited firms' ability to control the reported value of their pension assets.

Employers' latitude in controlling the size of their reported pension liabilities has been limited by ERISA's requirement that a plan's actuarial assumptions be certified by an enrolled actuary and approved by a certified public accountant. Firms still have considerable flexibility in determining the size of their annual pension expenses and liabilities for unfunded prior service costs, since these vary greatly depending on the funding method and actuarial assumptions used. Even so, ERISA has introduced an element of uniformity to these calculations.

ERISA's funding provisions were designed to require companies to accumulate funds for benefit accruals, to fund prior service costs, and to recognize and systematically amortize experience gains and losses. Those companies that fail to meet these minimum funding standards are subject to a 5 percent excise tax on the accumulated deficiency and a 100 percent excise tax if the deficiency is not corrected promptly.[21] The severe penalty for inadequate funding eventually should assure the accumulation of sufficient assets to finance pension claims. To protect these assets from abuse, ERISA introduced fiduciary standards that apply to any person who exerts some control over pension fund investments.

Fiduciary Responsibility

ERISA mandates "fiduciary responsibility" for pension plan trustees, for investment managers, and for any other person who may have control over the pension plan. The act states that fiduciaries must manage pension assets for the sole interest of the participants and beneficiaries and that they must invest with the skill and diligence of a "prudent man." More specifically, fiduciaries cannot use plan assets for their own benefit; allow business and investment transactions between the plan and "parties-in-interest," such as the sponsoring employer, plan participants, investment managers, or the unions involved; or invest more than 10 percent of the plans' assets in securities of the employer. The act also requires that the fiduciary diversify the pension portfolio in order to minimize investment risk. A fiduciary is personally liable to the plan for losses resulting from violations of his fiduciary obligations and, under

21. Ibid., p. 11.

certain circumstances, those of co-trustees. Moreover, ERISA author-
izes civil penalties for parties-in-interest who engage in prohibited
transactions. These provisions should prevent the type of financial
manipulation that sometimes occurred before the passage of ERISA.

Responsible financial management combined with strict funding
standards should assure a financially sound pension system in the future,
but the possibility exists that some plans may terminate with insufficient
assets to cover their benefit commitments. To protect plan participants
against this contingency, ERISA established the Pension Benefit Guaranty Corporation (PBGC).

The Pension Benefit Guaranty Corporation

From the perspective of corporate financial managers, the most
important part of the ERISA legislation was the establishment of the
PBGC. Before 1974 firms were not legally liable for the payment of
unfunded vested pension benefits. If a firm terminated its pension plan,
employees with vested pension claims would receive benefits only
insofar as the pension fund was adequate. Now the PBGC, an insurance
agency within the Department of Labor, guarantees the payment of
vested pension benefits even if a plan terminates with insufficient funds.[22]

Technically, the agency guarantees the payment of what it terms
"basic benefits," which are roughly equivalent to vested benefits. It
defines basic benefits as all retirement, death, and disability benefits of
current beneficiaries and, for vested current participants, the regular
retirement benefit payable under the normal annuity form. Basic benefits
do not include lump-sum and special supplementary benefits payable
under some plans to encourage early retirement, or death and disability
benefits not in current payment status. ERISA also imposes a limit on
the amount of basic benefit insured by the PBGC, which is adjusted
annually to reflect increases in the social security wage base. Originally
the maximum was $750 a month, but by 1982 the upward movement in
national wages had raised the limit to $1,381 a month. Finally, basic
benefits are fully insured only after benefit provisions have been in effect
for five years. This restriction prevents the PBGC from becoming liable
for benefit commitments made by newly established plans and by existing
plans that increase benefits just before termination.

22. Coverage for single-employer plans began in July 1974, while automatic insurance
for multiemployer plans was delayed until August 1980.

Plans terminate in a variety of ways. Most commonly an employer voluntarily terminates a pension plan, announcing that as of a specified date no further contributions will be made or benefits accrued under a plan covering workers in a particular plant or location. The key to this type of voluntary termination is the discontinuation of contributions, for according to PBGC guidelines a plan is not considered terminated so long as the employee remains subject to the minimum funding standards of ERISA, even though benefit accruals have been suspended or terminated.

The PBGC also has the authority to initiate a court action to force an involuntary plan termination. These terminations can be made for many different reasons, such as inadequate funding, inability to pay benefits, excessive distributions to substantial shareholders, or the creation of a large potential liability for the PBGC. In practice, the PBGC has not officially terminated any plan. Moreover, it appears unlikely that the agency would move to terminate even substantially underfunded plans sponsored by large companies such as Chrysler Corporation or International Harvester Company.

Once a plan is terminated, the primary financing for insured basic benefits is derived from the assets of the plan. But since not all benefits are insured by the PBGC, some procedure had to be devised for allocating plan assets between insured and uninsured benefits. The allocation procedure has important implications for all parties, since the greater the share of assets allocated to insured benefits, the smaller the unfunded liability for which the employer is responsible and the smaller the PBGC's responsibility. On the other hand, the greater the allocation of assets to insured benefits, the less likely that participants will receive any part of their uninsured benefits. Under current procedures the PBGC allocates assets first to those benefits financed by employee contributions, second to benefits in payment status (even if they exceed the insured limit of $1,381 a month), third to other insured benefits, fourth to noninsured vested benefits, and finally to all remaining benefit claims.

In 97 percent of plan terminations, both the sponsoring company and the pension fund are financially sound and plan assets are therefore sufficient to cover all insured benefits.[23] However, when a plan terminates without sufficient assets to pay guaranteed benefits, the PBGC can hold the sponsoring company liable for the underfunding up to an amount

23. Pension Benefit Guaranty Corporation, "Annual Report to the Congress, FY 79," p. 4.

equal to 30 percent of the company's net worth.[24] Initially it was unclear how a firm's net worth was to be determined. The PBGC has now specified that a company's market (rather than book) value is the best measure of its net worth and has listed various factors that can be used to establish a firm's fair market value. For companies that are to be sold at about the time of plan termination, the price set in the sales agreement provides a measure of market value. For publicly held companies, the market value of a firm's common stock often yields a useful measure of its net worth. For companies whose stocks are either not publicly traded or traded infrequently, some other factors, such as price-earnings ratios for similar firms, can be used to estimate net worth.[25] Finally, if plan termination is accompanied by bankruptcy, the value of the equity assumed in a plan of reorganization under chapter 11 of the U.S. Bankruptcy Code of 1978 can be used to establish the firm's net worth. Net worth is usually calculated as of the plan termination date, but to prevent abuse of the insurance program, the PBGC has the right to establish the net worth record date as many as 120 days before the actual plan termination.

The PBGC's claim to the firm's assets is awarded a high priority both in the case of an ongoing concern and in the event of bankruptcy. For ongoing concerns, if the employer refuses or fails to pay the PBGC's claim upon demand, the PBGC automatically acquires a lien upon all the property of the employer. In the event of bankruptcy, the PBGC's claim would be considered equivalent in priority to the federal government's claim for nonpaid taxes. The high priority implied by the PBGC's power to impose a tax lien, however, exaggerates the favorable treatment accorded PBGC claims. In reality, the agency can be considered subordinate to other corporate creditors, since it can appropriate 30 percent of only those assets in excess of corporate liabilities to defray the cost of unfunded pension benefits. If the bankruptcy does not involve corporate

---

24. ERISA also contained a section directing the PBGC to devise a scheme under which employers could insure themselves against the 30 percent contingent liability either through the agency or private insurance carriers. However, such provisions were rescinded by the Multiemployer Pension Plan Amendments Act of 1980, since they would allow firms to escape their liability by insuring against an event over which they have complete control. If this insurance had been introduced, corporations would have been in the same position as before ERISA, but the risk of inadequate funding would have been shifted from employees to the PBGC.

25. "Pension Benefit Guaranty Corporation," *Federal Register,* vol. 46, bk. 2, pt. 7 (January 28, 1981), p. 9527.

reorganization, the excess of assets over liabilities is zero and the PBGC's claim is worthless.

Any insured benefits that are not covered by a plan's assets, together with 30 percent of the sponsoring firm's net worth, are covered by PBGC revenues derived from these unfunded benefit obligations by the premiums assessed on employers. The premiums are uniform for all single-employer plans and were established initially at $1.00 a year per plan participant. This crude rate structure was adopted as a temporary measure, pending the availability of data to construct an actuarially sound premium structure. The PBGC, however, has had neither the data nor the resources to devise a more sophisticated scheme. Hence, when the initial premium proved inadequate, the agency maintained the simple, per participant rate structure and obtained congressional approval to increase the rate from $1.00 to $2.60.

In short, through a combination of the plan assets themselves, access to up to 30 percent of the sponsoring firm's net worth, and insurance financed by employer premiums, workers covered by single-employer plans are virtually assured of receiving vested retirement benefits up to $1,381 a month even if the pension plan is terminated. The fact that under ERISA employer obligations for benefit payments are no longer limited to accumulated pension assets has enormous implications for corporate financial management.

Financial Implications of ERISA

In the wake of ERISA a growing interest has developed in pension policy from a financial management viewpoint. Some experts have suggested that pension investment decisions should be considered in conjunction with other financial policies. In that way pension assets and liabilities would be treated as though they appeared on the balance sheet, and pension contributions would be viewed as a transfer from one corporate account to another. The unified approach not only provides a useful framework for analyzing the financial implications of ERISA, but has also led to controversial prescriptions for restructuring pension portfolios.

The Augmented Balance Sheet before ERISA

The concept of including pensions on the corporate balance sheet predates ERISA. Jack Treynor, editor of the *Financial Analysts Journal*, has argued for a decade that a firm's financial condition should be evaluated in terms of an augmented balance sheet, with pension obligations included in corporate liabilities and pension assets added to operating assets.[26] Treynor maintained that even though the beneficiary's legal claim was only against the pension fund, in practice the pension system usually functioned as if the claim extended to corporate assets. That is, as long as the company was solvent, it felt an obligation to draw down its own assets to meet pension claims. Therefore, although the corporate creditor was clearly senior to the pension claimant, the net assets of the company were effectively behind pension commitments.

While the augmented balance sheet is a straightforward concept, attaching an economic value to the corporation's pension liabilities is a complex task. Traditionally, a large discrepancy has existed between the value of pension claims as viewed by potential beneficiaries and the financial burden as perceived by the firm. Beneficiaries have regarded their claims as bona fide retirement funds, whereas sponsoring companies and their creditors have treated pension claims quite lightly.

The contractual value of the pension claim can be calculated by using the riskless rate of interest to discount future benefit payments back to the present.[27] This procedure yields an estimate of the market value of assets on which the plan participants must have a claim if they are not to be subject to investment risk. Treynor argues, however, that the relevant number for the augmented balance sheet is the economic value of the claim, which incorporates pension fund investment risk. Since pension claims are often not due for several decades, one cannot be certain that adequate funds will be available to pay benefits. This uncertainty makes the economic value of the pension claim always less than the contractual value, which is calculated at the riskless rate. In addition, because any increase in the value of the underlying assets accrues to the corporation, the economic value of the beneficiary's claim is always less than the value of the underlying assets.

26. Walter Bagehot, "Risk and Reward in Corporate Pension Funds," *Financial Analysts Journal*, vol. 28 (January–February 1972), pp. 80–84. (Bagehot is apparently a pseudonym for Jack L. Treynor.) Similar arguments appear in Treynor, Regan, and Priest, *Financial Reality of Pension Funding*, and Jack L. Treynor, "The Principles of Corporate Pension Finance," *The Journal of Finance*, vol. 32 (May 1977), pp. 627–39.

27. If the corporation is not required to protect beneficiaries against inflation, then the appropriate discount rate is the return on government obligations of comparable maturity. If the obligation is understood to be fixed in real value, then the appropriate rate is the riskless rate less inflationary expectations.

The discrepancy between the contractual and economic values of the pension claim can be interpreted as an option held by corporate shareholders to pay less than full benefits. This option, called a "pension put," represents a claim against pension plan participants and therefore an asset of the corporation.[28] The value of the pension put depends on the uncertainty surrounding the ultimate value of the underlying pension and corporate assets. Generally, the longer the period until benefits are payable, the greater this uncertainty and the larger the value of the pension put. In extreme cases—with forty years until the pension claim matures, a weak company, and an underfunded pension plan, for example—the value of the pension put may be nearly as large as the contractual value of the claim.

This type of option analysis can be incorporated in the construction of an economic balance sheet for the corporation. Treynor argues that the contractual value of pensions discounted at the riskless rate is a claim against the equity of the corporation and should therefore be included among other corporate liabilities. The market value of pension assets and the pension put, which reflects the claim against the pension beneficiary by the corporation, should both be included among the employer's assets. The economic balance sheet, with all the entries at market value, would appear as follows:

Assets	Liabilities
Corporate assets	Corporate liabilities
Pension assets	Pension liabilities
Pension put	Net worth

With an augmented balance sheet, employer contributions to the pension fund no longer represent an expense to the firm, nor do they necessarily improve the benefit security of plan participants. Although pension contributions increase pension assets, they generally leave the net value of total assets underlying the pension claim unchanged. On the

28. A put option is the right to compel another party to buy an asset sometime in the future at a predetermined price called the "exercise price." If the value of the underlying asset exceeds the exercise price at maturity, the put has no value and expires unused. But if the value of the underlying asset is less than the exercise price at maturity, it pays the holder of the option to purchase the asset in the open market, force the other party to buy the asset at the exercise price, and pocket the difference. For private pension plans the underlying assets are the sum of the net worth of the corporation and the pension assets; the pension put is the claim against the pension beneficiary by the corporate shareholders; and the exercise price is the contractual value of the claim. See Fischer Black and Myron Scholes, "The Pricing of Options and Corporate Liabilities," *Journal of Political Economy*, vol. 81 (May–June 1973), pp. 637–54.

other hand, pension contributions may increase the total risk associated with the underlying assets, since corporations usually finance the purchase of at least somewhat risky pension assets by reducing their holdings of a riskless asset, such as cash, or by increasing borrowing. Increasing the risk on the underlying assets raises the value of the put and reduces the net value of the pension claim. This analyis suggests that the establishment of minimum funding standards would actually reduce the net value of pension claims. Treynor therefore suggests that beneficiaries should concentrate their efforts on controlling payments, such as dividends, that reduce the assets securing their pension claims.

The augmented balance sheet and the put concept help to explain some widely observed features of pension plans before ERISA was enacted. First, corporations with underfunded plans would be likely to invest in relatively risky assets, since the increased risk would raise the value of the put. The burden of investment losses would be borne by pension participants, while investment gains would accrue to the employer. Second, corporate creditors historically may have been implicitly allowing for the offsetting effects of the pension put when they disregarded the pension plan in evaluating the financial health of an organization. In other words, unfunded pension liabilities as conventionally calculated may have significantly overstated claims on the firm. Finally, when employers' net assets barely exceeded the amount by which their pension plans were underfunded, any loss suffered from risky investments was borne by potential beneficiaries. It is therefore not surprising that even some vested pension claimants failed to recover full benefits.

The Implications of ERISA

To the extent that the Pension Benefit Guaranty Corporation can initiate involuntary plan terminations, ERISA has eliminated the pension put for most firms. If it appears that a plan's unfunded liability is about to exceed 30 percent of its net worth, the PBGC can terminate the plan and seize assets equal to 30 percent of the firm's net worth to pay the beneficiaries. Thus, regardless of the condition of the fund, plan participants are guaranteed receipt of basic benefits, equal in value to their face amount discounted by the riskless rate. The firm's liability equals the full amount of the unfunded guaranteed benefits, and there is no pension put on the firm's balance sheet. A pension put also does not appear as a liability on the balance sheet of the PBGC, since the PBGC can avoid liability by ordering termination of the pension plan. Of course, if a plan's unfunded liability already exceeds 30 percent of the sponsoring firm's net worth, the PBGC is liable for the difference and the corporation retains on its balance sheet a put of comparable magnitude.

The elimination of the put for firms whose unfunded liabilities are less than 30 percent of their net worth depends critically on the PBGC's authority and willingness to terminate plans with sufficiently large unfunded liabilities. If the PBGC allows firms to slip into bankruptcy before mandating termination of their plans, then its claim on the firm's assets will be worthless. Since the PBGC has shown no intention of terminating a plan simply because its unfunded guaranteed benefits exceed 30 percent of the sponsoring firm's net worth, some corporations retain a put option. But the option is now against the PBGC rather than against plan beneficiaries.

In most situations, however, ERISA has altered the distribution of risks associated with portfolio performance. Vested workers under established plans are now assured of receiving benefits up to the guaranteed level, and the liability for this guarantee is borne by the firm and the PBGC. Table 6-1 summarizes the apportionment of investment risk among the firm, the participants, and the PBGC before and after ERISA for plans with different initial funding positions.[29] Let

A = value of pension fund assets

B = total accrued benefits

G = basic benefits guaranteed by the PBGC; vested benefits before ERISA

W = market value of firm's net worth.

The first example represents a fully funded plan with sufficient assets to cover all benefits accrued to date. Both before and after ERISA, as long as $A > B$ the risk associated with poor investment performance is absorbed by the firm. Example 2 characterizes a fund with pension assets that are adequate to finance all vested or basic benefits but not to pay all accrued benefits. Here workers with nonvested benefit claims bear the risk of decline in the value of pension assets both before and after ERISA. By contrast, in the third example, where $A < G < (A + 0.3W)$, the distribution of risk has been changed by ERISA. Before the legislation

29. To precisely apportion the risk between the firm and the PBGC, one must take literally the mandate of the PBGC to terminate seriously underfunded plans. Table 6-3 is based on that assumption, although the agency would terminate a plan only if the funded ratio were deteriorating substantially.

Table 6-1. Apportionment of Investment Risk before and after ERISA

| | Risk bearer[b] | |
Funding status[a]	Before ERISA	After ERISA[c]
1. $A > B$	Firm	Firm
2. $B > A > G$	Nonvested worker	Nonvested worker
3. $A < G < (A + 0.3W)$	Vested worker[b]	Firm
4. $G > (A + 0.3W)$	Vested worker[b]	Pension Benefit Guaranty Corporation

Source: Author's calculations.
a. See text for explanation.
b. The bearer of the risk is defined as the party who will bear the financial consequences of a poor investment. Thus in cases 3 and 4, before ERISA the vested worker stood to lose from poor investment performance. Nonvested employees had already forfeited benefits, given the initial funding status, and are therefore not designated as bearers of the investment risk.
c. Distribution of risk is based on the assumption that the PBGC will terminate plans before the sponsoring companies slip into bankruptcy.

workers with vested claims stood to forfeit their benefits; they are now guaranteed the payment of their basic benefits. The portfolio risk associated with financing these benefits has been shifted to the firm. When the amount of guaranteed benefits exceeds pension assets plus 30 percent of the firm's net worth, as in the last case, the firm's liability is limited and the PBGC assumes any additional risk.

The PBGC's authority to pay all basic benefits has enormously improved the rights of pension participants. Simultaneously, the agency's power to reach beyond the pension fund assets to the assets of the company itself has changed the significance of pension liabilities for plan sponsors. The typical firm terminating its pension plan is a viable concern whose unfunded basic benefits are less than 30 percent of its net worth. This type of firm no longer holds a pension put; instead, it is liable for the full value of unfunded vested pension claims. The financial reality of these claims in the wake of ERISA provides support for including pensions in corporate financial planning.

Pension Investment Strategy in Corporate Financial Planning

Building on Treynor's contention that companies should be evaluated according to a consolidated balance sheet, Fischer Black argues that corporate financial managers should hold only bonds in their pension funds and that they should seek ways to maximize their pension contributions.[30] Bonds, unlike corporate equities, allow for tax arbitrage, since

30. Fischer Black, "The Tax Consequences of Long-Run Pension Policy," *Financial Analysts Journal*, vol. 36 (July–August 1980), pp. 21–28. Similar arguments have been made by Irwin Tepper, "Taxation and Corporate Pension Policy," *The Journal of Finance*, vol. 36 (March 1981), pp. 1–13.

the firm earns tax-exempt interest on its pension fund assets but pays tax-deductible interest on its outstanding corporate debt.

After selling all the stock in their pension funds and buying bonds, firms, according to Black, should issue new bonds of their own and use the proceeds to purchase some of their own stock, to acquire another company, or to expand operations. In other words, a company should sell bonds and buy its own stock at the same time that its pension fund does just the reverse—sells stocks and buys bonds. The trade-offs between the corporate and pension fund purchases and sales are not one-for-one, however, since pension fund contributions are tax deductible.

To understand how Black's plan would work, consider a pension fund that will pay all benefits at the end of the year. Assume that (1) the interest rate is 10 percent, (2) the firm's marginal tax rate is 50 percent, and (3) stocks that might be held by the pension fund perform as well as the firm's own stock. Suppose that the benefits to be paid at the end of the year total $220 million and that the fund at the beginning of the year holds 2 million shares of $100 stock, or total assets of $200 million. If the pension fund continued to hold stock and the value of the stock rose from $100 to Y during the year, the fund would pay the $220 of benefit commitment and would return to the firm $(2Y - 220)$ million. After taxes this would be worth $(Y - 110)$ million to the firm.

Under Black's scheme, however, the pension fund would sell its $200 million in stocks and purchase one-year bonds. The firm would then issue $100 million in one-year bonds from its corporate account and would use the proceeds to buy $100 million of its own stock.[31] By the end of the year the bonds in the pension fund would produce enough interest to pay promised pension benefits. On the corporate side, the firm could sell the million shares of its own stock at Y a share and pay off the bonds for $100 million plus $10 million interest. Again the firm would experience a net gain of $(Y - 110)$ million. But in this case the firm would also receive a tax saving of $5 million from the $10 million interest deductions on its own debt. Thus the firm would earn an extra $5 million after taxes for the year, and all capital structure changes would be reversed, restoring the firm's balance sheet to its initial position.

31. Since pension contributions are tax deductible and the marginal income tax rate is assumed to be 50 percent, $1.00 of pension assets are equivalent to 50 cents on the corporate side of the ledger. Hence a company that shifted pension investments from stocks to bonds would not issue the same amount of bonds to buy its own stock. Rather, the company would issue 50 cents of bonds for every $1.00 switched from stocks to bonds in the pension fund.

Given the gains to holding bonds in the pension fund, Black argues that corporate financial managers should maximize pension contributions rather than follow the common strategy of minimizing them. However, full funding yields tax benefits only if the funds are invested in bonds; the same principles do not apply to stock investments by the pension fund, since these can be protected within the corporation. For example, the potential benefits of stock investments in the pension fund can be duplicated if the firm purchases its own stock or approximated if the firm purchases shares in a mutual fund that converts capital gains to dividends. The firm would incur no tax liability by holding its own stock, and because of the 85 percent dividend exclusion, it would be taxed on only 15 percent of a mutual fund's dividends. Although the effective 7.5 percent tax rate on mutual fund dividends is higher than the zero rate on a firm's own shares, it is still much lower than the tax a firm would have to pay on bonds held in its corporate account. Since the amount of assets that may be held relatively tax free is limited and since stock may be held tax free elsewhere, incremental tax gains arise only if bonds are held in the pension fund.

In the aggregate, companies held $176 billion of stock in their pension funds at the end of 1980.[32] If they were to shift those funds into bonds, issue new bonds at, say, 10 percent interest in the amounts Black suggests ($88 billion), and repurchase their own stock, corporate taxes would fall by $4.4 billion a year. Black sees such savings as essentially riskless, since the newly issued bonds that give rise to the tax deductions would be balanced by newly purchased bonds in companies' pension funds. He estimates that the stock market would capitalize the tax saving at firms' after-tax cost of borrowing—in this example 5 percent. A $4.4 billion per year tax savings would then increase the value of all companies' stock by $8.8 billion, or roughly 3 percent of their total value.

The tax savings and stock price gains available to individual companies depend on their current tax liabilities and the amount of stock in their pension funds relative to the market values of their own shares outstanding. Companies that pay no taxes, like Chrysler Corporation in 1980–81, would gain nothing by switching to an all-bond pension fund portfolio. But a recent *Fortune* article estimates that the benefits could be enormous for some other companies. Using Black's strategy, Inland Steel Com-

32. Securities and Exchange Commission, *Monthly Statistical Review*, vol. 40 (May 1981), p. 10.

pany, for instance, could boost the value of its stock by as much as $10.50 a share, or 36 percent.[33]

Despite the potential for significant savings and the widespread acknowledgment that Black's proposal is logically correct, most corporate pension executives reject its implementation on practical grounds. The principal objection is that bond-rating agencies might not recognize changes in the pension fund portfolio and might therefore lower a company's bond rating in response to the higher debt–equity ratio that would appear on the conventional corporate balance sheet. The rating agencies claim that they would consider pension fund changes, but would weight them less heavily than transactions on the corporate side of the balance sheet.[34] But Black argues that even if a firm's credit were lowered, only the cost of new debt would be affected. It is inconceivable, he claims, that a firm's increased borrowing costs would offset the benefits of the tax arbitrage.

Pension executives also object to Black's suggestion that a company deal in its own securities, a practice that has traditionally been approached very cautiously. Moreover, a company sacrifices diversification when it sells a portfolio of stocks from the pension fund and buys its own shares for the corporate treasury. If the company were to perform poorly, it could lose far more than it made through the tax arbitrage. But it could maintain a diversified portfolio by buying a selection of stocks on the corporate side and still capture most of the tax savings. Even though the company would be taxed on capital gains and 15 percent of dividends received, the amount would be much less than the tax savings on its newly issued bonds.

A more fundamental impediment to implementing Black's provocative proposal is that pension fund assets are not identical to corporate assets.[35] Under ERISA pension assets are segregated from the company's capital structure and are not available to satisfy general corporate obligations. The company is essentially the caretaker for the funds of plan participants, who increasingly are taking a more active interest in the investment of pension fund monies. Participants and unions concerned with issues of social investing might actively resist the company's effort to switch from stocks to bonds.

33. A. F. Ehrbar, "How to Slash Your Company's Tax Bill," *Fortune* (February 23, 1981), p. 122.

34. Ibid., p. 124.

35. "Pension Executives Cautious about Bond Arbitrage Approach," *Pensions and Investments* (November 10, 1980), p. 3.

Pension Funding and the Corporation

While theoretically it may be optimal for firms to fund their pension obligations as quickly as possible, recent surveys indicate that a portion of vested pension liabilities are unfunded. This section explores the extent of underfunding among large corporations, summarizes the available evidence on the effect of unfunded pension liabilities on corporate equity prices, and discusses the implications of these results for national saving, the stock market, and the Pension Benefit Guaranty Corporation.

Measuring Unfunded Pension Liabilities

Before 1980 companies generally reported two measures of unfunded pension liabilities. All companies included the first measure, the value of "unfunded accrued vested benefits," in a footnote to their financial statements. Publicly held companies were also required by the Securities and Exchange Commission to disclose on the 10-K forms the second measure, the amount of their "unfunded prior service cost." These two measures are based on very different concepts. The value of unfunded vested benefits is calculated from benefits actually earned by present and former employees, based on salary histories and creditable service before the valuation date. Unfunded prior service costs are equal to that part of the total future benefit liabilities not covered by current assets plus scheduled normal cost contributions. An examination of these alternative approaches to measuring unfunded liabilities is useful for evaluating the pension information actually reported by various companies.[36]

UNFUNDED PRIOR SERVICE COST. "Unfunded prior service cost," "unfunded actuarial liability," and "unfunded past service liability" are terms used interchangeably to describe that portion of future benefit liabilities for which no funds have been allocated.[37] To understand the meaning of this number, one must first understand how the actuary calculates it.

36. The SEC requirement to report unfunded prior service costs was eliminated in 1980.

37. The following discussion is based on an article by Paul A. Gewirtz and Robert C. Phillips, "Unfunded Pension Liabilities: The New Myth," *Financial Executive*, vol. 46 (August 1978), pp. 18–24.

His calculation begins with an estimate of the "present value of prospective benefits," which is based on the benefit provisions of the plan, characteristics of current workers and retirees such as age, sex, length of service, and salary, and actuarial assumptions about the likelihood that a person will live to receive benefits and about the duration of benefit payments. The actuary discounts this estimated future benefit stream back to the present, using an assumed interest rate (see figure 6-1). The resulting present value of benefit payments will vary, depending on the assumptions used by the actuary.

The difference between the present value of projected benefits and the assets on hand determines the total future contributions required by the plan sponsor (see figure 6-1, part B). The actuarial cost method is then used to establish a schedule on which contributions should be based. Annual pension contributions generally consist of two components (see figure 6-1, part C). First, the "normal cost" payment represents the contribution required to cover the costs of benefits accrued during a given year. The present value of the normal contributions constitutes the firm's total commitment to accruing future benefits. Second, an amortization payment is required to eliminate the firm's "unfunded actuarial liability," which is that portion of benefit costs not covered by current assets or scheduled normal-cost contributions. The unfunded actuarial liability is usually amortized over a fixed period of years so that it is paid off like a home mortgage.

The size of a plan's unfunded actuarial liability will vary according to the cost method used by the actuary (see figure 6-1, parts D–E). The "entry-age normal cost" method and the "unit credit" method are the two most popular techniques, the choice between them usually depending on how the plan sponsor wants to make contributions over time. Under the unit credit method benefits are funded as they accrue.[38] Although contributions for the individual employee increase each year, the entry of enough younger and lower-paid members into the plan can keep the sponsor's overall contribution rate reasonably level.[39] Under the entry-age normal cost method, projections are made of the contributions needed each year to finance an employee's benefits. The

38. For most defined benefit plans each year of service yields equal credit in calculating the employee's benefit. The pension benefit therefore accrues at an even pace throughout the member's participation in the plan.

39. Even though benefits accrue at an even pace under most defined benefit plans, contributions increase each year because the older the worker, the less time available for the contribution to earn an investment return.

Figure 6-1. Unfunded Actuarial Liability

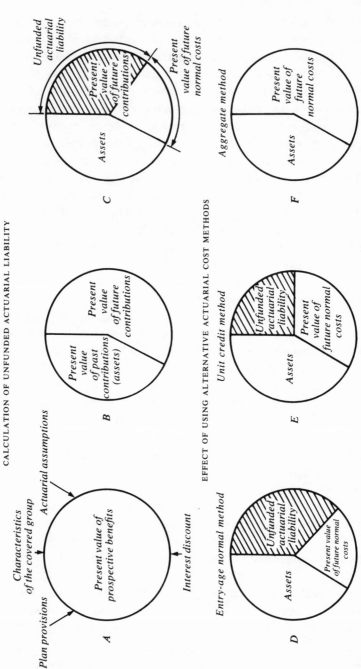

CALCULATION OF UNFUNDED ACTUARIAL LIABILITY

EFFECT OF USING ALTERNATIVE ACTUARIAL COST METHODS

Source: Paul A. Gewirtz and Robert C. Phillips, "Unfunded Pension Liabilities: The New Myth," *Financial Executive*, vol. 46 (August 1978), pp. 19, 20, 21.

sponsor's total required contributions are then leveled over the entire period of plan membership, starting with the age at which the employee began to accrue benefits and ending with his retirement. The plan sponsor's total contribution rate, averaged over all members, tends to remain stable if the average entry age remains unchanged. Since this method does not require a growing plan membership to maintain a stable contribution rate, it is preferable for a company with a static or declining work force. The entry-age normal cost method is the most common funding method in the United States, and the unit credit method the most common in Canada.

A numerical example may help clarify the meaning of normal cost and unfunded actuarial liability under the two methods.[40] Suppose an actuary calculates that for a particular employee $15,000 must be contributed over the next five years. Under the unit credit method, pension benefits would be funded as they accrue and contributions would increase each year—say $1,000 in the first year, $2,000 in the second year, $3,000 in the third year, $4,000 in the fourth year, and $5,000 in the fifth year. Under the entry-age normal cost method, the actuary would level the required contributions over the entire period of the employee's plan membership, so that the plan sponsor would have a normal cost of $3,000 a year for five years.

To determine the unfunded liability under the two methods, consider the status of the plans after two years of funding. Assume that the actuary still projects that $15,000 will be required for the employee when he retires three years hence. Under the unit credit method, future normal cost contributions would be $3,000, $4,000, and $5,000 for a total of $12,000. Since a total of $15,000 would be needed and $12,000 would come from future normal cost contributions, a $3,000 fund would be enough to ensure future benefit payments. If the fund, for some reason, accumulated $4,000, the actuary would declare a $1,000 surplus. Under the entry-age normal method, the normal cost contributions of $3,000 a year for the next three years would provide $9,000. Since $15,000 is required and $9,000 would come from future normal cost contributions, $6,000 should be in the fund after two years. If the fund had only $4,000, then there would be an unfunded actuarial liability of $2,000.

40. This example assumes a zero rate of interest and is based on D. Don Ezra, "How Actuaries Determine the Unfunded Pension Liability," *Financial Analysts Journal*, vol. 36 (July–August 1980), pp. 43–50.

Since the unit credit method allocates a larger portion of required future contributions to normal costs than the entry-age normal method, it usually yields a smaller actuarial unfunded liability than the second approach. An extreme case arises when the aggregate cost method is used. This approach yields no unfunded actuarial liability whatsoever, since normal costs include payments both to cover the accrual of future benefits and to eliminate the accrued liability over the lifetime of current workers. Thus the wide range of acceptable actuarial cost methods complicates comparisons of unfunded actuarial liabilities among plans.

UNFUNDED ACCRUED VESTED BENEFITS. The alternative to evaluating the financial status of total projected benefits is to determine the funding of benefits earned to date. As shown in figure 6-2, the present value of prospective benefits can be divided into those already accrued and those to be accrued in the future. Benefits accrued to date can be further divided into vested and nonvested claims. The vested category includes those benefits insured by the PBGC and some that are not insured by that agency.[41] The value of a firm's unfunded accrued vested benefits is simply the difference between the values of vested benefit claims and plan assets. For example, in part D of figure 6-2 plan assets do not fully cover vested benefits, and the firm therefore has a small unfunded liability for accrued vested benefits.

The funding status of benefits earned to date is certainly a more precise concept than the actuarial liability that emerges from projecting benefits. However, the value of unfunded accrued benefits is relevant only if a plan terminates, and most plans do not. On the other hand, since the calculation of unfunded accrued vested benefits does not require using an actuarial cost method, it does provide a more consistent basis for comparing funding among plans. For this reason, the Financial Accounting Standards Board required that beginning in 1980 firms report their funding status in terms of the actuarial present value of accrued vested benefits, accrued nonvested benefits, net assets available for benefits, and the interest assumption used to value benefits.[42]

41. Noninsured vested benefits may include benefits that are attributable to plan improvements made in the last five years that have not been fully phased in under PBGC regulations and benefits that exceed specified dollar maximums.

42. *Disclosure of Pension Information*, Financial Accounting Standards Board Statement 36 (New York: FASB, 1980).

Figure 6-2. Unfunded Accrued Vested Benefits

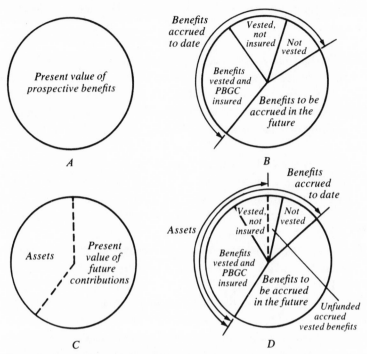

Source: Gewirtz and Phillips, "Unfunded Pension Liabilities," pp. 19, 23.

The Funding Status of Private Plans

A 1981 survey summarized the funding status of pensions sponsored by the nation's large corporations.[43] Funding information was extracted from 1980 annual reports to shareholders for 386 of the Fortune 500 industrial corporations and for 168 of the 200 corporations that comprise the Fortune 50 largest nonindustrial commercial banking, retailing, transportation, and utility organizations. The results of the sample may overstate the adequacy of funding, since large plans tend to be better funded than small ones. Nevertheless, the sample comprises a large part of the U.S. pension system; the combined plan assets of these industrial and nonindustrial corporations amounted to about $200 billion, roughly half the nation's total private pension reserves of $408 billion in 1980.

43. Johnson and Higgins, *Funding Costs and Liabilities of Large Corporate Pension Plans.*

The survey showed that plans sponsored by the 386 companies in the industrial group held assets that covered 86 percent of total accrued liabilities and 91 percent of vested liabilities. Individual companies were distributed widely around the mean figures, since 46 percent (176 companies) had net assets equal to or greater than total accrued liabilities and 58 percent (222 companies) had assets in excess of vested liabilities. In fact, the averages somewhat understate the degree of funding, because the figures were constructed by limiting the assets of overfunded plans to 100 percent of accrued benefits. Without this adjustment, the group as a whole would have more than enough assets to cover vested benefits, since the companies had vested pension liabilities of $151 billion and total pension assets of $154 billion. Considering nonvested as well as vested benefits, the pension assets would cover 93 percent of the $165 billion total accrued liability. The average interest assumption used to value accrued benefit liability was 7.2 percent.[44]

The degree of funding varied substantially by industry. Three industry groups had funded less than 80 percent of their vested liabilities, lowest among them being the shipbuilding, railroad, transportation equipment industry, at 70.1 percent. Rubber manufacturers were next lowest (79.5 percent), followed by motor vehicles (79.8 percent). High funding levels were evident in the publishing, chemical, aerospace, cosmetic, scientific equipment, and sporting goods industries (99 percent or more).[45]

If vested liabilities are used as a serviceable approximation for PBGC-guaranteed benefits, the ratio of unfunded vested liabilities to net worth roughly indicates whether corporate assets would be adequate to cover PBGC-insured benefit commitments. On average, unfunded vested liabilities amounted to 2.7 percent of net worth for the sample of Fortune 500 industrials. About 2 percent of the companies had unfunded vested liabilities in excess of 30 percent of net worth—the maximum amount that the PBGC could claim to pay for a plan's unfunded basic benefits. The highest ratio was found in the motor vehicle industry, in which unfunded vested liabilities averaged 17.6 percent of net worth. Rubber manufacturers registered the next highest ratio—13.6 percent—and shipbuilding, railroad, transportation equipment firms followed with 10.0 percent.[46]

The nonindustrial firms tend to have more fully funded pensions than the industrials. Plan assets accounted for 99 percent of vested liabilities

44. Ibid., pp. 34–41.
45. Ibid.
46. Ibid., p. 42–45.

in commercial banking, 88 percent in retailing, 86 percent in transportation, and 98 percent in the utilities. For this nonindustrial group as a whole, unfunded vested liabilities averaged only 1.2 percent of net worth. Moreover, the nonindustrials use a slightly lower interest rate, 7.0 percent, to value accrued benefit liabilities.

Some have argued that the unfunded liabilities for accrued benefits reported by some firms can be attributed primarily to the use of conservative interest rate assumptions, and that once current higher long-term rates are introduced these plans appear to be fully funded.[47] Technically, this argument is correct. If a firm is about to terminate a plan under which it must pay $100 million for accrued benefits, the firm can fulfill its obligations by setting aside a smaller sum of money if the interest rate is assumed to be 15 percent rather than 5 percent. Beyond this narrow concept of termination liability, however, the effect of changing interest rates on a firm's pension liability is much less pronounced. When the liability is valued on the basis of plan continuation, the inflation that caused interest rates to rise will also be reflected in salary increases.

For instance, assume that the initial $100 million termination liability was for 5,000 workers forty years old who are entitled to 20 percent of final pay at age sixty and who will die at age seventy. If these workers were currently earning $10,000, then termination liability would be calculated as 20 percent of $10,000, or $2,000 per worker per year for ten years. When the liability is valued on a plan continuation basis, the relevant final pay is no longer current salary but rather projected earnings at age sixty. With an inflation rate of 10 percent that is passed on in the form of salary increases, final pay would be $66,000 rather than $10,000. Thus even without further benefit accruals, the firm's liability would be increased to $13,200 (20 percent of $66,000) per employee per year, for a total liability of $660 million over the assumed ten-year retirement period.[48]

47. Jeremy I. Bulow, "The Effect of Inflation on the Private Pension System," Conference Paper 103 (National Bureau of Economic Research, March 1981).

48. This example is merely intended to be illustrative. While the effect of inflation on salary increases will offset the higher interest rate over employees' work lives, the net impact during the retirement period depends on the degree to which benefits are indexed to reflect cost-of-living changes. In the example, the present value of the liability is roughly equal over the twenty-year period up to retirement. But because the example ignores the indexing issue, the present value of benefits over the entire thirty-year period is actually less with inflation than without it. Nevertheless, the point is valid that in most situations market interest rates should be used only if salary increases are included in the calculation.

Since most pension plans base benefits on final earnings and are unlikely to terminate, the concept of vested pension benefits based on projected final salary is probably a more reasonable measure of the firm's pension liability. The low interest rates used to calculate vested pension liabilities can be considered as partially offsetting the omission of projected inflation in final pay. Simply applying today's high market rates to calculations based on current salaries significantly understates a company's pension commitment. Moreover, in evaluating the status of funding among U.S. firms, it is important to note that pensions sponsored by smaller companies are likely to be less well funded than the Fortune 500 and that, in general, accrued nonvested benefits are not funded at all.

The Effect of Unfunded Liabilities on Equity Prices

Unfunded vested pension obligations represent a claim by plan participants against the earnings of the firm. Since unfunded pension benefits, unlike other claims, are not recorded on the corporate balance sheet, the portion of the firm's net worth credited to shareholders tends to be overstated. For some firms the amount of overstatement can be sizable. The question is whether the market recognizes and values pensioners' claims in pricing the firm's common stock.

To determine whether common stock values reflect pension obligations, investigators have adopted a model proposed by Franco Modigliani and Merton Miller, which yields an equation that expresses the market value of a firm's common stock as a function of several financial variables.[49] To this traditional equation subsequent researchers have added a variable for the firm's unfunded vested pension obligations. If each dollar of unfunded vested liability reduced the price of the firm's stock by one dollar, then the coefficient on the pension variable would be -1.

Whether a dollar-for-dollar offset should be expected depends on whether unfunded vested benefits, as published in the firm's financial statement, overstate or understate the company's total unfunded pension obligations. On the one hand, contributions to the pension fund are tax deductible, so that $1.00 contributed out of corporate income reduces

49. Franco Modigliani and Merton H. Miller, "The Cost of Capital, Corporation Finance, and the Theory of Investment," *American Economic Review*, vol. 48 (June 1958), pp. 261–97, and "Corporate Income Taxes and the Cost of Capital: A Correction," *American Economic Review*, vol. 53 (June 1963), pp. 433–43.

the firm's equity by about 50 cents. Hence unfunded vested benefits overstate the potential drain on stockholder wealth. Similarly, the lack of post-retirement indexing means that real pension liability may be lower than the magnitude implied by unfunded vested benefits. Moreover, failure to take account of the PBGC provisions that limit the firm's liability to 30 percent of net worth will overstate the liability of firm owners. On the other hand, unfunded vested benefits may seriously understate the firm's liability. First, since some nonvested benefits will eventually become vested, they would also be expected to reduce equity values. Second, since vested pension obligations are based on current rather than projected salaries, in an inflationary environment they understate true pension liabilities.[50] The net effect of these offsetting biases is theoretically indeterminate.

The first empirical analysis of the effect of a firm's unfunded vested pension benefits on its share price was performed by George Oldfield. He found that for 166 manufacturing firms in 1974 the coefficient on unfunded vested benefits was negative, was significantly different from zero, and hovered around -1.5.[51] His estimates indicate that each $1.00 of unfunded vested liability reduces share prices by $1.50, which implies that, according to the stock market, the unfunded liability for vested benefits somewhat understates the firm's true unfunded pension obligations. Nearly identical results were reported by Martin Feldstein and Stephanie Seligman, who estimated a similar equation using inflation-adjusted financial data for 1976 and 1977.[52] In a recent study Mark Gersowitz estimated an equation like Oldfield's, but allowed for a separate estimation of the coefficient for unfunded vested benefits in excess of the PBGC limit.[53] His results indicate that equity values appear unaffected by the portion of unfunded vested benefits above 30 percent

50. The impact of future inflation on wages and benefits could be incorporated in the pension valuation either by correctly forecasting nominal benefits and discounting by the corresponding nominal rates of return or by forecasting real benefits and using the real rate of return. In practice, vested pension liability is calculated using real benefits and an interest rate that reflects expected returns on the pension portfolio; it therefore partially incorporates the effects of inflation.

51. George S. Oldfield, "Financial Aspects of the Private Pension System," *Journal of Money, Credit and Banking,* vol. 9 (February 1977), pp. 48–54.

52. Martin Feldstein and Stephanie Seligman, "Pension Funding, Share Prices and National Saving," Working Paper 509 (National Bureau of Economic Research, July 1980).

53. Mark Gersovitz, "Economic Consequences of Unfunded Vested Pension Benefits," Working Paper 480 (National Bureau of Economic Research, May 1980).

of the firm's net worth. With this improved specification, however, the coefficient on unfunded vested benefits becomes even more negative (-2.3), which implies that, according to the stock market, pension liabilities are greatly understated in financial statements.

The finding that unfunded vested pension liabilities have a depressing effect on the market value of a firm's stock has implications for national saving, stock market performance, the magnitude of PBGC claims, and the potential impact of revised accounting procedures. As discussed in chapter 4, the extent to which unfunded pension liabilities affect stock market values influences the degree to which private pensions affect aggregate saving.[54] If pension liabilities lower stock values on a dollar-for-dollar basis, the savings disincentive arising from the promise of an additional dollar of unfunded benefits to potential pensioners should be offset by the stockholders' incentive to increase saving in response to a dollar reduction in stock values. Aggregate saving would then be totally unaffected by private pension plans.

The depressing effect of unfunded liabilities on stock values may have contributed somewhat to the poor performance of the stock market between 1969 and 1979, when Standard and Poor's index fell 47 percent in real terms. The impact was probably small, however, since unfunded vested pension benefits amounted to only 3 percent of the market value of equities during that period.[55] Moreover, in a rational stock market equity values would always be reduced by the value of unfunded benefit obligations. But the quantitative impact may have been greater in the 1970s than in previous decades because ERISA made unfunded vested benefits a binding obligation of the firm, whereas before 1973 the firm's liability was limited to the assets in the pension fund. ERISA undoubtedly also increased investors' awareness of private pension obligations.

Unfunded liabilities also affect the magnitude of the PBGC's claim on firm assets. As described earlier, the PBGC can hold a firm liable for unfunded guaranteed benefits up to an amount equal to 30 percent of its

54. Martin Feldstein, "Do Private Pensions Increase National Savings?" *Journal of Public Economics,* vol. 10 (December 1978), pp. 277–93.

55. Vested benefits in 1979 were assumed to be 90 percent funded, based on the 92 percent figure for 1980 provided by the 1981 Johnson and Higgins survey. Pension assets in 1979 totaled $350.5 billion, implying an unfunded vested benefit liability of $38.9 billion. The market value of total stock outstanding was $1,188.3 billion. See table 2-1, note b; Securities and Exchange Commission, *Monthly Statistical Review,* vol. 40 (May 1981), p. 10; American Council of Life Insurance, *Life Insurance Fact Book, 1981,* p. 54; and Board of Governors of the Federal Reserve, *Flow of Funds Accounts: Assets and Liabilities Outstanding, 1957–1980* (The Board, 1981), p. 39.

net worth, where net worth is frequently measured by the market value of the firm's stock. The size of the PBGC claim, however, is reduced if the market value of the firm's stock already reflects the pension liability. For example, if a firm has $100,000 of assets and no corporate liabilities, the PBGC can claim up to $30,000 of the firm's net worth. But if the firm has a $40,000 pension liability that reduces the market value of the stock to $60,000, the PBGC's claim will be only $18,000. Thus the PBGC's claim on corporate assets is less than 30 percent of corporate net worth when the market value of the firm's equity already reflects unfunded vested pension liabilities.

Finally, investor awareness of pension liabilities and of the impact of these unfunded liabilities on stock prices somewhat diffuses the current debate over the proper accounting for pensions. If a firm's unfunded liabilities are already incorporated in the valuation of its shares, then explicitly including pensions assets and liabilities on the corporate balance sheet should have little effect on the behavior of corporate managers or investors.

Accounting for Pension Costs

Although pension items do not appear on the balance sheet, the accounting profession has consistently attempted to introduce uniformity into the disclosure of pension costs. This section summarizes the evolution and limitations of current accounting practices, the interim standards recently adopted by the Financial Accounting Standards Board, and the current debate over the place of pensions on the corporate balance sheet.

Evolution of Present Practices

In 1948 the accounting profession made its first formal pronouncement on pension plans; namely, on the proper accounting for past service costs—that is, pension costs attributed under an actuarial method to the years before the plan started.[56] The accountants expressed the view that

56. American Institute of Accountants, Committee on Accounting Procedure, "Pension Plans: Accounting for Annuity Costs Based on Past Services," Accounting Research Bulletin 36 (November 1948). Past service cost is similar to prior service cost except that the latter also includes the additions to the accrued actuarial liability resulting from retroactive benefit increases after the plan has been in operation.

since plans were usually introduced to improve the future productivity of the company, past service costs should be charged to current and future income, not to surplus. But they did not require that past service costs be recognized for accounting purposes, nor did they indicate how periodic pension costs should be reflected in the income statement of the employer.

With the continued expansion of pensions and the growing recognition that pension promises are ongoing commitments, a 1956 pronouncement addressed the entire subject of accounting for pensions. It was argued that the accounting be done on an accrual basis, not in the old way that listed on the firm's financial statement only those sums actually transferred to the pension fund.[57] It was also suggested that past service costs be amortized over some reasonable period. This pronouncement, however, had little effect, since the accrual concept was applied only to vested benefits and at that time few plans had vesting provisions.

Employers therefore continued to adopt widely divergent methods of accounting for pension costs, which seriously complicated the interpretation of corporate financial statements. As a result, the Accounting Principles Board commissioned a comprehensive study of pension cost accounting, which formed the basis for APB Opinion 8, issued in 1966.[58] This opinion officially endorsed and prescribed the accrual basis of accounting; thereafter a firm was required to reflect on its books a pension charge at least equal to the normal cost of the plan plus interest on the firm's unfunded actuarial liability.[59] Much flexibility remained, however, since employers could adopt a wide range of actuarial cost methods and use various approaches to amortize unfunded liabilities. The opinion of the accounting board did not prescribe that unfunded liabilities appear on the employer's balance sheet unless required accruals had not been funded.

Interest in accounting for pension costs was rekindled by the enactment of ERISA, which imposed a new legal liability on employers with

57. American Institute of Accountants, Committee on Accounting Procedure, "Accounting for Costs of Pension Plans," Accounting Research Bulletin 47 (September 1956).

58. The Accounting Principles Board authorized a study by Ernest L. Hicks, *Accounting for the Cost of Pension Plans,* Accounting Research Study 8 (New York: American Institute of Certified Public Accountants, 1965). The board concurred with most of the study's conclusions and recommendations and therefore incorporated them into *Accounting for the Cost of Pension Plans,* APB Opinion 8 (New York: AICPA, 1966).

59. An additional funding contribution was required to reduce any unfunded liability for vested benefits.

inadequately funded plans. The accounting hierarchy established task forces to explore four fundamental questions: (1) how to determine the amount of pension expense to be charged to the employer for each accounting period; (2) how plan assets should be valued; (3) whether the unfunded liability should appear on the balance sheet; and (4) whether plan costs should be calculated in the same way for the plan as for the sponsoring company.

At about the same time, the Pension Research Council, a private group of pension experts, commissioned two partners of Arthur Andersen and Company, one of the "big eight" accounting firms, to try to resolve the foregoing issues within a "coherent, theoretical framework." The resolution reached by the authors, William D. Hall and David L. Landsittel, was clearly considered controversial, since the eighty-page study was published with fifty-six pages of dissenting comments by the actuary members of the council.[60] Nevertheless, the study and dissenting comments probably constitute the most comprehensive summary of the technical and philosophical issues that surround pension accounting.

Hall and Landsittel generally endorsed the principle embodied in APB Opinion 8 that the costs of a pension plan should be charged to the accounting period in which they accrue, whether or not they are funded.[61] At the same time, however, they felt that the opinion allowed employers excessive latitude in calculating accrued pension costs, since the various equally acceptable actuarial cost methods produce widely different results under identical economic circumstances.

As a first step in narrowing the wide range of acceptable actuarial methods, Hall and Landsittel tried to define the rate at which pension costs accrue. Since pension obligations are incurred when services are performed and services are rewarded by wages and salaries, they concluded that the accrual of a pension obligation should be measured in

60. William D. Hall and David L. Landsittel, *A New Look at Accounting for Pension Costs* (Irwin, 1977).
61. At the outset the authors stated that the purpose of financial statements should be to communicate information about the nature and value of the economic resources of an entity as of a specified date, the interests of various parties in such reserves as of that date, and changes in the nature and value of those resources from period to period (ibid., p. 3). Two corollaries follow from this objective. First, only economic resources that are useful, scarce, and exchangeable should be recognized as assets. Intangible assets and deferred charges, items that do not have a value separable from the business, should not appear on the balance sheet. Second, changes in net economic resources should be reflected in the income statement as they occur. From these conclusions the authors endorsed APB Opinion 8.

terms of the employee's compensation, no matter how the benefit is determined under the plan's provisions. The authors then explored two ways of correlating the accrual of pension costs with employee compensation; they chose the one that would assign to each year of service a proportion of the total projected benefit that reflects the ratio of the employee's compensation in that year to total expected compensation.[62] The authors chose this approach even though it yields employer costs that increase over time for the individual employee, and, in some cases, for all covered workers. While an alternative actuarial cost method that would produce level annual cost accruals was considered, it was rejected because it would yield actuarial liabilities above the actuarial value of benefits actually earned. On balance, the authors concluded that it was more important for the balance sheet to reflect realistic values than for the income statement to be insulated against fluctuating pension cost accruals.

Once accrued pension benefits have been calculated, the value of assets in the pension fund must be determined in order to calculate the employer's unfunded liability. Hall and Landsittel concluded that plan assets should be valued at market for accounting purposes, since the balance sheet is designed to provide a "snapshot" of the firm's resources and liabilities at a given time. The valuation of pension liabilities should also reflect market considerations through periodic changes in the investment return used to calculate the present value of pension commitments. The authors acknowledged that funding policies may be based on different principles from those underlying accounting practices and that for funding purposes it may be desirable to smooth asset market values.

Hall and Landsittel concluded that the unfunded liability for all benefits accrued to date should appear as a liability on the firm's balance sheet.[63] The argument for including nonvested as well as vested benefits rests on the assumption that the pension plan will continue indefinitely.

62. The alternative approach considered would allocate the total projected benefit to the employees' prospective years of service in such a way that pension *cost* accruals constitute a level percentage of compensation.

63. For the time being, the authors would allow the liability for unfunded benefits to be offset by an asset labeled "deferred charges," so that the employers' net worth would not be reduced suddenly by the unfunded pension obligations. Deferred charges, however, are not a valid asset according to the guidelines that follow from the financial statement objectives established at the outset of the Hall and Landsittel study. They are not

Since benefits promised will ultimately be paid, they represent a claim on the economic resources of the employer. On the other hand, the authors maintained that full consolidation of the assets and liabilities of the plan into the financial statements of sponsoring employers would not be appropriate, since the funded assets of a pension plan are not available to pay the general claims of the creditors of the employer.

Finally, Hall and Landsittel argued for symmetry between the method of accounting for pension benefits used by a pension plan and that used by the sponsoring employer in recognizing pension costs. They maintained that a pension plan has no economic substance apart from the sponsoring employer, because the plan is merely a vehicle for discharging the employer's pension obligations. Thus costs and liabilities should be computed in the same way for the pension plan and the employer.

Most of the opposition to Hall and Landsittel's recommendations centered on the idea of including unfunded accrued benefits as a liability on the balance sheet. The main arguments against such a change were (1) that not all accrued pension benefits are legal obligations of the employer; (2) that pension costs arising from benefit improvements applied to prior service should not be attributed to an earlier period, because they are usually instituted to improve current and future labor performance; and (3) that including prior service costs on the balance sheet would discourage benefit liberalizations and the establishment of new plans. Also criticized was the proposal to value plan assets at market. The actuaries argued that since pension plans are ongoing concerns, some measure of the average value of assets would be more appropriate than market value as of a particular date. The market value of plan assets at a given time is relevant only if the pension plan is to be terminated on that same date. Finally, several members of the Pension Research Council objected to the actuarial method proposed by Hall and Landsittel, some opposing the adoption of a single method and others opposing particular elements of their proposal, such as the rising and unstable costs and the relation of benefit accrual to compensation regardless of the plan's provisions.

---

exchangeable, since they are not separable from the business, nor can they be sold or exchanged for other assets or used to satisfy claims of creditors. Hence, in the future, the authors' preferred solution would be to expense any increase in the unfunded liabilities during the year in which the plan is adopted or amended, thereby eliminating the need for deferred charges.

Recent Developments in Accounting for Pension Costs

Although it is still too early to determine whether the Hall-Landsittel recommendations will be adopted, recent developments from the Financial Accounting Standards Board indicate that the accounting profession is moving in that direction. In 1980 the board issued statements 35, *Accounting and Reporting by Defined Benefit Pension Plans,* and 36, *Disclosure of Pension Information,* as interim measures to improve the reporting and disclosure of pension information until the major study of pension accounting that is in progress can be completed. This comprehensive review was initiated in early 1981 with the circulation of a discussion memorandum that raised many fundamental issues about accounting for pensions.[64]

Statement 36 was designed to immediately improve the quality of pension data disclosed on employers' financial statements. The board concluded that unfunded prior service costs, which the Securities and Exchange Commission requires on its form 10-K, are not useful in evaluating the impact of pension plans on the financial condition of the employer, since the value of those costs can vary considerably depending on the actuarial method selected. The board also felt that too much latitude existed in calculating the value of unfunded accrued vested benefits, which appears on corporate financial statements, because APB Opinion 8 did not specify the basis that should be used for valuing pension assets. To remedy these deficiencies, statement 36 required all firms to disclose the actuarial present value of all accumulated plan benefits and the market value of plan assets available to pay those benefits. Employers must disclose the assumed rate of return used in calculating the present value of benefits and the date as of which the benefit information was determined. Moreover, they must present any changes in actuarial cost method, actuarial assumptions, or plan provisions that affect the comparability of reported data from one period to another.

Statement 35, which pertains to the financial statements of the pension plans, specifies how the present value of vested and nonvested accumulated benefits and of the plan assets are to be determined. The statement defines participants' accumulated benefits as those future benefit payments that are attributable under plan provisions to the

64. Financial Accounting Standards Board, "An Analysis of Issues Related to Employers' Accounting for Pensions and Other Postemployment Benefits," FASB Discussion Memorandum, February 19, 1981.

employees' service rendered up to the valuation date. This measurement is based primarily on employees' past salaries and service; future salary changes and future years of service are not considered.[65] Plan assets are to be evaluated by the accrual basis of accounting, that is, presented at fair market value. Hence much of the ambiguity surrounding the disclosure of pension plan data has been eliminated.

The discussion memorandum is the first step in a complete review of how employers should account for obligations and costs incurred in connection with post-employment benefits. The review will eventually yield a statement that supersedes APB Opinion 8. Although the entire review will be long and complex, the Financial Accounting Standards Board has limited the current discussion memorandum to eight basic issues:[66]

—What part, if any, of the obligation to provide future benefits should be recognized as a liability on the employer's balance sheet?

—What amount should be recognized as a pension benefit expense in the employer's income statement?

—How should liabilities and expenses be allocated to various time periods?

—How should a change in an existing plan or the introduction of a new plan be accounted for?

—How should experience gains and losses be recognized?

—What disclosures should be required in addition to items recognized on the balance sheet and income statement?

—How would the answers to these issues differ for (a) pension plans based on final salary and other plans, for (b) plans covered by ERISA and noncovered state and local plans, and for (c) funded plans and unfunded plans?

—How should post-employment benefits other than pensions be accounted for?

To further simplify the analysis, the memorandum focuses on traditional single-employer plans. Thus the consideration of multiemployer plans, insured plans, and foreign plans has been deferred. Also postponed for later discussion are issues surrounding actuarial assumptions, such

65. Future years of service are considered only in determining employees' expected eligibility for particular types of benefits, such as early retirement, death, or disability.

66. Besides these explicit questions, a major issue addressed repeatedly throughout the discussion memorandum is the distinction between pension expense and pension funding. The memorandum questions whether the current practice of most employers to fund and expense the same amount is necessarily appropriate.

as the desirability of adopting uniform assumptions for plan valuations. Nevertheless, despite its somewhat narrow focus, the current memorandum will undoubtedly spur some provocative changes in the accounting for pension costs.

Conclusion

A 1965 cabinet committee report on the status of the U.S. private pension system cited many examples of overstrict participation and vesting requirements, lack of coverage for workers who change jobs frequently, inadequate pension funding, mismanagement of pension assets, and plans that terminated without enough assets to fulfill benefit commitments.[67] The passage of the Employee Retirement Income Security Act roughly a decade later eliminated most of these problems. In doing so, ERISA greatly increased the legal responsibility of the corporation for these pension benefits. Its impact was actually threefold. First, ERISA's participation and vesting standards have created pension commitments that would not have existed without the legislation. Second, the funding requirements have led to pension contributions that would not otherwise have been made. Finally, the authority of the Pension Benefit Guaranty Corporation to assess companies for up to 30 percent of their net worth means that corporate assets are committed to financing pension benefits that were not so committed before ERISA. The magnitude of these increased liabilities for any particular employer depends on the pre-ERISA characteristics of that employer's plan. Large corporations with well-established plans may have been relatively unaffected by the passage of ERISA, whereas other corporations with smaller plans have probably been affected very much.[68]

67. See President's Committee on Corporate Pension Funds and Other Private Retirement and Welfare Programs, *Public Policy and Private Pension Programs: A Report to the President on Private Employee Retirement Plans* (Government Printing Office, 1965).

68. A study prepared for the Business Roundtable in 1979 concluded that over 89 percent of the small plans in operation two and one-half years after the passage of ERISA had to extend pension coverage to additional workers and to increase the vested status of some previous participants. See Arthur Andersen and Co., *Cost of Government Regulation Study for the Business Roundtable* (New York: The Business Roundtable and Arthur Andersen and Co., March 1979), pp. 40–41. These costs may have contributed to the relatively large number of post-ERISA terminations among small plans. During the three years after ERISA's enactment there was a 5 percent net reduction in the number of single-

For the corporate community as a whole, however, ERISA has established pensions as serious commitments whose fulfillment is backed not only by pension fund assets but also by the assets of the corporation. Although ERISA provided for the explicit separation of pension assets from corporate assets, at the same time it made the pension plan an integral part of corporate activity. And now many financial analysts and accountants are arguing that the corporation and the pension plan should be evaluated on a consolidated basis.

---

employer defined benefit plans, as 16,500 plans were terminated between October 1974 and September 1977. Most of these terminations were of small plans, which have a termination rate roughly twenty times greater than large plans. See Pension Benefit Guaranty Corporation, *Analysis of Single Employer Defined Benefit Plan Terminations, 1977* (PBGC, 1978), pp. 4, 17.

chapter seven **Private Pensions
in an Inflationary Environment**

Inflation has become the most serious economic problem of the 1980s. Yet it is often argued that no one need be hurt by continually rising prices because, in theory, all monetary transactions could be indexed. Private pension benefits are of particular interest in this regard, since it appears virtually impossible to protect workers' pensions from the erosive effect of inflation without restructuring the whole private pension system.

This chapter examines private pensions in an inflationary environment. The first section explores current provisions designed to ensure that accrued benefits keep pace with inflation until the employee retires. Because final earnings plans are increasingly common, more workers will receive benefits that reflect inflation and productivity growth over their careers. But even with such plans the benefits of workers who change jobs frequently will be eroded by inflation. The second section focuses on the existing provisions for post-retirement cost-of-living adjustments. While these provisions have compensated somewhat for rising prices, in general they have only partly offset the impact of inflation on retirees' benefits. In the third section a model is discussed that summarizes the investment performance required of pension funds if private plans are to provide full cost-of-living adjustments both before and after retirement. According to the model, the full indexation of benefits to inflation would require that nominal interest rates fully reflect increases in the price level. Since real rates of return declined during the 1970s in response to inflation, pension funds currently have not had access to investments that satisfy this criterion. Alternative approaches to indexing are explored, including the issuing of index bonds for pension funds. The fourth section describes the new British pension system, which has greatly improved portability and ensured full indexing of both public and private pension benefits. The chapter concludes that although full indexing may not be possible without major innovations, partial indexing is both desirable and possible.

Preserving the Value of Benefits until Retirement

To preserve the value of benefits that accrue over a person's working years, his pension must be based on earnings that reflect the increases in productivity and the price level during those years. For private plans the real value of benefits will depend on the period used to calculate a worker's average earnings and the degree of continuing participation in a particular plan. Conversely, social security, which has virtually universal coverage and revalues past wages to reflect inflation and productivity gains, preserves the full value of benefits until retirement.

Private Pension Plans

Employer-sponsored private plans are divided into two main categories: defined contribution and defined benefit plans. Under the first the employer is obliged to set aside funds on a specified basis; under the second the employer provides benefits according to a specified formula. Thus under defined contribution plans the employee's benefit is determined by the value of accumulated contributions made on his behalf and by the investment earnings on those contributions. To what degree this benefit replaces current wages will depend on the investment performance of accumulated assets. Under defined benefit plans benefits are determined by a formula relating the pension to compensation or length of service or both. In this case the compensation base determines whether the worker's initial benefit reflects productivity and inflation-induced wage increases. The following discussion focuses on the effect of inflation on defined benefit plans, since most pension plan participants were covered by such plans.[1]

1. Forms for 1975 filed by plan administrators with the Department of Labor indicate that over 85 percent of coverage is in defined benefit plans, about 10 percent in profit-sharing plans, and less than 5 percent in money purchase plans. Defined benefit plans predominate because of the circumstances surrounding the introduction of private plans. During the 1950s, when most modern-day pension plans were being formed, benefit schemes were so constructed that, to achieve equity among employees, employers could blanket in older workers for whom little or no contributions had been paid. The defined

Defined benefit formulas can be either a flat or a unit type. Under a flat benefit formula the pension varies with years of service but not with employee compensation. For instance, if a worker were to accrue $100 for each year of service, after thirty years he would be entitled to an annual benefit of $3,000. Plans that use flat benefit formulas used to be called pattern plans, and this terminology is still used in the Bankers Trust studies.[2]

Under the more common unit formula, benefits depend on both compensation and length of service; that is, a specified percentage of compensation accrues to the employee for each year of creditable service. For example, an employee may earn 1.5 percentage points a year and after thirty years be entitled to a benefit equal to 45 percent of preretirement compensation. Plans using this type of benefit formula have traditionally been called conventional plans.[3]

---

benefit plan facilitated the granting of retroactive credits more easily than plans based on defined contributions. The importance of retroactive coverage is confirmed by a 1974 Bureau of Labor Statistics survey of about 1,500 pension plans, showing that 70 percent of workers covered by defined benefit plans had received full retroactive credits when the plan was introduced and almost all the remaining 30 percent had received some partial service credit. BLS, Office of Wages and Industrial Relations, 1974 Defined Benefit Pension Plan Study, datatape, 1977.

The proportion of workers covered by defined benefit plans may decline somewhat in the future. Because ERISA imposed strict funding and extensive reporting requirements on those plans, most plans established after 1974 have been ones with defined contributions. In fact, between 1976 and 1978, 70 to 85 percent of all participants in newly formed pensions were covered by defined contribution plans. Despite this trend, however, most workers with pension coverage today belong to defined benefit plans. See James H. Schulz, Thomas D. Leavitt, and Leslie Kelly, "Private Pensions Fall Far Short of Preretirement Income Levels," *Monthly Labor Review,* vol. 102 (February 1979), p. 32, n. 4; Peter M. Mieszkowski and Alicia H. Munnell, "Retroactive Coverage on Funding Private and Public Retirement Systems: To Fund or Not to Fund," in Peter Mieszkowski and George E. Peterson, eds., *Public Sector Labor Markets* (Washington, D.C.: Urban Institute, 1981), pp. 129–63; and press releases, Internal Revenue Service, July 1, 1977, March 24, 1978, and February 8, 1979.

2. These have been adopted by some international unions and negotiated with minor variations by individual companies or groups of companies. Under pattern plans inflation and wage growth are reflected in adjustments in the flat dollar accrual rates. According to the Bankers Trust studies, the median accrual rate for the pattern plans was $66 during 1965–70, $108 for 1970–75, and $144 for 1975–80. William J. Mischo, Sook-Kuen Chang, and Eugene P. Kaston, *Corporate Pension Plan Study: A Guide for the 1980s,* Bankers Trust Company, Employee Benefit Division (New York: Bankers Trust, 1980), p. 39; and Bankers Trust Company, *Study of Corporate Pension Plans, 1975* (Bankers Trust, 1975), p. 26.

3. These plans apply to most salaried workers and to some collectively bargained situations.

For a worker covered by a conventional defined benefit plan who remains with the same employer throughout his working life, the extent to which the benefit reflects inflation and productivity growth depends on the compensation base used in the benefit calculation. This base can be an average of earnings over the worker's entire career, part of his career, or his final year of employment. The longer the averaging period, the more years of relatively low earnings it will include, and therefore the lower the base. Unless the benefit formula is liberalized periodically, the purchasing power of benefits calculated on career average earnings will be eroded by inflation. Conversely, the more the compensation base emphasizes final pay in any given benefit formula, the better the worker's benefit will be protected from inflation over his working years.

In response to the high inflation of the 1970s, more of the conventional plans included in the Bankers Trust studies began calculating benefits on some form of final earnings. Whereas only 39 percent of the plans surveyed based all benefits on final pay during the period 1965–69, 76 percent did so during the period 1975–79. Over these same periods the proportion of plans with all benefits based on career earnings declined from 35 to 15 percent (see table 7-1).

At the same time final pay plans tended to shorten the number of years over which earnings are averaged. By 1979, 83 percent of such plans were based on average compensation in the last five years of employment. But with 10 percent annual wage growth, even a five-year average plan pays benefits about 17 percent below the worker's salary in his final year. If all wage growth were due to inflation, a worker in a plan based on final five-year pay would receive a benefit worth only 83 percent of the benefit he would have received without inflation. In short, the only formula that preserves on a contractual basis the value of pension benefits as they accrue is one that bases benefits on the final year of pay.

For workers who change jobs frequently, the ability of even final earnings plans to offset the effects of inflation is limited. Consider a worker who enters the labor force at twenty-five and changes jobs every ten years until he retires. Even if all his employers sponsor final earnings plans and his benefits are fully vested, his final pension will resemble that of a career average plan. Table 7-2 shows the ratio of benefits for workers with continuous and discontinuous employment under various rates of inflation and wage growth. Even though this example assumes that all employers have identical plans, it is clear that the mobile employee is severely penalized. If inflation were 6 percent, the pension

Table 7-1. Compensation Base of Conventional Private Pension Plans, 1950–79
Percent of Plans

Compensation base	1950–52	1953–55	1956–59	1960–64	1965–69	1970–74	1975–79
Career average	72	62	56	45	35	22	15
Final average	18	26	27	31	39	54	76
Regular benefits, career average; minimum benefits, final average	4	6	12	16	20	16	5
Part on career average and part on final average	0	1	2	5	6	8	4
Other	6	5	3	3	0	0	0
Addendum *Average length of compensation base*[a]							
Three years	n.a.	n.a.	0	0	1	2	16[b]
Five years	n.a.	n.a.	53	57	77	93	83
Ten years	n.a.	n.a.	41	37	15	4	0
Other	n.a.	n.a.	6	6	7	1	1

Sources: William J. Mischo, Sook-Kuen Chang, and Eugene P. Kaston, *Corporate Pension Plan Study: A Guide for the 1980s,* Bankers Trust Company Employee Benefit Division (New York: Bankers Trust, 1980); Bankers Trust Company, *Study of Industrial Retirement Plans, 1965* (Bankers Trust, 1965); and Bankers Trust Company, *Study of Industrial Retirement Plans, 1956* (Bankers Trust, 1956).
n.a. Not available.
a. Includes all pension plans that use a final average compensation base.
b. Includes a small number of plans with four-year average or final year's compensation.

received by the worker who had held four jobs during his work life would equal 51 percent of the pension received by the worker who had been continuously employed by one firm. If inflation were 10 percent, the relative position of the mobile employee would deteriorate further, so that his benefit would be worth only 40 percent of that awarded to the one-job worker. Thus the higher the rate of inflation, the more discontinuous employment reduces the real value of benefits. This erosion of benefits occurs because benefits are not indexed between termination of employment and retirement.[4]

Preserving the value of pension benefits between termination and retirement cannot be accomplished merely by increasing portability.

4. Similar problems, of course, emerge under flat benefit formulas. A vested pension of $100 for an employee who terminates employment at age thirty would have the purchasing power of only $55 by age sixty-five if annual inflation were 4 percent; with an inflation rate of 8 percent, purchasing power would be reduced to $32.

Nevertheless, from the point of view of plan participants, portability or reciprocity agreements, which allow the transfer of accrued pension credits among plans, are desirable provisions, since they protect employee rights and complement vesting provisions. Whereas vesting protects a plan participant who changes jobs before retirement against the loss of accrued benefit rights, portability enhances the employee's chances of becoming vested. Allowing workers to transfer accrued credits from one plan to another helps them to accumulate enough credits to meet minimum standards for plan coverage and entitlement to benefits. Through the aggregation of credits in two or more plans, benefits may be paid where otherwise they would not be.

With minor exceptions, provisions for portability do not exist in the United States.[5] Several proposals have been made over the years to create a central clearinghouse to permit workers to transfer accrued pension credits.[6] But these proposals have usually had limited goals, such as preserving retirement benefits that might otherwise be cashed out. None of the proposals seeks to maintain the value of pension benefits between termination and retirement. For even with complete portability—for instance, if all private pensions were identical defined benefit plans and workers could easily transfer credits from one plan to another—preserving benefit values in an inflationary environment would still be problematic.

To protect the value of pension benefits for the mobile employee it is

5. Portability is usually associated with collectively bargained, multiemployer plans in industries where employees can be expected to work for many different employers and in several geographical areas during the course of their working lives. Hence provisions for portability are especially prevalent in the building and construction industries. Also, the International Brotherhood of Teamsters has stressed reciprocity. Portability also exists in the nonprofit sector. Under the Teachers Insurance and Annuity Association–College Retirement Equities Fund (TIAA-CREF) professors who work for a number of participating colleges will have all their contributions added to a single account. Approximately 4,000 employers in the health and welfare field have formed the National Health and Welfare Retirement Association, which combines the vested pensions earned by member employers and pays the retiree a single pension. See Dan M. McGill, *Preservation of Pension Benefit Rights* (Irwin for the Pension Research Council of the Wharton School of Finance and Commerce, 1972), p. 182.

6. Merton C. Bernstein, *The Future of Private Pensions* (London: Free Press of Glencoe, 1964), pp. 270–96; President's Committee on Corporate Pension Funds and Other Private Retirement and Welfare Programs, *Public Policy and Private Pension Programs: A Report to the President on Private Employee Retirement Plans* (Government Printing Office, 1965); and Donald S. Grubbs, Jr., "Pension Portability," *National Pension Policies: Private Pension Plans,* Hearings before the Subcommittee on Retirement Income and Employment of the House Select Committee on Aging, 95 Cong. 2 sess. (GPO, 1978), pp. 529–65.

Table 7-2. Comparison of Benefits for a Four-Job Worker and a One-Job Worker over Forty Years of Employment, at Different Rates of Inflation and Wage Growth[a]

Item	Compensation base: final pay (dollars)[b]	Compensation rule (percent of salary)[c]	Benefits (dollars)	Ratio of benefits: four-job/ one-job worker
Inflation rate: 0 percent				
Four-job worker[d]				
Job 1	10,000	10	1,000	. . .
Job 2	10,000	10	1,000	. . .
Job 3	10,000	10	1,000	. . .
Job 4	10,000	10	1,000	. . .
Total	. . .	40	4,000	1.00
One-job worker	10,000	40	4,000	
Inflation rate: 6 percent				
Four-job worker[d]				
Job 1	17,908	10	1,790	. . .
Job 2	32,071	10	3,207	. . .
Job 3	57,435	10	5,744	. . .
Job 4	102,857	10	10,286	. . .
Total	. . .	40	21,027	0.51
One-job worker	102,857	40	41,143	
Inflation rate: 8 percent				
Four-job worker[d]				
Job 1	21,589	10	2,159	. . .
Job 2	46,609	10	4,661	. . .
Job 3	100,626	10	10,063	. . .
Job 4	217,243	10	21,724	. . .
Total	. . .	40	38,607	0.44
One-job worker	217,243	40	86,897	
Inflation rate: 10 percent				
Four-job worker[d]				
Job 1	25,937	10	2,594	. . .
Job 2	67,275	10	6,728	. . .
Job 3	174,494	10	17,449	. . .
Job 4	452,593	10	45,259	. . .
Total	. . .	40	72,030	0.40
One-job worker	452,593	40	181,037	

Source: Author's calculations.

a. Assumes a consistent annual increase in wages to compensate for inflation, and no growth in wages due to productivity.

b. Base salary is $10,000, and benefit is calculated on earnings in last year of employment.

c. Assumes annual benefit accrual of 1 percent a year.

d. Assumes worker stays at each job for ten years.

Table 7-3. Purchasing Power of $100 Vested Benefits at Age Sixty-five, at Varying Inflation Rates and Age at Job Termination
Dollars

	Annual inflation rate		
Age at job termination	6 percent	8 percent	10 percent
30	13	7	4
40	23	15	9
50	42	32	24

Source: Author's calculations.

necessary to index benefits between termination and retirement. Although final earnings plans provide implicit indexation for people who work until retirement, employers resist indexing vested benefits for terminated employees. Rapidly rising wages combined with declining real yields on pension assets would significantly raise the required level of pension contribution. The firm can shift part of this additional cost to active employees by slowing the rate of wage growth, but it would be forced to bear the full burden for terminated employees. Furthermore, by providing lower benefits to mobile employees, the firm can perhaps reduce employee turnover and retain skilled workers. Without post-termination indexing, however, the mobile employee suffers a substantial loss in the value of his pension benefit because of inflation (see table 7-3).

Social Security

The social security system presents an interesting contrast to private pension plans, since all U.S. workers covered by social security are now institutionally protected against erosion of benefits over their lifetime. Because social security coverage is virtually universal, workers continue to accrue benefit credits despite changes in employment. Moreover, although social security benefits are based on career average compensation rather than final earnings, periodic liberalization of the benefit formula before 1977 compensated for inflation and productivity growth, and, more recently, indexation of earnings histories and the benefit formula have ensured that benefits keep pace with inflation and real wage increases over the employee's working years.[7]

7. The benefit for a person retiring at age sixty-five in 1982 is based on earnings after 1950, in the highest n calendar years, where n is the number of years after 1950 and before the year of attaining age sixty-two (1979), minus 5 years. Thus benefits for such a person retiring in 1982 would be based on twenty-three years of earnings. Present legislation provides that in the future the number of years be increased by one each calendar year until the averaging period reaches thirty-five for those attaining age sixty-five in 1993.

Before the 1972 amendments, adjustments for inflation and wage growth were made by ad hoc increases in the benefit formula. After 1950 and up to and including 1972, the benefit formula was adjusted eight times, yielding a 142 percent cumulative increase in the level of initial benefit payments. These increases more than compensated for the effect of inflation over the period, since the consumer price index rose by only 74 percent. In fact, the cumulative increase in benefits closely approximated the 158 percent growth in average wages between 1950 and 1972.[8]

In an effort to introduce automatic adjustments that would keep benefits in line with productivity growth and inflation, the 1972 amendments overindexed the benefit structure for workers about to retire, thereby authorizing benefits that represented an increasing proportion of preretirement income. The 1977 amendments corrected the overindexing through a procedure that maintains a constant ratio of benefits to preretirement earnings. This procedure explicitly adjusts both the worker's prior earnings and the social security benefit formula for increases in the average nationwide wage.[9] By calculating benefits on past earnings that have been revalued to reflect increases in prices and productivity up to age sixty-two and increases in prices thereafter, the social security program now protects the value of benefits against inflation over the worker's career.

Preserving the Value of Benefits after Retirement

Maintaining the value of pension benefits between termination and retirement will only partly protect pensions against inflation. Unless there are post-retirement cost-of-living adjustments, retirees' living standards will decline in retirement as inflation erodes the purchasing power of their benefits.[10] Since the future pattern of price increases cannot be predicted, no amount of preplanning can ensure total protection from inflation. Therefore, the only way to insulate retirees from the erosion of

8. *Social Security Bulletin: Annual Statistical Supplement, 1976*, p. 15. The consumer price index (1967 = 100) was 125.3 in 1972 and 72.1 in 1950. Average weekly earnings in private nonagricultural employment were $136.90 in 1972 and $53.13 in 1950. *Economic Report of the President, January 1980*, pp. 245, 259.

9. Without annual adjustments, the progressivity of the benefit formula would result in declining replacement rates as the level of wages increases.

10. For a comprehensive discussion of indexation, see Robert J. Myers, *Indexation of Pension and Other Benefits* (Irwin, 1979).

their pension benefits is to provide cost-of-living adjustments that compensate for increases in the price level. Without such adjustments a retiree's economic welfare depends entirely on the vagaries of the economy—a situation that undermines the establishment of a rational retirement system.

Automatic cost-of-living adjustments during retirement will maintain the worker's standard of living by preserving his command over goods and services. Nevertheless, the retiree's economic position will decline relative to that of current workers because those still in the work force receive adjustments for any improvements in productivity as well as for any increase in prices. Indexing pension benefits to the average wage rather than to the price level would both permit retirees to share in the growth of the economy and insulate them from inflation. Such an arrangement would prevent a deterioration in their position relative to that of employed workers.

Although most people recognize the need for inflation adjustments, many oppose adjusting retirement benefits to reflect productivity growth. Resistance centers on two points: (1) the desirability of extending rewards for gains in productivity to those who did not earn them and (2) the ability of society to afford such increases. Moreover, the philosophical debate over whether standards of living should be measured in real or relative terms is as yet unsettled. But the fact that social security ties post-retirement increases to inflation means that price adjustments are regarded as the relevant criterion against which to evaluate the performance of private plans.

The debate has been muted in recent years, since the traditional relationship between the growth in wages and the growth in prices has been reversed. Between 1950 and 1970, money wages grew at an annual rate of 4.2 percent, 1.8 percent attributable to productivity gains and 2.4 percent to rising prices. During the 1970s average money wages increased 7.0 percent annually, while prices increased 7.8 percent. Prices rose faster than wages in that decade because productivity growth averaged −0.8 percent annually. Because of the reversal of the traditional relationship between wage growth and price growth, some analysts have proposed that benefit adjustments for social security retirees be limited to the rate of wage growth. It would seem inequitable for workers to pay taxes to ensure that retirees keep pace with inflation when workers themselves are falling behind. On the other hand, a system that forces retirees to share in productivity losses without allowing them to benefit from productivity gains would also seem inequitable. A compromise was suggested by the National Commission on Social Security whereby automatic benefit increases would be limited to wage growth when the consumer price index rose faster than wages for a two-year period, but a "catch-up" provision would enable beneficiaries to recoup the reduction once wage growth began to exceed price increases.[11]

The Choice of an Index

While the current consensus is that retirees' income should be adjusted for increases in prices and not productivity, considerable controversy has surrounded the appropriate price index to be used for adjusting benefits. The consumer price index, prepared by the Bureau of Labor Statistics, is the most widely known and is used to adjust social security benefits.[12] The index had been criticized for not accurately reflecting the total level of inflation, primarily because of its treatment of homeownership. In response to the extensive criticism, the bureau announced in late 1981 that a new index would be issued based on a revised procedure for estimating the changes in the cost of owner-occupied housing. The new index would be applied to indexing social security benefits beginning in January 1985.

Before the new index was announced, some economists suggested that the implicit deflator for personal consumption expenditures (PCE) would serve as a more accurate measure of inflation than the CPI. The present CPI and the PCE deflator differ conceptually in many ways, most notably in their weighting procedures and the treatment of housing. These differences tend to make the CPI increase more rapidly than the PCE deflator during periods of accelerating inflation. The bias is symmetrical, however, so that the index would understate inflation as the rate of price increase declines. As shown in table 7-4, the two indexes increased at roughly the same rate from 1950 to 1972, when inflation was

11. National Commission on Social Security, *Social Security in America's Future*, Final Report (NCSS, 1981), pp. 163–67. The commission's proposal would apply only when the increase in the CPI exceeded 5 percent.

12. Since January 1978 the Bureau of Labor Statistics has published official consumer price indexes for two population groups: (1) a new CPI for all urban consumers (CPI-U), which covers 80 percent of the total noninstitutional population, and (2) a revised CPI for urban wage earners and clerical workers (CPI-W), which covers about 45 percent of the population. Despite its narrower coverage, the CPI-W is used to index social security benefits and serves as the basis for cost-of-living adjustments under most collectively bargained wage agreements. In the following discussion, however, references to the consumer price index refer to the CPI-U unless otherwise indicated.

Table 7-4. Change in the Consumer Price Index for All Urban Consumers and in the Personal Consumption Expenditure Deflator, 1950–80
Percent

Year or period	CPI	PCE deflator	Percentage point difference
1950–72	2.5	2.6	0.1
1973–76	8.6	7.6	1.0
1977	6.5	6.0	0.5
1978	7.7	6.8	0.9
1979	11.3	8.9	2.4
1980	13.5	10.2	3.3
1960–80	4.2	3.9	0.3

Sources: Data for CPI is from Department of Labor, Bureau of Labor Statistics; implicit PCE deflator is from *Survey of Current Business*, vol. 61 (September 1981), p. 19, and preceding issues.

low, but as the inflation rate rose from 1973 to 1976 the CPI began increasing more rapidly. When inflation subsided somewhat in 1977 and 1978, the discrepancy between the two indexes narrowed, but as soon as inflation accelerated in 1979 and 1980 the CPI increased over 3 percentage points more than the PCE deflator.

This upward bias occurred in part because the CPI is a fixed-weight index while the PCE deflator uses current-period weights. The CPI reflects the monthly cost of buying a fixed basket of goods and services, which includes about 300 items weighted according to expenditure patterns reported in consumer expenditure surveys conducted in the 1972–74 period. The market basket is deliberately kept constant in order to isolate price changes from changes in living standards. A fixed-weight index, however, tends to overstate increases in the cost of living, since it fails to take into account the possibility of substituting less expensive goods for goods whose prices are rising rapidly. In contrast, the PCE deflator uses the current period's expenditure weights to construct the index by pricing current consumption both at current prices and at base-period prices. The deflator tends to understate cost-of-living increases by assuming that individuals sacrifice no satisfaction by changing their consumption patterns. Any discrepancy caused by the differences in weighting procedures appears relatively small. A comparison of the PCE deflator using 1972 weights and the PCE deflator using 1979 weights indicates that both yielded similar measures in 1980—10.9 and 10.5, respectively.[13]

13. Janet L. Norwood, "Two Consumer Price Index Issues: Weighting and Home-ownership," *Monthly Labor Review*, vol. 104 (March 1981), p. 58.

Whereas the choice of the market basket has a relatively small effect, the treatment of housing introduces a large upward bias in the present CPI during periods of rising prices and interest rates. In table 7-5 the housing component of the PCE deflator is compared with the various parts of the rent and homeownership component of the CPI. The difference between the PCE deflator and the CPI stems from both the weight attached to housing in the two indexes and the actual price increases registered by the individual components. The housing component represents 17.6 percent of the weight in the PCE deflator, as against a 30.9 percent weight for rent plus homeownership in the CPI. The increase in the PCE housing component in 1979 was only 9.0 percent, compared with a weighted average of 15.7 percent for rent and home-ownership in the CPI. This discrepancy arises from three characteristics of the CPI treatment of housing: (1) the overweighting of the home purchase and mortgage interest component, (2) the treatment of existing mortgage contracts as though they were variable-rate rather than fixed-rate mortgages, and (3) the failure to subtract from the higher home prices and mortgage rates the benefits consumers receive from tax deductions of interest and from capital gains due to appreciation in house values.[14]

The PCE deflator estimates the cost of homeownership by the rental equivalence method; that is, the actual market data on rental transactions are used to calculate the implicit rent on owner-occupied homes. Although this method has its own shortcomings insofar as the character-istics of rental units may differ considerably from those of owner-occupied houses, it avoids the bias created by the treatment of housing in the CPI. An experimental index (CPI:X1) constructed by the Bureau of Labor Statistics, which included the rental equivalence for the

14. The overweighting of the home purchase and mortgage interest components stems from two sources. First, the Bureau of Labor Statistics procedure assumes that the home purchase and mortgage interest payments are separate transactions. The CPI includes the house price once as the weight for house price changes, then counts most of it again by including the sum of all mortgage interest payments due over the first half of the mortgage. In addition to this double counting, housing receives a large weight because the base period, 1972–73, exhibited strong housing construction. So even though there is little activity in today's mortgage market, today's higher housing prices and interest rates enter with the weights established in the early 1970s, when the housing and mortgage markets were very active. For further discussion of the problems associated with the treatment of housing in the consumer price index, see Robert J. Gordon, "The Consumer Price Index: Measuring Inflation and Causing It," *The Public Interest*, no. 63 (Spring 1981), pp. 112–34; and Alan S. Blinder, "The Consumer Price Index and the Measurement of Recent Inflation," *Brookings Papers on Economic Activity, 2: 1980*, pp. 539–65.

Table 7-5. Rent and Homeownership Components: CPI and PCE Deflator Weights and Price Increases, 1979–80

Percent

Item	Weight in total index, December 1980	Increase in prices December 1979– December 1980
PCE deflator housing component	17.6	9.0
CPI housing components		
Residential rent	5.1	9.0
Homeownership	25.8	16.8
Home purchase	10.3	13.8
Contractual mortgage interest cost	9.8	21.8
Property taxes	1.6	3.5
Property insurance	0.6	13.6
Maintenance and repairs	3.6	9.0

Sources: Implicit PCE deflator is from Bureau of Economic Analysis; CPI components are from the Bureau of Labor Statistics.

homeownership component, produced year-to-year changes very similar to the PCE deflator for the 1960–80 period.[15] In October 1981 the bureau announced plans to adopt the experimental index on a permanent basis. The CPI for all urban consumers (CPI-U) was slated for change in January 1983, and the CPI for urban wage earners and clerical workers (CPI-W) was scheduled for revision in January 1985.

Because the original CPI was constructed to measure the change in the price of a fixed market basket of goods and services for urban wage earners and clerical workers, it has sometimes been criticized as being inappropriate for pensioners. For instance, retirees would be expected to spend considerably less than workers on household furnishings, clothing, and transportation. However, attempts to reweight the CPI to reflect the spending patterns of the elderly have shown that an index for retirees would not differ significantly from the published consumer price index.[16] Moreover, the present CPI for all urban consumers, who constitute about 80 percent of the population, is probably a better measure of retirees' consumption patterns than the earlier index based only on the spending patterns of workers. In short, once the housing

15. "Indexing Federal Programs: The CPI and Other Indexes," excerpt from the Council of Economic Advisers and the Office of Management and Budget, *Report on Indexing Federal Programs* (GPO, 1981), in *Monthly Labor Review,* vol. 104 (March 1981), p. 64.

16. Janet L. Norwood, "Cost-of-Living Escalation of Pensions," *Monthly Labor Review,* vol. 95 (June 1972), pp. 22–23.

component is revised to the rental equivalence basis, the CPI will probably provide a reasonably accurate measure of the price increases faced by the retired worker.

To the extent that their benefits do not keep pace with increases in the price level, retirees will experience a decline in their standard of living. In this regard, the key difference between social security and private pension benefits is that the former is automatically indexed for inflation and the latter is not. It would be misleading, however, to imply that social security can index benefits without increasing program costs, since the costs of benefit indexing have been partly responsible for payroll tax increases in recent years. Nevertheless, the fact remains that the need for post-retirement indexing has been recognized in the public sector but has not been adequately addressed by plan sponsors in the private sector.[17]

Private Pension Plans

Private plans, however, have been aware of the erosive power of inflation and have usually provided some adjustments to beneficiaries. The 1980 Bankers Trust study indicates that during the 1975–79 period roughly 70 percent of the 325 plans surveyed extended a cost-of-living adjustment to some or all of their beneficiaries.[18] But nearly three out of five plans that provided adjustments did so only once during the period. Under conventional plans, which account for three-quarters of the Bankers Trust sample, most firms increased pensions by a stated percentage for each year of retirement. The most common figure was 2 or 3 percent, so that a person who retired in 1975 would have received an 8 to 12 percent increase in his pension over the 1975–79 period. Other firms increased pensions by a flat percentage, usually 10 percent. And some other firms simply increased benefits by a fixed percentage that depended on the employee's retirement date; for example, 15 percent if he retired before 1966, 10 percent if he retired between 1966 and 1970, and 5 percent if he retired between 1971 and 1975. Under pattern plans an increase of a flat dollar amount or dollar increase for each year of

17. Even the President's Commission on Pension Policy placed relatively little emphasis on the effect of inflation on private pension benefits. The commission recommended that "greatest emphasis should be placed on expanding pension coverage rather than providing full inflation protection to some at this time." *Coming of Age: Toward a National Retirement Income Policy* (GPO, 1981), p. 51.

18. Mischo, Chang, and Kaston, *Corporate Pension Plan Study*, pp. 5, 7.

service was most common. According to Bankers Trust calculations, the average cost-of-living adjustment over the 1975–79 period for persons who retired in January 1975 was equivalent to a *one-time* increase in their pension of $480, or 9 percent, under a conventional plan and $660, or 8 percent, under a pattern plan.[19] Since the CPI rose 48 percent and the PCE deflator rose 39 percent over the same period, most retirees experienced a substantial decline in their living standards.[20]

Moreover, the Bankers Trust study focuses on the plans of the country's largest employers, who tend to provide more generous pensions. Other surveys suggest that even the meager cost-of-living adjustments described above are less prevalent than the Bankers Trust study would lead one to believe. A 1980 Hewitt Associates survey of 501 companies with defined benefit plans indicated that 57.5 percent had made no post-retirement increases to salaried employees since 1973; a similar survey, by Hay Associates of 700 large corporations found that 42 percent were making no adjustments in retirees' pensions.[21]

Social Security

In contrast to private pensions, social security benefits are increased annually to reflect price increases. According to the 1972 amendments, when the consumer price index rises by 3 percent or more, beneficiaries receive an automatic cost-of-living adjustment. For example, because the CPI increased 11.1 percent between the first quarter of 1980 and the first quarter of 1981, social security benefits were increased by an equivalent amount in June 1981. This automatic adjustment prevents the erosion of purchasing power over the beneficiary's retirement years and makes social security benefits considerably more valuable than an equivalent initial benefit from most private pension plans as they now exist.

Under normal circumstances, when wages grow faster than prices, the payroll tax under a pay-as-you-go system will generate, without an increase in the tax rate, sufficient revenues to finance the cost-of-living

19. Ibid., pp. 52–55.
20. The CPI and the PCE deflator rose from 155.4 and 121.5, respectively, in December 1974 to 229.9 and 169.3, respectively, in December 1979.
21. See "Inflation Is Wrecking the Private Pension System," *Business Week* (May 12, 1980), p. 96; and *1981 Hay-Huggins Non-Cash Compensation Comparison* (Philadelphia: Hay Associates, 1981).

adjustments.[22] In recent years, however, the benefit increases required to keep pace with inflation have far exceeded the payroll tax revenues generated from the slower growing earnings base, which has caused serious cash flow problems for the social security program. In 1980 the 14.3 percent increase for beneficiaries was particularly burdensome; average wages had grown by less than 8 percent and high levels of unemployment further reduced payroll tax revenues.[23]

Indexed Benefits for Private Pensions?

Although private pension plans do not currently provide fully indexed benefits, their future depends, at least partly, on their ability to protect workers from the erosive effects of inflation. An important issue, therefore, is the ability of private pensions to provide more or less fully indexed benefits and remain actuarially sound in an inflationary environment.

The model presented in appendix C abstracts from the difficulties of preserving the pension benefits of mobile employees. Instead, it addresses the more basic issue of benefit indexation, assuming that the private pension system is a giant, universal, uniform pension plan covering all workers.

The model is designed to determine what the rate of return on pension assets must be to enable a plan that is actuarially sound in the absence of inflation (that is, the present discounted value of benefits equals the present discounted value of contributions plus current assets) to remain actuarially sound without any change in contribution rates during inflationary periods. The model was applied to plans with benefits based on career average earnings and to plans with benefits based on final pay, with and without post-retirement indexing.

22. Payroll tax rates will be forced to increase if the ratio of retirees to workers increases, but inflation alone will have no impact on the tax rate unless prices rise more than wages. Since the taxable earnings base is increased in line with the growth in annual wages, the tax base rises with inflation and productivity.

23. The slow growth in the total taxable wages occurred despite significant increases in the maximum taxable earnings base. The Social Security Amendments of 1977 accelerated the increase in the base to $22,900 in 1979, $25,900 in 1980, and $29,700 in 1981. Without the legislated increases, the base for 1981 would have been only $22,200 under the automatic adjustment provision. See National Commission on Social Security, *Social Security in America's Future*, p. 71.

The relevant case to compare with social security is a final earnings plan with post-retirement cost-of-living adjustments. The model shows that for this type of plan to remain actuarially sound, without increasing contribution rates and while providing benefits based on final earnings and post-retirement indexing, the nominal rate of return on plan assets must reflect a full inflation premium. Even in this ideal hypothetical system the goal of providing benefits that fully keep pace with inflation will be unattainable unless pension funds have access to investments whose nominal yields fully reflect the rate of price increases.

The Effect of Inflation on Pension Assets

In order for the nominal yield on pension assets to increase by the full amount of inflation, the real return must be unaffected by inflation. Most of the recent evidence in the economic literature, however, suggests that the real returns on corporate equities and fixed-income securities decline when the rate of inflation increases.

The inverse relationship between equity values and inflation is evident in figure 7-1, which depicts the real value of the Standard and Poor's index of 500 stocks during a period of accelerating price increases. The long-run negative correlation between stock prices and the rate of inflation has been confirmed in several statistical studies.[24] Other research has shown that the returns to equity—which may be reflected in equity values—are also negatively affected by inflation.[25] But some controversy surrounds the mechanism by which inflation affects equity prices. Although the general uncertainty created by an inflationary economy may have been largely responsible for the poor performance of the stock market, many economists have also found that the unindexed tax structure has been an important factor.[26]

24. See Franco Modigliani and Richard A. Cohn, "Inflation, Rational Valuation and the Market," *Financial Analysts Journal,* vol. 35 (March–April 1979), pp. 22–44; Bruno A. Oudet, "The Variation of the Return on Stocks in Periods of Inflation," *Journal of Financial and Quantitative Analysis,* vol. 8 (March 1973, *Papers and Proceedings, 1972*), pp. 247–58; and John Lintner, "Inflation and Security Returns," *Journal of Finance,* vol. 30 (May 1975), pp. 259–80.

25. Eugene F. Fama, "Stock Returns, Real Activity, Inflation and Money," working paper (University of Chicago, Graduate School of Business, 1979).

26. Richard W. Kopcke, "Are Stocks a Bargain?" *New England Economic Review* (May–June 1979), pp. 5–24, and Kopcke, "The Decline in Corporate Profitability," *New England Economic Review* (May–June 1978), pp. 36–60; Martin Feldstein, "Inflation and the Stock Market," Working Paper 276 (National Bureau of Economic Research, 1979);

Figure 7-1. Inflation and Real Stock Prices, 1955–81

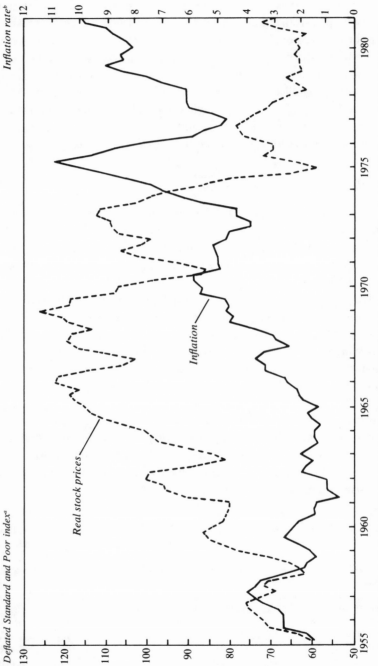

Sources: Marcelle Arak, "Inflation and Stock Values: Is Our Stock Structure the Villain?" *Federal Reserve Bank of New York Quarterly Review*, vol. 5 (Winter 1980–81), pp. 4,6. GNP implicit price deflator is from Department of Commerce, Bureau of Economic Analysis.
a. Standard and Poor's index of 500 stocks, deflated by the implicit GNP price deflator.
b. Percent change in GNP price deflator from four quarters earlier.

Both the federal personal income tax and the corporate income tax have features that cause the real tax burden to vary with inflation. As to the personal income tax, individuals are subject to "bracket creep" as inflation pushes their income into higher marginal brackets and they pay capital gains taxes on appreciation due solely to inflation. At the corporate level the tax burden rises because nominal inventory profits are taxable and allowable depreciation is based on original rather than replacement cost. On the other hand, corporate shareholders benefit from inflation, since the decline in the real value of outstanding liabilities (such as bank loans, bonds, and accounts payable) is not included in taxable income.[27]

The net impact of the offsetting effects depends on the particular inflation situation. For instance, a one-time unexpected increase in the price level of 4 percent would have only a small negative impact on equity values (see table 7-6). Inflation would give rise to a once-and-for-all inventory profit on which taxes must be paid and a one-time loss in the real value of depreciation allowance.[28] But these losses would be almost offset by the reduction in the firm's outstanding debt.[29] In an alternative situation—and one more consistent with recent experience—the rate of inflation increases unexpectedly by 4 percentage points and is expected to remain at that level. The increased taxes due to inventory profits and the loss in the value of depreciation allowances reoccur each year. In addition, individuals face increased tax liabilities from taxes on nominal gains. The reduction in the real value of oustanding debt would

Martin Feldstein, Jerry Green and Eytan Sheshinski, "Inflation and Taxes in a Growing Economy with Debt and Equity Finance," *Journal of Political Economy*, vol. 86 (April 1978), pp. S53–S70; Marcelle Arak, "Can the Performance of the Stock Market Be Explained by Inflation Coupled with Our Tax System?" Research Paper 7820 (Federal Reserve Bank of New York, 1978); and T. Nicolaus Tideman and Donald P. Tucker, "The Tax Treatment of Business Profits under Inflationary Conditions," in Henry J. Aaron, ed., *Inflation and the Income Tax* (Brookings Institution, 1976), pp. 33–80.

27. Moreover, real after-tax debt servicing costs may decline if the nominal interest rises only enough to maintain the real after-tax earnings to the interest recipient. See Marcelle Arak, "Inflation and Stock Values: Is Our Tax Structure the Villain?" *Federal Reserve Bank of New York Quarterly Review*, vol. 5 (Winter 1980–81), p. 6.

28. New equipment purchased at the higher price level would yield depreciation allowances proportional to those in the preinflation environment.

29. The estimates in table 7-6 assume that stock prices fall by as much as the real return to stockholders. For this to take place, an infinite supply of alternative investments must exist whose real returns have remained at preinflation levels. If there were few alternative assets and people wanted to maintain the same stock of wealth despite the lower returns, they would not shift out of equities. Equity prices would not fall, and the public would simply be forced to accept a lower return.

Table 7-6. Percent Change in Equity Values Due to the Effect of Inflation on Real Tax Burden

Component of tax system	An unexpected once-and-for-all rise in the price level of 4 percent	An unexpected 4 percentage point rise in the inflation rate that is expected to continue
Tax on inventory profits	−0.6	−5.4
Tax on understated depreciation allowances	−0.9	−10.9
Effect on nominal debt and debt servicing	1.1	4.8
Capital gains tax (in personal income tax code)	0.0	−5.3
Total	−0.4	−16.8

Source: Marcelle Arak, "Inflation and Stock Values: Is Our Tax Structure the Villain?" *Federal Reserve Bank of New York Quarterly Review*, vol. 5 (Winter 1980–81), p. 8.

offset a portion of these losses, but, as shown in table 7-6, inflation in this case would have a significant negative effect on equity values.[30]

The return on corporate bonds will also be adversely affected by inflation. Holders of outstanding corporate liabilities suffer capital losses as inflation increases, since they are locked into the preinflation nominal yields. Some ambiguity exists about the yields on new issues, but considering the decline in corporate profitability, firms will probably not be able to offer yields that fully compensate for inflation.[31]

One could argue that declining real rates of return after the initial unanticipated inflation has become expected are a short-run phenomenon and that, over time, in response to these lower yields the capital stock will decline relative to the labor force until the previous real rate of return is restored. There are two problems with this sanguine view. First, with a smaller capital stock total compensation (including pensions) would be lower than it would have been without the decline in corporate profitability. Second, the transition period during which the capital stock adjusts to restore former yields can be quite long. It is not clear that

30. Kopcke, "Are Stocks a Bargain?" calculated the effect of the same tax elements and found estimates about 50 percent larger than Arak's. Feldstein, Green, and Sheshinski, "Inflation and Taxes in a Growing Economy," used a different approach and found that a 6 percent difference in inflation leads to a 21 percent difference in the rate of return on equity, slightly less than Arak's results.

31. Richard W. Kopcke, "Why Are Interest Rates So Low?" *New England Economic Review* (July–August 1980), pp. 24–33.

workers would tolerate inadequate pensions or that companies could afford the rising benefit costs while this adjustment was being made.

Solutions to the Indexing Problem

Without financial assets whose real rates of return are unaffected by inflation and whose nominal yields fully incorporate an inflation premium, private pension plans cannot offer fully indexed benefits. However, there are two alternative ways to solve the indexing problem: performance indexing and index bonds.

PERFORMANCE INDEXING. Under this method inflation-augmented or "excess" investment earnings above a statutory real rate would be used to escalate the value of pensions in force.[32] For even if equities and fixed income securities fail to incorporate a full inflation premium, interest rates usually tend to be higher in periods of rapidly rising prices. During the 1970s the yield on short-term Treasury bills has fairly well mirrored inflation. Longer-term bonds appear to include a large inflation premium, although they also subject the holder to possible capital losses.[33] Without post-retirement indexing, these excess interest earnings over a real interest rate represent profit to the plan and result in lower stated costs. Performance indexing would require that firms' liability for benefits in payment status be valued at the real rate of return, say 2 or 3 percent, and any excess of the actual return over this amount would be used for indexing pensions. Although this approach would not result in fully indexed benefits, it would ensure that the plan sponsor provides at least as much inflation protection as plan participants could achieve on their own. Performance indexing will naturally produce higher costs, since plan sponsors are currently appropriating actuarial gains from inflation to reduce their required contributions. It is important to note, however, that performance indexing will not impose more real costs on the plan sponsor than would have been incurred in a noninflationary environment.

INDEX BONDS. Full indexing would become a feasible alternative to performance indexing only if a financial instrument were introduced whose nominal yield fully incorporated the effects of inflation. The availability of index bonds—bonds that guarantee a real rate of return

32. Performance indexing has been proposed by Myers, *Indexation of Pension and Other Benefits*, pp. 145–47.
33. See *Economic Report of the President, January 1981*, pp. 293, 308.

plus an inflation premium—would enable private plan sponsors to provide benefits that keep pace with inflation during participants' post-retirement years.[34] Equivalently, life insurance companies could offer plan sponsors indexed annuities sold on the basis of a real rather than nominal rate of interest. The question is whether either private firms or the federal government are capable of issuing this type of security.

Despite a case for index bonds and the likelihood that they could be issued at a lower ex ante cost than traditional bonds, firms have made no effort to initiate this form of financing.[35] The private sector's lack of innovation is not surprising in light of the negative impact of inflation on corporate profitability.[36] If firms were to issue index bonds, the inverse relationship between inflation and profitability would worsen, since corporations would forfeit the mitigating effect of the decline in the value of outstanding liabilities as inflation increased. Apparently, issuing index bonds would become an attractive alternative to private firms only if the corporate income tax were levied on inflation-adjusted income.

If the private sector is unable to issue index bonds, the only other source of these securities is the federal government. Indeed, the governments of Israel and Brazil introduced index bonds in 1954 and 1964, respectively, after periods of exceptionally high inflation.[37] More

34. The yield required on a competitively priced index bond providing a risk-free real rate of return may be approximately zero, since it has been shown that the expected return on the portfolio whose real return has minimum variance (Treasury bills hedged against unanticipated inflation by a small position in a diversified portfolio of commodity futures) is approximately zero. See Zvi Bodie, "Purchasing-Power Annuities: Financial Innovation for Stable Real Retirement Income in an Inflationary Environment," Working Paper 442 (National Bureau of Economic Research, 1980).

35. Stanley Fischer, "The Demand for Index Bonds," *Journal of Political Economy,* vol. 83 (June 1975), pp. 509–34; and Alan S. Blinder, "Indexing the Economy through Financial Intermediation," in Karl Brunner and Allan H. Meltzer, eds., *Stabilization of the Domestic and International Economy,* Carnegie-Rochester Conference Series on Public Policy 5 (Amsterdam: North-Holland, 1977), pp. 69–105. See also James E. Pesando, "Private Pensions in an Inflationary Climate: Limitations and Policy Alternatives," Discussion Paper 114 (Ottawa: Economic Council of Canada, 1978). This article provides an excellent summary of the academic literature on index bonds.

36. Several articles have been written recently that explore alternative reasons for the nonissuance of index bonds. See Stanley Fischer, "Corporate Supply of Index Bonds," Working Paper 331 (National Bureau of Economic Research, 1979); and Nissan Liviatan and David Levhari, "Risk and the Theory of Indexed Bonds," *American Economic Review,* vol. 67 (June 1977), pp. 366–75.

37. For an excellent discussion of the limited experience with index bonds in other countries, see Pesando, "Private Pensions in an Inflationary Climate," pp. 35–39. In both Brazil and Israel, index bonds were introduced after periods of very high inflation in which interest rate ceilings would have inevitably led to the collapse of the capital markets.

recently, the government of Great Britain issued £1 billion worth of bonds that guarantee a 2 percent real rate of return and that have a nominal yield tied to the retail price index.[38] Were the U.S. Treasury to substitute index bonds for long-term securities in its annual financing, it could issue about $10 billion in index securities each year.[39] Even if the purchase of these securities were limited to private pensions, plan sponsors would only gradually be able to acquire enough of these securities to provide fully indexed pensions and remain actuarially sound.

On the other hand, since index bonds would eliminate the risk of capital losses due to inflation, their existence might result in a shift in the maturity mix of Treasury offerings toward long-term securities. If the government issued index bonds to meet all its financing needs, the annual increase would be substantial, and private pensions could rapidly accumulate an adequate amount to finance indexed pensions.[40] But such a large volume of federal index bonds might disrupt markets for existing assets.

A more modest scheme, which would address only the problem of indexing benefits after retirement, would be to allow all persons sixty-two or older to transfer accumulated pension assets—perhaps up to some limit, such as three times the social security earnings base—to the government in exchange for an index bond.[41] To increase equity between those persons covered by private plans and those not covered,

38. "Index Bonds New U.K. Securities?" *Pension and Investment Age* (May 11, 1981), pp. 2, 70.

39. The $10 billion figure was derived by adding the $6.4 billion increase in net long-term borrowing between 1976 and 1977 and an estimated $4 billion for refinancing existing long-term debt, assuming an average maturity of 10 years and an inflation rate of 8 percent. *Federal Reserve Bulletin,* vol. 64 (June 1978), p. A32.

40. The net annual increase in total public debt between 1974 and 1977 averaged about $70 billion. In addition, short-term securities are constantly maturing and could be reissued in the form of index securities.

41. Robert W. Hartman of the Brookings Institution has proposed a far more extensive program whereby everyone would be allowed to make tax-deductible contributions of 10 percent of earnings up to a maximum of $7,500 into an account similar to an individual retirement account. At retirement, one could exchange the accumulated balance in this account (up to a limit of three times the social security earnings base) for a government-issued index bond yielding 1 percent real interest annually. Under this plan the government would not only assume the interest rate and inflation risks but also introduce a new way for people to defer taxation until retirement. Since in 1978, 72 percent of the deductions for IRAs and 93.5 percent of the deductions for Keogh plans were made by persons with incomes over $20,000, the Hartman plan would primarily benefit those with high incomes. See "Inflation Insurance for Retirement," working paper (Washington, D.C., September 1979).

perhaps all assets of the elderly up to some specified limit could be eligible for exchange for an index bond.

Issuing index bonds for any purpose could create serious political problems. Any administration introducing this type of financial instrument might be accused of "throwing up its hands" about eliminating inflation. Moreover, issuing index bonds to help pension funds improve benefits would raise the question whether further government support of private pension funds is appropriate. Private pension plans already receive a considerable subsidy through the tax system, yet coverage is far from universal and benefits are concentrated among higher-paid workers. If the government were to assume the risks associated with inflation, a more equitable scheme would be one that did not discriminate between those covered and those not covered by a private pension plan.

The British Pension System

In the United Kingdom the government has assumed the inflation risk for both public and private plan benefits up to a specified limit, which roughly approximates the benefits provided under the U.S. social security program. Workers are protected against the erosion of deferred vested benefits in their preretirement years and are assured fully indexed benefits in retirement.

Until recently the British pension system consisted of a universal state plan that paid a flat benefit plus modest additional earnings-related benefits.[42] Occupational pensions, which covered about half the work force, could either supplement the state benefit or contract out to provide the entire earnings-related portion.[43] In 1978 a new system was introduced that essentially maintained the flat benefit but greatly expanded the mandatory level of earnings-related benefits. Under the new system, therefore, the pension consists of two parts: (1) the basic component, which is defined as 100 percent of earnings up to a base level, and (2) the

42. The National Insurance Act of 1959 introduced the concept of an earnings-related supplement to the basic state pension. See David Callund, *Employee Benefits in Europe, 1978* (London: Callund and Co., 1979), p. 349.

43. In 1971, 46 percent of workers in the United Kingdom were covered by occupational pension schemes. See E. A. Johnston, "The Effects of Inflation and Currency Instability on Pension Schemes in the United Kingdom," in International Labour Office, *Pensions and Inflation: An International Discussion* (Geneva: ILO, 1977), p. 97.

additional component, which is defined as 25 percent of earnings between the base level and a ceiling equal to seven times the base level.[44] Benefits are calculated on the worker's twenty years of highest earnings revalued in line with average wage growth. After retirement the basic component is indexed in line with average wage growth or prices, whichever is higher, while the additional component is indexed by prices.

Both the basic and earnings-related components are financed on a pay-as-you-go basis by contributions from employers, employees, and the general fund. The large increase in earnings-related benefits under the new scheme required considerably higher contributions from all three sources. But employers may contract their employees out of the earnings-related part of the state pension scheme if their own pension plans provide benefits no less generous than those provided by the second tier of the state plan. Contracting out greatly reduces the required taxes for both the employer and employee.[45]

To allow contracting out, the occupational pension scheme must provide benefits of at least 1.25 percent of "pensionable pay" for each year of service. Pensionable pay may be based either on final earnings or on career average earnings that are revalued each year to reflect the growth in wages. But employers who contract out are not required to provide post-retirement cost-of-living adjustments. Rather, at retirement the state plan will calculate a total state pension for the employee as if he had never been contracted out and pay cost-of-living increases on this calculated amount. Thus workers who remain with the state system or who remain with an employer who has contracted out will receive

44. This formula applies to persons retiring after the new pension scheme has been in operation for twenty years. For those retiring before then, the additional component will be a pension of 1.25 percent of earnings between the base level and the ceiling for each year of service in the new scheme. If the new scheme were currently in effect, data for 1978 would provide an idea of the magnitude of the benefits. At that time, the basic component of the state pension was £17.50 ($40.25) a week, or $2,093 a year. Anyone earning at that level would be entitled to a pension equal to 100 percent of preretirement earnings. The ceiling, which is set at seven times the base level was £122.50 ($281.75) a week, or $14,651 per year. A worker earning at the ceiling would be eligible for a benefit of $5,233 ($2,093 of basic component and [$14,651 − $2,093] × 0.25 = $3,140 of earnings-related benefits), that is, 36 percent of preretirement earnings. Since over 95 percent of workers earned below the $14,651 ceiling in 1978, the new pension scheme provides substantial benefits for most employees.

45. The difference between contracted-in rates and contracted-out rates in April 1978 was 7 percent. This difference is expected to decline to 4.50 percent over the next thirty years.

benefits that reflect productivity growth and inflation over their work lives and that will be indexed for inflation after retirement.[46]

The new British system also provides for the mobile employee, who is particularly hurt by inflation in the United States. Mobile employees in Britain are divided into two groups—those with less than five years of service and those with five or more years of service with a particular employer. An employee with at least five years of service whose employer has contracted out is entitled to a pension at retirement no less favorable than a member who remained in service until retirement. This "preservation" requirement implicitly assures that the earnings on which the benefit is calculated will reflect both inflation and productivity growth between termination and retirement. When an employee moves from one contracted-out scheme to another, his preserved pension benefits are transferred in a lump sum. When the employee moves to an employer who is not contracted out, his former employer makes a lump-sum payment to the state plan.

When an employee with less than five years of service terminates employment, the employer who has contracted out may either (a) preserve the guaranteed minimum pension, 1.25 percent of earnings between the base level and the ceiling for each year of service, or (b) transfer to the state scheme an amount equal to contributions that would have been paid had the employer not contracted out. If funds are returned to the state, the earnings on which the contributions were based will be automatically revalued to calculate the employee's ultimate benefit. If the employer does not return the funds to the state, he must provide for indexation between termination and retirement in one of three ways: (a) increase the guaranteed minimum pension in line with the growth in average wages; (b) increase the pension by 5 percent a year and pay a "limited revaluation premium" to the state, which will then bear the cost of any increase in excess of 5 percent; or (c) increase the guaranteed minimum pension at a fixed rate of 8.5 percent each year.[47]

Although it is too early to know the full implications of the new British pension system, it shows the possibility of designing a scheme that permits full portability and that fully protects workers' benefits from inflation both over their working lives and in retirement, provided the

46. See ILO, *Pensions and Inflation*, pp. 101–02. As noted earlier, the basic component is also indexed to reflect productivity growth if this approach yields more favorable results.

47. Jack R. S. Revell, "Great Britain," in Introduction to George M. von Furstenberg, ed., *Social Security versus Private Saving* (Ballinger, 1979), p. 29.

government is willing to accept considerable responsibility for designing and financing the system.

Conclusion

While the increase in the proportion of private pensions that base benefits on final earnings is a step toward preserving the value of benefits over employees' preretirement years, post-retirement cost-of-living adjustments under private plans are still rare and usually fail to compensate fully for increases in prices. Until private pensions are responsive to the problems created by worker mobility and inflation, they will not be providing employees with the real benefits they have earned.[48]

For private plans to provide benefits that fully keep pace with inflation, they must be able to earn a return on fund assets that fully reflects increases in the price level. In other words, pension funds must have access to investments whose real rate of return is not affected by inflation. Recent studies, however, suggest that the real return on corporate securities declines when inflation increases. Reforming the corporate income tax so that the prices of capital goods and inventories are adjusted to reflect increases in the price level would eliminate the rise in the corporate tax rate on real profits during inflationary times and avoid the decline in real corporate rates of return. This would enable pension funds to invest in an inflation-proof security—corporate stock.

Alternatively, pension funds could be permitted to invest in index bonds—bonds whose nominal rate of return includes an inflation premium. But government provision of index bonds to aid pension funds would require a further subsidy to private plans, which already receive substantial benefits from federal income tax provisions. Moreover, since private pension coverage is far from universal, higher-paid workers would be the primary beneficiaries of federally issued index bonds. If the government were willing to accept the risks involved, a more equitable solution would be to make index bonds available to all persons over a certain age.

In the absence of major tax reform or index bonds, serious consideration should be given to encouraging or mandating performance indexing

48. For an interesting discussion of how indexing would affect the employment contract, see James E. Pesando, "Employee Valuation of Pension Claims and the Impact of Indexing Initiatives," working paper (University of Toronto, January 1981).

for benefits in the post-retirement period. Any inflation premium reflected in higher yields should be passed on to the plan participants rather than appropriated by the plan sponsor to reduce employer contributions. Performance indexing would ensure that beneficiaries received roughly the same inflation protection as they could have secured by investing on their own and requires no additional costs to plan sponsors beyond those that would have been incurred in a noninflationary environment.

The failure of private plans to provide meaningful benefits in an inflationary environment has created a vacuum. Either private plans must improve their benefits or political pressure will develop for government action. This action may take the form of mandatory cost-of-living adjustments or, perhaps, an expansion of social security. Without indexing, the role of private pensions in the provision of retirement income can be expected to decline in the future.[49]

49. According to the President's Commission on Pension Policy, even if private pension plans provide post-retirement cost-of-living adjustments equal to one-third the inflation rate, their share of total retirement benefits will decline from 18 percent in 1975 to 7 percent by 2000 if inflation stays at 8 percent. *Working Papers: Retirement Income Goals* (The Commission, 1980), p. 50.

chapter eight **The Future of Private Pensions**

The U.S. retirement system is a recent development reflecting the shift away from individual thrift and toward organized saving plans in the wake of the Great Depression. Although a few private plans were introduced in the last quarter of the nineteenth century, the modern pension movement followed the passage of social security in 1935 and was spurred by the high taxes and wage controls introduced during World War II. Since then, both public and private plans have grown at a tremendous rate (see table 8-1). Retirement benefits as a percent of personal income have increased from less than 1 percent in the 1940s to more than 8 percent in 1980. As a result of this growth, the incidence of poverty among the aged has declined relative to that among the population as a whole (see table 8-2).

Private pension plans have played a major role in the growth of this retirement system. Benefits provided by these plans increased from 11 percent of total benefit payments in 1955 to 20 percent in 1980. Whether private plans will continue to grow in importance or be dwarfed by the social security system largely depends on the resolution of the following issues.

Coverage

Less than half the private nonfarm work force is currently covered by private plans. As shown in table 8-3, the largest percentage of covered workers is found in the highly unionized manufacturing, mining, and transportation industries and the lowest percentage in the nonunion service and retail trade industries. The relatively small size of establishments in services and retail trade, as well as their lack of unionization, contribute to the dearth of pension plans in these industries. Recent data

199

Table 8-1. Retirement Benefits under Social Security and Public and Private Plans, Selected Years, 1940–80 [a]

Millions of dollars

Year	Social security [b]	Public plans [c]	Private plans	Total	Total as percent of personal income
1940	35	328	140	503	0.6
1945	274	446	220	940	0.6
1950	961	833	370	2,164	1.0
1955	4,968	1,602	850	7,420	2.0
1960	10,677	2,997	1,720	15,394	3.9
1965	16,737	4,975	3,520	25,232	4.7
1970	28,796	9,607	7,360	45,763	5.7
1975	58,509	21,820	14,810	95,139	7.6
1980	105,074	37,379 [d]	35,177 [e]	177,630	8.2

Sources: *Social Security Bulletin: Annual Statistical Supplement, 1976*, pp. 56, 74; Alfred M. Skolnik, "Private Pension Plans, 1950–74," *Social Security Bulletin*, vol. 39 (June 1976), p. 4; Martha Remy Yohalem, "Employee-Benefit Plans, 1975," *Social Security Bulletin*, vol. 40 (November 1977), p. 27; *Social Security Bulletin*, vol. 44 (May 1981), p. 43; and ICF, Inc., *A Private Pension Forecasting Model*, submitted to the Department of Labor, Office of Pension and Welfare Benefit Programs (October 1979).

a. Includes retirement, survivor, and lump-sum payments.
b. Benefits paid under the OASI portion of the OASDHI program.
c. Includes federal, state, and local employees and those covered under the Railroad Retirement Plan.
d. Author's estimate.
e. Author's estimate derived from the ICF, Inc., 1980 estimate of the ratio of benefits to contributions and the author's 1980 projection of employer contributions to private plans.

indicate that 79 percent of noncovered employees work in firms that employ fewer than 100 people.[1]

Because of the influence of industry structure on pension coverage, the percentage of the work force covered by pension plans is not expected to increase significantly in the future. Industries with traditionally high pension coverage, such as manufacturing, are expected to employ a declining share of workers, while employment in industries with low pension coverage, such as retail trade and services, is projected to increase. Moreover, small businesses, which employ the bulk of non-covered workers, are unlikely to adopt pension plans. These businesses operate on a very small profit margin in a highly competitive environment and cannot afford the additional cost of a pension plan, especially since the relative cost of establishing such a plan tends to be higher for small firms. Moreover, the progressivity of the corporate income tax, which ranges from 16 percent to 40 percent for firms earning less than $100,000 as against 46 percent for larger corporations, reduces the value to small

1. President's Commission on Pension Policy, *Coming of Age: Toward a National Retirement Income Policy* (Government Printing Office, 1981), p. 28.

Table 8-2. Percentage of People below Poverty Level among Total Population and among Those Sixty-five and Over, Selected Years, 1959–80

Year	Total population	People sixty-five and over	Percentage point difference in poverty rate
1959	22.4	35.2	12.8
1967	14.2	29.5	15.3
1968	12.8	25.0	12.2
1969	12.1	25.3	13.2
1970	12.6	24.5	11.9
1971	12.5	21.6	9.1
1972	11.9	18.6	6.7
1973	11.1	16.3	5.2
1974	11.2	14.6	3.4
1975	12.3	15.3	3.0
1976	11.8	15.0	3.2
1977	11.6	14.1	2.5
1978	11.4	14.0	2.6
1979	11.6	15.1	3.5
1980	13.0	15.7	2.7

Sources: Bureau of the Census, *Currrent Population Reports, Consumer Income,* series P-60, no. 119, "Characteristics of the Population Below the Poverty Level: 1977" (GPO, 1979), pp. 13, 19; and Bureau of the Census, Population Division, unpublished data.

Table 8-3. Percentage of All Workers Covered by a Pension Plan, by Age and Industry, 1979

Industry	Age	
	25–64	16 and over
Mining	74	70
Construction	46	37
Manufacturing	73	66
Transportation	70	66
Trade	41	29
Finance	58	50
Services	36	30
All private, nonfarm	55	46

Source: President's Commission on Pension Policy, *Coming of Age: Toward a National Retirement Income Policy* (GPO, 1981), p. 27.

firms of the tax deduction for pension contributions. And in addition to cost considerations, the high turnover rate among small businesses precludes long-term commitments like a pension plan.

Since saving through pension plans is subsidized by the federal tax system, this lack of universal participation is an issue of public policy.

The Treasury estimates that the subsidy in 1981 amounted to a tax expenditure of $15 billion. Although the benefits of this subsidy accrue to higher-paid workers covered by private plans, all taxpayers must pay higher taxes to make up the forgone revenues. ERISA introduced the individual retirement account and increased contribution limits on Keogh plans to broaden the group eligible for favorable tax treatment on retirement saving, but participation in these alternative saving schemes also appears to be concentrated among higher-paid workers.

Since voluntary expansion of pension coverage through tax incentives appears unlikely, the President's Commission on Pension Policy in 1981 recommended the establishment of a minimum universal pension system funded by employer contributions equal to 3 percent of payroll.[2] The proposed system would cover all employees over twenty-five with one year of service. Benefits earned under the system would be vested immediately. To reduce costs for small businesses, all employers would be eligible for a tax credit of 46 percent of contributions.

This provocative proposal generated much controversy, particularly regarding the costs of such a program and its predicted effects on small businesses.[3] One issue not discussed, however, was whether those not currently covered by a pension plan want to participate in a plan in order to supplement their social security retirement benefits. This issue becomes particularly important once it is recognized that workers usually forgo some wage income to participate in a pension plan and that two-thirds of noncovered workers earned less than $10,000 in 1978.[4] Low-paid workers may have little interest in trading a portion of current income for future retirement benefits. Yet without universal coverage low-paid, noncovered workers will continue to subsidize through their tax payments the pension saving of higher-paid, covered workers.

Tax Provisions

The equity issue surrounding the tax expenditure would be eliminated by universal coverage, but an efficiency issue would remain. The justification for the deferral of taxation on contributions to private plans

2. Ibid., pp. 42–45.
3. "Commission Ignores Voters," *Pension and Investment Age* (February 6, 1981), p. 12; "Commission Report Runs into Criticism," *Pension and Investment Age* (March 16, 1981), pp. 4, 38; "EBRI Man Rips Commission Data," *Pension and Investment Age* (May 25, 1981), p. 53.
4. President's Commission on Pension Policy, *Coming of Age*, p. 28.

rests on the supposition that such favorable tax treatment encourages retirement saving. Although the tax provisions have stimulated the growth of private plans, the accumulation of assets in private pension funds is not equivalent to a net increase in aggregate saving. The limited empirical evidence on the response of covered workers indicates that they reduce other saving to offset a substantial portion of their accrued pension benefits. If so, the bulk of pension assets must be viewed as a reallocation of saving, not as an increase in the aggregate.

Much of the net annual increase in pension assets can be attributed to the immaturity of the private pension system. Newly established plans tend to have a low ratio of beneficiaries to active participants, since only a small percentage of newly covered workers are eligible for retirement. Hence contributions in young plans far exceed benefit payments, and the stock of pension assets grows rapidly. Over time, the system matures as workers with pension coverage reach retirement age, the beneficiary–worker ratio rises, and the excess of contributions over benefits declines. At the limit, contributions and benefits could be equal, yielding a net pension saving of zero. As shown in table 8-4, the ratio of benefits to contributions and of beneficiaries to contributors has been rising steadily. Therefore, the pension saving attributable to the immaturity of the system will decline over time. If the substantial tax expenditures do not stimulate saving, they represent a relatively high-cost, low-benefit use of federal tax revenue.

The 1977 Treasury proposal for reform of the tax treatment of private plans would not only recoup most of the revenue loss from the present tax provisions but would also improve employee rights.[5] Under this plan both employee and employer contributions would be deductible from income, benefits would be taxed upon receipt, and pension fund earnings would be included in the income of vested employees. Earnings not assignable to plan participants would be included in employers' income. Such an approach would make the tax structure more equitable as well as eliminate the bias in favor of employer-financed plans.

Protection of Employee Rights

When pensions are financed by employers, employees have no immediate claim on contributions, even though they may have accepted

5. Department of the Treasury, *Blueprints for Basic Tax Reform* (GPO, 1977), pp. 56–58.

Table 8-4. The Maturation of the Private Pension System, Selected Years, 1940–80

Year	Contrib-utors (thousands)	Benefici-aries (thousands)	Ratio of beneficiaries to contributors	Contributions (millions of dollars)	Benefits (millions of dollars)	Ratio of benefits to contributions
1940	4,100	160	0.04	310	140	0.45
1945	6,400	310	0.05	990	220	0.22
1950	9,800	450	0.05	2,080	370	0.18
1955	14,200	980	0.07	3,840	850	0.22
1960	18,700	1,780	0.10	5,490	1,720	0.31
1965	21,800	2,750	0.13	8,360	3,520	0.42
1970	26,300	4,750	0.18	14,000	7,360	0.53
1975	30,300	7,050	0.23	29,850	14,810	0.50
1980	35,800[a]	9,100[a]	0.25	68,970[b]	35,177[c]	0.51[a]

Sources: Skolnik, "Private Pension Plans, 1950–74," p. 4; Yohalem, "Employee-Benefit Plans, 1975," p. 27; and ICF, Inc. *Private Pension Forecasting Model.*
    a. Estimate from ICF, Inc., *Private Pension Forecasting Model.*
    b. Author's projection, based on actual employer contributions of $54,899 million in 1979 as reported by the Department of Commerce, Bureau of Economic Analysis. Projections assume that employer contributions grew at the same rate from 1979 to 1980 as over the 1975–79 period and that in 1980 employers made 94 percent of total contributions to private plans.
    c. Author's estimate derived from the ICF, Inc., 1980 estimate of the ratio of benefits to contributions and the author's 1980 projection of employer contributions.

lower wages in return for pension coverage. Rather, entitlement to benefits based on employer contributions hinges on specific provisions of the pension plan. Even though employees' rights were significantly improved by the participation and vesting standards established under ERISA, many workers covered by private plans who fail to complete the ten-year vesting requirement will not receive benefits.

If employees were to finance their own pensions through tax deductible contributions, as suggested by the Treasury proposal, the trade-off between pension coverage and wages would be made explicit. The employee would also have an immediate right to the accumulated contributions even if ultimate entitlement to benefits remained contingent on satisfying a ten-year vesting standard. Accumulated contributions could then be transferred either to an IRA or to a new plan when the employee changed jobs. Thus employee-financed plans would reduce the forfeiture of earned pension rights and would probably lead to greater portability within the private pension system.

If plans were financed by employees, the inequities surrounding the current IRS integration guidelines would become obvious. These provisions currently allow plans to pay few or no benefits to low-paid workers. If these workers, like their higher-paid counterparts, were to receive lower wages in exchange for deferred pension income, there would be no justification for denying them benefits at retirement.

Employee contributions would clarify the issue: either low-paid workers
would contribute and become eligible for benefits, or they would make
no contributions and rely solely on social security for retirement income.

Inflation

Inflation, more than any other factor, will determine the future role of
private pensions in the provision of retirement income. Unless benefits
are indexed over the worker's employment and in retirement, their value
will be reduced dramatically by inflation. The recent trend toward final
earnings plans has somewhat offset the erosive effect of inflation during
the employee's working years. Problems still remain, however, with
mobile employees, since inflation greatly reduces the real value of
pension benefits in the period between termination and retirement.
Moreover, private plans provide little in the way of post-retirement cost-
of-living adjustments. When high rates of inflation are combined with
earlier retirement and increased longevity, the value of an unindexed
pension diminishes rapidly.

If plan sponsors could earn a return on plan assets that includes a full
inflation premium, full indexing of pension benefits both over the
employee's work life and in retirement would be possible at no additional
real cost to the employer. But if real rates of return decline in response
to accelerating inflation—as they have in recent years—nominal yields
will not fully reflect the rate of price increases. So plan sponsors cannot
offer fully indexed benefits without incurring higher real costs. On the
other hand, although the returns on assets do not fully incorporate the
effects of inflation, nominal yields do rise as the rate of price increases
accelerates. Plan sponsors currently appropriate the partial inflation
premium incorporated in asset yields to reduce their contributions, so
that the real costs of providing pensions are lower than would be required
in the absence of inflation. As a compromise to indexing, plan sponsors
could value the firm's liability for benefits in payment status at a real rate
of return of 2 or 3 percent and use anything above this amount to provide
partial post-retirement cost-of-living adjustments. This form of indexing
will not impose any more real costs on plan sponsors than would be
incurred in a noninflationary environment and will ensure beneficiaries
roughly the same inflation protection as they could have secured on their
own.

If employers are unwilling or unable to finance at least partial indexing, pressure will develop for government intervention. Either the government may mandate cost-of-living adjustments for private plans, or public support may increase for an expansion of social security. Many European countries, such as Great Britain, France, and West Germany, have shifted away from funded private plans toward government-sponsored pay-as-you-go pensions because of persistent high levels of inflation.[6]

Conclusion

In the early 1980s the future of private pension plans appears uncertain. Some plans are under serious financial pressure as a result of ERISA funding provisions, a decade of poor returns on fund assets, and increased liabilities caused by shifts from career average to final pay plans. In addition, there is the prospect of future cost increases if plans are to provide post-retirement inflation adjustments. At the same time the justification for tax-subsidized plans that cover only half the work force and primarily benefit higher-paid workers is being subjected to increased scrutiny.

6. International Labour Office, *Pensions and Inflation: An International Discussion* (Geneva: ILO, 1977).

appendix A Empirical Analysis of the Interaction of Social Security and Private Pensions

The empirical analysis of the interaction of private pensions and social security is based on a stock-adjustment model in which people are assumed to alter their accumulations in private pension plans and their other savings so that their combined retirement assets (including social security) will ensure a desired level of retirement income. The model is designed to test the hypothesis that social security and private pensions have acted as almost perfect substitutes in the provision for retirement income.[1] Saving for retirement in any period is a function of the gap between desired retirement assets ($RASS^*$) and the existing stock ($RASS_{t-1}$):

$$(1) \qquad RS_t = f(RASS^* - RASS_{t-1}).$$

The desired level of retirement assets is, in turn, a function of the target level of retirement income (RY^*) and the number of years the person expects to live in retirement (*Years*):

$$(2) \qquad RASS^* = f(RY^*, Years).$$

Desired retirement income is assumed to depend on permanent income, which is approximated by current and lagged disposable income (YD_t and YD_{t-1}), and the rate of unemployment (RU):

$$(3) \qquad RY^* = f(YD_t, YD_{t-1}, RU).$$

The existing stock of retirement assets includes the reserves in private pension funds ($PENASS$),[2] accumulated social security benefits (SSW)—

1. The analysis is based on aggregate economic variables and therefore ignores the differences in tax treatment and coverage between private pensions and social security.
2. To the extent that private pensions are not fully funded, pension reserves understate accumulated pension benefits.

207

since Social Security is financed on a pay-as-you-go basis, this value must be represented as the present discounted value of future benefits— and the net nonpension wealth of consumers that will be allocated for retirement $\lambda_1(W - PENASS)$:

$$(4) \quad RASS_{t-1} = SSW_{t-1} + PENASS_{t-1} + \lambda_1(W - PENASS)_{t-1}.$$

Retirement saving (RS) is composed of the net increase in the assets of private pension funds (PS), contributions to social security ($OASI$)[3] and some fraction, λ_2, of other saving (SO):[4]

$$(5) \quad RS_t = PS_t + OASI_t + \lambda_2 SO.$$

Therefore, combining equations 1 through 5, retirement saving can be expressed as follows:

$$(6) \quad RS_t = PS_t + OASI_t + \lambda_2 SO = f[YD_t, YD_{t-1}, RU,$$
$$Years, (SSW + PENASS)_{t-1}, \lambda_1(W - PENASS)_{t-1}].$$

Expressing the relationship in terms of pension saving, the equation becomes

$$(7) \quad PS_t = f[YD_t, YD_{t-1}, RU, Years, (SSW + PENASS)_{t-1},$$
$$\lambda_1(W - PENASS)_{t-1}] - OASI_t - \lambda_2 SO_t.[5]$$

The Data

The dependent variable, pension saving (PS), is defined as the net increase in the book value of pension fund reserves during the calendar year. This figure is equivalent to the contributions of employers and

3. Social security taxes are an imperfect measure of retirement saving, since the system is financed on a pay-as-you-go basis and future benefits are not strictly related to current contributions.

4. Retirement saving also occurs through other public pensions, such as civil service, military, and state and local retirement systems. These systems have been excluded from the empirical analysis because they generally are either unfunded or only partly funded and therefore no "wealth" data are available.

5. Including other saving as an independent variable clearly introduces simultaneity bias, since this value is determined by the same factors that influence total retirement saving. If appropriate instruments were available, equation 7 should be estimated by some limited information technique. However, the use of inadequate instruments can introduce more bias than that resulting from the use of an ordinary least squares estimator. Therefore, the equation will be estimated directly by ordinary least squares and the resulting coefficient will be biased. The equation is reestimated excluding the SO_t variable.

employees plus investment earnings (excluding capital gains) minus payments to beneficiaries and administrative expenses.

Permanent income is represented by the current and lagged values of disposable income, as defined in the national income accounts, and the unemployment rate, measured by the average unemployed percentage of the civilian labor force. Data on the average number of years in retirement are unavailable; therefore, the labor force participation rate for men sixty-five and over was included as a proxy for the lengthening of the retirement period to reflect the trend toward early retirement.[6] The variable is entered with disposable income, since a multiplicative relationship is implied in the formulation of desired retirement assets.

The existing stock of retirement assets includes pension reserves, social security wealth, and an unknown fraction of other nonpension wealth of consumers. Pension assets include the reserves in private pension funds at book value as of the end of the year. The wealth series (W) is the net worth of consumers at market prices as originally presented by Ando-Modigliani and updated from wealth data based on the same definitions from the MIT-Penn-SSRC econometric model.[7] Pension assets are subtracted from the net worth data to calculate nonpension net worth of consumers ($W - PENASS$). Social security wealth ($SSWG$) is an estimate of the present discounted value of future benefits outstanding to current workers and retirees, taking into account the probabilities of living long enough to receive them. The value of social security wealth has increased rapidly and is now almost equivalent to the net worth of consumers. Since it is unclear whether people perceive their future payroll tax payments as an offset to future benefits or whether they view the social security tax as similar to any other government levy, a net social security variable was also constructed. Net social security wealth ($SSWN$) is calculated by subtracting the present discounted value of future taxes from the gross wealth.[8]

6. Whether this trend will continue under the demographic characteristics of the next century is subject to debate.

7. Albert Ando and Franco Modigliani, "The 'Life Cycle' Hypothesis of Saving: Aggregate Implications and Tests," *American Economic Review*, vol. 53 (March 1963), pp. 55–84.

8. Data on the net worth of consumers was obtained from the Board of Governors of the Federal Reserve System. Series for social security wealth and social security taxes were obtained from Dean R. Leimer and Selig D. Lesnoy, "Social Security and Private Saving: A Reexamination of the Time Series Evidence Using Alternative Social Security Wealth Variables," ORS Working Paper Series 19 (Social Security Administration, Office of Research and Statistics, 1980).

Table A-1. The Effect of Social Security on Private Pensions, Regression Results[a]

Equation	Independent variable										Summary statistic	
	YD_t	YD_{t-1}	RU_t	$(LF65 \cdot YD)_t$	$(W - PENASS)_{t-1}$	$(SSWG + PENASS)_{t-1}$	$(SSWN + PENASS)_{t-1}$	$OASI_t$	SO_t	Constant	$\bar{R}^2$	Durbin-Watson
1930–40, 1947–77												
8-1	0.126 (0.032)	-0.032 (0.027)	-0.053 (0.101)	-0.106 (0.069)	-0.002 (0.005)	-0.001 (0.004)	...	-0.728 (0.314)	-0.175 (0.033)	-0.018 (0.053)	0.66	1.77
8-2	0.128 (0.032)	-0.028 (0.027)	-0.050 (0.100)	-0.112 (0.067)	-0.003 (0.005)	...	-0.002 (0.004)	-0.739 (0.318)	-0.171 (0.033)	-0.014 (0.052)	0.66	1.77
1947–77												
8-3	0.171 (0.039)	-0.020 (0.032)	0.325 (0.179)	-0.192 (0.100)	-0.011 (0.005)	-0.015 (0.006)	...	-0.546 (0.329)	-0.133 (0.029)	0.008 (0.015)	0.78	1.76
8-4	0.161 (0.039)	-0.027 (0.032)	0.369 (0.184)	-0.170 (0.102)	-0.010 (0.005)	...	-0.012 (0.006)	-0.738 (0.369)	-0.133 (0.030)	0.006 (0.013)	0.77	1.74

a. The numbers in parentheses are standard errors. All variables are expressed in per capita 1972 dollars. The dependent variable is pension saving, in other words, the net increase in pension fund reserves. Social security wealth is estimated as of January; therefore, current rather than lagged values were used to calculate the lagged stock of retirement assets.

The other forms of retirement saving included as independent variables are social security contributions and an unknown portion of other saving. Social security contributions represent the net total contributions to the old-age and survivors insurance ($OASI$) trust fund. The other saving variable (SO) is simply national income accounts personal saving less pension saving (the net increase in pension reserves).

All variables were converted to constant 1972 dollars (deflated by the GNP deflator for consumption) and have been divided by the total civilian population to obtain per capita values. The final equation to be estimated is

$$(8) \quad PS_t = \alpha_0 + \alpha_1 YD_t + \alpha_2 YD_{t-1} + \alpha_3 RU + \alpha_4 (LF65 \cdot YD)_t +$$
$$\alpha_5 (SSW + PENASS)_{t-1} + \alpha_6 (W - PENASS)_{t-1} + \alpha_7 OASI_t + \alpha_8 SO_t.$$

Two variants of equation 8 were estimated for each of the time periods, 1930–77 (excluding the war years) and 1947–77. The social security variable entered the equation first as a gross value ($SSWG$), then as a net value ($SSWN$).

The stock-adjustment model implies specific coefficients for each variable. Retirement assets $[(SSW + PENASS)_{t-1}]$ should have a negative coefficient, since an increase in the existing stock implies a reduction in the gap between desired and actual assets and therefore less pension saving. Nonpension wealth should also have a negative effect on pension saving, although this coefficient should be significantly smaller than that of other retirement assets, since only a fraction of consumer net worth is designated for retirement. Social security contributions ($OASI$) should have a coefficient of -1 because the model implies that pension saving and social security payments are perfect substitutes. Other savings (SO) should have a negative coefficient but less than one, because this form of saving is undertaken for purposes other than retirement. The coefficient of $(LF65 \cdot YD)_t$, the labor force participation rate of males aged sixty-five and over (multiplied by current disposable income), should be negative, because a decline in participation indicates an increase in the prevalence of retirement and therefore an increase in the need for pension saving.

Results

The estimates of equation 8 for 1930–77 (excluding the war years) and 1947–77 are presented in table A-1. Since private pensions were relatively unimportant in the American economy before World War II, the results for the 1947–77 period probably deserve the most attention. The coefficients of the variables are generally consistent with the stock-adjustment model.

The main focus of the empirical analysis centers on the impact of the social security program on private pensions. The empirical results are consistent with the hypothesis that social security contributions and private pension saving are close substitutes. It was found that individuals generally reduce their savings through pension plans by roughly 75 cents for each dollar contributed to social security.

The other important explanatory variables are the labor force participation and other saving. The coefficient of SO should be interpreted in terms of the original model as the value of λ_2, the percentage of nonpension saving allocated for retirement. Since retirement saving is only one of many motives for accumulating wealth and other saving excludes increases in private pension reserves, a coefficient of 0.13 seems reasonable. Excluding SO from the equations does not significantly affect the results.

The labor force participation variable was introduced to reflect the trend since World War II toward early retirement, due in part to the availability of social security and private pension benefits, the spread of compulsory retirement policies that accompanied the growth of these programs, and the social security earnings test. Earlier retirement implies a shorter working life and a longer period of dependency on retirement benefits, and therefore should stimulate retirement saving. The results are consistent with this view. To the extent that social security is responsible for either directly or indirectly lengthening the retirement period, this positive influence on pension plan growth must be considered as an offset to the negative impact of OASI benefits and social security wealth.

appendix B Classifying Private Pension Plans

The roughly 450,000 private plans found in the United States today vary greatly in structure, financing, breadth of coverage, and benefit provisions.[1] While it is difficult to generalize about these plans, this appendix attempts to outline the framework of the private pension system by describing several broad categories into which private plans can be classified.

Structure

Employers make pension commitments in the form of either defined benefits or defined contributions. In defined benefit plans the employer's pension commitment is defined by the benefit he agrees to pay plan participants.[2] In defined contribution plans the employer's commitment is expressed as the level of pension contributions that he agrees to make on an employee's behalf. While defined benefit plans account for only 29 percent of total plans, they cover 65 percent of total participants.[3]

Defined Benefit Plans

The benefit amounts that employers agree to pay plan participants under defined benefit plans are determined by fixed benefit formulas.

This appendix was prepared by Jennifer B. Katz and Laura E. Stiglin, former research assistants at the Federal Reserve Bank of Boston.

1. Department of Labor, *Preliminary Estimates of Participant and Financial Characteristics of Private Pension Plans, 1977* (Government Printing Office, 1981).

2. James H. Schulz, Thomas D. Leavitt, and Leslie Kelly, "Private Pensions Fall Far Short of Preretirement Income Levels," *Monthly Labor Review,* vol. 102 (February 1979), p. 32, note 4.

3. See Department of Labor, *Preliminary Estimates of Participant and Financial Characteristics of Private Pension Plans, 1977.*

Although these formulas vary considerably, they may be classified into two broad categories: unit benefit formulas and flat benefit formulas. Plans using unit benefit formulas are sometimes referred to as conventional plans; those using flat benefit formulas may be termed pattern plans. This terminology is used in the Bankers Trust pension studies discussed below, one of the few data sources that describe current pension plans and their benefit provisions.

When a unit benefit formula is used, the employee is credited with some specified unit of benefit for each year of service with the employer. Sometimes this benefit unit is expressed as a specific dollar amount, particularly in plans where the range of hourly wage rates among participants is relatively narrow. A more common procedure, used particularly for salaried workers, is to credit the employee with a specified percentage of compensation for each year of service. For example, the employee may earn 1.5 percentage points a year and after thirty years of service receive a benefit equal to 45 percent of preretirement compensation.

Flat benefit formulas assume a variety of forms. One commonly used formula pays retirees a specified flat percentage of their earnings, usually 20 to 40 percent, regardless of their length of service. Another formula pays a flat dollar amount for each year of service. Under this type of formula a worker might accrue $150 for each year of service and after thirty years of service be entitled to an annual pension of $4,500. Finally, a small number of plans use a flat amount formula that pays the same benefit to all eligible retirees, regardless of age, service, or compensation.

Defined Contribution Plans

Whereas defined benefit plans emphasize the value of the ultimate pension to be paid to the retiree, defined contribution plans (also known as money-purchase plans) stress the value of the periodic contributions made to the pension fund. Under this type of arrangement the retiree's benefit depends on the amount of contributions plus investment earnings accumulated on his behalf. Contributions to these plans are generally based on some target level of benefits and may be made either solely by the employer or jointly by employer and employee. Under the traditional defined contribution plan the employer makes all pension contributions, and these are equal to a specified percentage of each participant's current earnings. For example, the employer might make monthly contributions equal to 10 percent of each participant's salary. When a worker retires, his benefit is equal to the fixed annuity that can be purchased with the accumulated contributions plus investment earnings.

Integration

As discussed in chapter 2, the pensions paid by many employer-sponsored defined benefit plans are integrated with social security, that is, reduced to take into account the portion of retirement income that pensioners receive from social security benefits. Of the large corporate pension plans surveyed by the Bankers Trust Company in 1980, almost no pattern plans were integrated with social security, whereas 86 percent of conventional plans were integrated.[4] Among integrated conventional plans 56 percent used the offset method of integration, whereby a specified percentage of the basic social security benefit is subtracted from the gross pension. The rest of the plans used some form of excess method, either allowing pension benefit accrual only on compensation above a certain level or establishing benefit accrual rates that are higher above this compensation level than below it.

Some studies have indicated that small pension plans are more likely to be integrated than large plans. A 1974 survey conducted by the Congressional Research Service indicated that 64 percent of small plans (plans with fewer than twenty-six members) were integrated, whereas only 29 percent of large plans were integrated.[5] A 1978 study performed for the Department of the Treasury indicated that 84 percent of small plans were integrated, as against 62 percent of large plans.[6]

Qualified and Nonqualified Plans

A pension plan that meets the participation and vesting standards designated in the Internal Revenue Code is referred to as a qualified plan and, as such, receives certain tax advantages not available to nonqualified plans.[7] Compensation in the form of employer contributions to qualified plans is deductible by the employer when contributions are

4. William J. Mischo, Sook-Kuen Chang, and Eugene P. Kaston, *Corporate Pension Plan Study: A Guide for the 1980s,* Bankers Trust Company, Employee Benefits Division (New York: Bankers Trust, 1980), pp. 39, 41.

5. Raymond Schmitt, "Integration of Private Pension Plans with Social Security," in *Studies in Public Welfare,* paper 18: *Issues in Financing Retirement Income Studies,* studies prepared for the Subcommittee on Fiscal Policy of the Joint Economic Committee, 93 Cong. 2 sess. (GPO, 1974), p. 175.

6. "Results of A. S. Hansen Study of Pension Plans," Department of the Treasury, *News,* April 25, 1978.

7. For a more detailed discussion of the tax treatment of private plans, see chapter 3.

made, but not taxed to the employee until benefits are distributed from the plan. As discussed in chapter 3, qualified plans, by allowing the worker to defer taxes until retirement, offer substantial tax advantages over nonqualified plans.

The Financial Structure of Pension Funds

Source of Financing: Contributory versus Noncontributory Plans

The favorable tax treatment accorded employer contributions to qualified pension plans has encouraged the growth of plans that are primarily employer financed. During the late 1940s and early 1950s management and labor debated whether private plans should be contributory (financed at least partially by employees) or noncontributory (financed by employers). Management usually took the position that contributory plans would make employees more aware of pension costs and hence more responsible in their pension demands. Union leaders held that only a noncontributory pension plan could be made compulsory and that compulsory participation was the only way to ensure that employees would not postpone joining a pension plan until they were approaching retirement age.[8] A precedent was finally set in 1949, when the Basic Steel Industry Fact Finding Board recommended noncontributory plans.[9] This decision was based in part on the fact that each dollar of a tax-deductible employer contribution yields more benefits than a dollar of employee contribution, which is first taxed under the federal income tax. Since the 1940s the trend toward noncontributory plans has been widespread. As illustrated in table 2-1, employer contributions increased from 58 percent of total private pension contributions in 1940 to 94 percent in 1980.

Investment of Funds: Pension Trusts and Life Insurance Companies

A pension plan is usually funded either through a group annuity contract offered by a life insurance company or through a trust established by the employer and administered by a bank or trust company.[10]

8. Merton C. Bernstein, *The Future of Private Pensions* (London: Free Press of Glencoe, 1964), p. 221.
9. Basic Steel Industry, 13 Lab. Arb. H6 at 90 (1949).
10. Some plans may split their portfolios and provide through both a trust and an insurance company.

Plans funded through an insurance company are sometimes referred to as insured plans, while those funded through a bank or trust company are sometimes called trusteed or noninsured plans.

Pension trusts, the dominant vehicle for funding private plans, held 63 percent of pension assets in 1980. Under the trust fund arrangement pension contributions are deposited with a trustee who invests the money to earn a return. Benefits may be paid either directly from the trust or through the sponsoring company's pension plan administrator. Many large companies manage their own pension funds by establishing in-house pension trusts. Since economies of scale are present in pension fund management, smaller companies tend to relinquish these responsibilities, most often to a commercial bank trust department.

In the case of pension funds held by life insurers, the employer uses pension contributions to purchase annuity contracts, either on a group or an individual basis, from an insurance company. Group annuity pension plans are more prevalent than individual contracts and, as shown in table B-1, in 1980 they accounted for over three-quarters of insured plan assets and covered 19 million people. Group annuity contracts can be administered in two ways. Under the first approach pension contributions are accumulated in a pooled account, and money is withdrawn from the accumulated funds to buy an annuity when the employee retires. Alternatively, the employer can purchase a paid-up deferred annuity for each plan member each year, and the employee's retirement benefit will equal the sum of the deferred annuities purchased on his behalf. Individual contracts, often used by small firms with too few employees to qualify for coverage under a group annuity contract, generally involve the purchase of a whole life, endowment, or retirement-income policy for each person under the plan.

As discussed in chapter 5, the portfolio composition of pension trusts is very different from that of funds held by life insurers. For example, in 1980, 51 percent of pension trust assets were invested in stocks and 35 percent in bonds and government securities. Pension assets held by life insurance companies were invested quite differently—44 percent in bonds and government securities and only 11 percent in stocks. Until the early 1960s the historical tendency of life insurance companies to invest conservatively was reinforced by state laws limiting their holdings of corporate stock. But since then most states have passed legislation allowing life companies to hold pension assets in separate accounts, which may be invested partially or completely in corporate equities. In 1980, 20 percent of pension assets with life insurers—or $33.4 billion—

Table B-1. Assets and Coverage of Pension Plans with Life Insurers, 1980

	Assets		People covered	
Type of plan	Amount (billions of dollars)	Percent of total	Number (millions)	Percent of total
Group annuities[a]	127.2	76.7	19.2	73.6
Individual policy pension trusts[b]	7.6	4.6	2.2	8.4
Tax-sheltered annuities	10.3	6.2	1.8	6.9
Terminal funded group plans	4.3	2.6	0.2	0.8
Keogh plans	2.5	1.5	0.5	1.9
Individual retirement accounts	3.0	1.8	1.1	4.2
Other plans	11.0	6.6	1.1	4.2
Total	165.8	100.0	26.1	100.0

Source: American Council of Life Insurance, *Life Insurance Fact Book, 1981* (Washington, D.C.: ACLI, 1981), p. 54.
Figures are rounded.
  a. Includes immediate participation guarantee and deposit administration plans.
  b. Includes group permanent plans and profit-sharing plans.

were held in separate accounts; 47 percent of these assets were invested in common stock.[11]

Under separate accounts funding, the insurer establishes one or more special accounts for the sole purpose of investing pension funds. Usually these accounts are used to invest the pooled assets of two or more pension plans. The insurer normally establishes at least one separate common stock account but sometimes maintains two or more such accounts with differing investment objectives. Various other separate accounts may also be used, such as real estate mortgage accounts and publicly traded bond accounts. Of course, the insurer may establish a separate account for an individual employer, with whatever asset mix the employer specifies. This procedure is less common, though, since it is only practical for a large employer with sufficient funds to permit asset diversification.

Breadth of Coverage

Multiemployer Plans versus Single-Employer Plans

Pension plans can be classified, according to the employee units that they cover, as single- or multiemployer plans. These two types of plans

11. American Council of Life Insurance, *Pension Facts, 1981* (Washington, D.C.: ACLI, 1981), p. 17.

differ in their funding, vesting provisions, and benefit levels, each being suited to particular industries.

The first pension plans were sponsored almost exclusively by individual employers, who paid benefits to employees who retired in accordance with specific plan requirements. While the provisions of these single-employer plans were appropriate for many workers, they failed to address the needs of workers in industries with seasonal and irregular employment and high job-turnover rates. Many workers in such industries as construction, service, and apparel did not work for one employer long enough to qualify for pension benefits. The failure of single-employer plans to provide benefits to these workers gave rise to the concept of collectively bargained multiemployer pension plans.

Multiemployer plans are sponsored by a group of employers, usually within the same industry, who agree to provide benefits for all the eligible workers in any of the participating firms. Employers pay into the plan at an agreed-upon rate, usually expressed in cents per hour of covered employment. These contributions are accumulated in a pooled fund governed through equal board representation of employers and unions. Benefits are paid from the fund to all eligible workers regardless of which employer (or employers) they have worked for. While multiemployer plans usually provide less generous benefits than single-employer plans, they offer workers retirement income security by allowing them to retain pension credits as they move among participating employers. Moreover, they protect a worker's benefit even through his employer may leave the plan.

Although multiemployer pension plans were introduced in the 1940s, the major collective bargaining advancements in these plans began in the mid-1950s. Since then the number of workers covered by such plans has grown rapidly, increasing from 3.3 million in 1959 to 8.0 million in 1980.[12] The number of workers covered by multiemployer plans as a percentage of workers covered by all plans has also increased dramatically. Multiemployer plans covered 9 percent of private plan participants in 1950, 16 percent in 1959, and 22 percent in 1980.[13] According to the latest

12. Pension Benefit Guaranty Corporation, "Program Overview" (PBGC, September 1981), p. 1.

13. Harry E. Davis, "Multiemployer Pension Plan Provisions in 1973," *Monthly Labor Review,* vol. 97 (October 1974), p. 10. The 1980 figure reflects the fact that out of the 33 million workers covered by private pension plans only 8 million were covered by multiemployer plans. See Pension Benefit Guaranty Corporation, "Fact Sheet" (PBGC, January 1981), and table 2-1 in this volume.

survey, 23 percent of multiemployer plan participants worked in manufacturing, 28 percent in construction, 21 percent in motor transportation, and the remaining 29 percent in other nonmanufacturing industries.[14]

Keogh Plans and Individual Retirement Accounts

Keogh plans and individual retirement accounts (IRAs) are two kinds of individual retirement savings plans available to workers. A Keogh plan is a tax-deferred retirement savings program that allows self-employed persons and proprietors of small unincorporated businesses to establish individual accounts for themselves and their employees. Congress authorized Keoghs as defined contribution plans in 1962, allowing tax-deductible annual contributions of 10 percent of annual income, up to a maximum of $2,500.[15] The Employee Retirement Income Security Act of 1974 (ERISA) increased this contribution limit to 15 percent of income, up to a maximum of $7,500. The maximum deductible contribution was increased to $15,000, effective January 1, 1982, by the Economic Recovery Tax Act of 1981. As a result of ERISA, defined benefit Keogh plans have also been authorized. The benefit formula in these plans is based on a guideline table of retirement income stated in the law as a percentage of current salary, the percentage decreasing with age.

To establish a Keogh plan for his own retirement, the owner or partner of a business must do the same for any full-time employees with three or more years of continuous service. The percentage of salary contributed on behalf of these employees must be at least equal to the percentage of salary contributed for the self-employed person. Moreover, a person who is self-employed part-time can establish a Keogh plan based on his additional earnings even if he is covered by another pension plan. In all cases, contributions made to Keogh plans are fully vested immediately.

The 1974 ERISA legislation also created the individual retirement account (IRA) to encourage workers who are not currently covered by retirement savings plans to set aside pension funds on their own. The 1981 Economic Recovery Tax Act, liberalized the provisions so that any full- or part-time employee, including those covered by private pension plans, may contribute as much as 100 percent of compensation

14. Pension Benefit Guaranty Corporation, *Multiemployer Study Required by P.L. 95 214* (PBGC, 1978), app. 2, p. 3.
15. H.R. 10, enacted as the Self-Employed Individuals Tax Retirement Act of 1962.

Table B-2. Contributions to Individual Retirement Accounts and Keogh Plans, by Adjusted Gross Income, 1980

Adjusted gross income (thousands of dollars)	Individual retirement accounts		Keogh plans	
	Amount (millions of dollars)	Cumulative percent distribution	Amount (millions of dollars)	Cumulative percent distribution
0–5	14.5	100.0	7.9	100.0
5–10	85.1	99.6	10.8	99.6
10–15	215.2	97.1	36.6	99.0
15–20	324.3	90.8	60.9	97.0
20–30	832.1	81.2	118.2	93.8
30–50	1,213.6	56.9	485.4	87.5
50–100	602.6	21.3	774.8	61.5
100–200	101.8	3.6	302.0	20.0
200 and over	22.0	0.6	70.9	3.8
Total	3,411.2	. . .	1,867.5	. . .

Source: Internal Revenue Service, Statistics Division, *Statistics of Income, Individual Income Tax Returns, 1980, Advanced Data* (GPO, 1981). Figures are rounded.

into an IRA (up to a limit of $2,000 a year) and deduct the contribution from taxable income. This legislation also increased the maximum deductible contribution for a spousal IRA from $1,750 to $2,250.

At the end of 1980 IRAs and Keogh plans held combined assets of over $30 billion.[16] As shown in table B-2, the bulk of contributions to these plans comes primarily from higher-income persons. For example, in 1980, 81 percent of the tax-deductible contributions to IRAs were made by persons with annual incomes of $20,000 or more. Because the self-employed are concentrated in higher-income brackets, the trend for Keogh plans is even more exaggerated. Persons with incomes of $20,000 and over made 94 percent of the total tax-deductible contributions to Keogh plans in 1980.

Benefit Provisions

Normal Retirement

The "normal" retirement age is not the age at which employee retirement is mandatory but the earliest age at which an employee is

16. American Council of Life Insurance, *Pension Facts, 1981,* p. 14.

eligible to receive full pension benefits. Some plans may have several different retirement schedules and, consequently, several normal retirement ages. Historically, the normal retirement age in most plans has been sixty-five. But a 1974 study by the Bureau of Labor Statistics estimated that while 63 percent of the workers in defined benefit plans had an age requirement of sixty-five for normal retirement, the rest usually had lower retirement ages.[17] ERISA has reinforced this trend by stipulating that the normal retirement age should not be later than sixty-five unless a worker has participated in the company's pension plan for less than ten years.

Many private plans require participants both to attain a specified normal retirement age and to complete a service requirement in order to receive full retirement benefits. Of the defined benefit plans examined in the Bureau of Labor Statistics study, 71 percent had some service requirement. Data from the Bankers Trust pension studies indicate that, at least in large, single-employer defined benefit plans, service requirements have been liberalized over time. The proportion of pattern plans allowing full retirement benefits after only ten years of service increased from 53 percent in 1955 to 100 percent in 1980. During the same period, the percentage of conventional pension plans with similarly liberalized service requirements increased from 79 to 100 percent.[18]

Data for multiemployer pension plans reveal more stringent service requirements. Of those with service requirements, 39 percent require ten years or less of service, 32 percent require eleven to fifteen years, and 29 percent require sixteen to thirty years of service.[19]

Early Retirement

Many pension plans allow workers to retire before reaching normal retirement age, provided that they have attained a specified early retirement age and completed any early retirement service requirements. Ninety-five percent of the covered workers included in the 1974 Bureau of Labor Statistics defined benefit plan study were in plans that provided

17. Bureau of Labor Statistics, Office of Wages and Industrial Relations, 1974 Defined Benefit Pension Plan Study, datatape, 1977; the study surveyed 1,467 defined benefit plans before the enactment of ERISA.

18. Mischo, Chang, and Kaston, *Corporate Pension Plan Study,* p. 37; and Bankers Trust Company, *Study of Industrial Retirement Plans, 1960* (New York: Bankers Trust, 1960), pp. 10, 12.

19. BLS, 1974 Defined Benefit Plan Study.

early retirement benefits. But only 1 percent of these workers were in plans that pay full normal retirement benefits to early retirees; in all other cases early retirees qualified for reduced benefits.

Normal retirement benefits are calculated on the assumption that employees will not collect benefits before normal retirement age and that accumulated pension contributions will therefore earn interest until that date. Thus if an employee elects early retirement, his pension benefit is usually reduced for two reasons. First, the assets used to finance his pension benefits will accumulate to a smaller sum owing to loss of investment earnings. Second, since pension payments will be made over a longer retirement period, the annual benefit provided by each dollar of accumulated assets will be smaller.

Early retirement benefits that are lowered by a certain percentage to reflect the extended retirement period and the loss of investment earnings are said to be actuarially reduced. The percentage by which an employee's pension is reduced for early retirement depends on the mortality and interest rate assumptions used to calculate benefits under the plan. For example, under a given set of assumptions, the reduction in a worker's benefit for each year of early retirement might be 9 percent. A worker retiring at age sixty-four, therefore, would receive a pension equal to 91 percent of the benefit payable at age sixty-five. Although not all plans reduce early retirement benefits in strict accordance with the actuarial method, most use some approximation of an actuarial reduction.

According to the Bankers Trust study, provisions for early retirement benefits have been liberalized over time. In 1955, 70 percent of the pattern plans and 92 percent of the conventional plans examined by Bankers Trust had some early retirement provisions. In more than half of these plans, however, the company's consent was required before the employee could claim an early pension. By 1980 almost all plans surveyed by Bankers Trust gave employees the option to retire early and receive immediate pensions at their own election.[20] Moreover, early retirement benefits have become more generous in recent years. Pattern plans providing early retirement benefits greater than their actuarial equivalents increased from 52 percent in 1970 to 90 percent in 1980. Similarly, the portion of conventional plans offering early retirement benefits larger

20. Bankers Trust Company, *Study of Industrial Retirement Plans, 1960,* pp. 14–15; and Mischo, Chang, and Kaston, *Corporate Pension Plan Study,* pp. 18, 21.

than their actuarial equivalents rose from 47 percent in 1970 to 90 percent in 1980.[21]

Disability Retirement

Most pension plans provide early retirement benefits for workers who are permanently unable to work because of injury or disease. For example, 80 percent of the plans examined in the 1980 Bankers Trust study extended some disability retirement provision. And the 1974 Bureau of Labor Statistics study indicated that 81 percent of workers covered by a pension plan received some form of disability coverage. The percentage of plans providing disability protection has increased over time. In 1955, 46 percent of the conventional and 80 percent of the pattern plans examined by Bankers Trust had disability retirement provisions. By 1980, 75 percent of conventional and 98 percent of pattern plans provided these benefits.[22]

Eligibility criteria for disability retirement benefits vary among private plans, yet there is a general trend toward less stringent age requirements and more stringent service requirements than for normal retirement eligibility. According to the 1974 study, 94 percent of the workers covered by disability retirement provisions were required to fulfill some service requirement, but in almost all cases the service requirement was no more than fifteen years and for roughly half the workers it was ten years or less. Since age requirements for disability benefits are less common, only about one-fifth of these workers were required to attain some minimum age before claiming disability benefits.

The coordination of disability benefits and normal retirement benefits differs among private plans. Many plans provide a disability benefit until the disabled worker reaches the specified normal retirement age and thereafter pay the worker's normal retirement benefit. But this practice varies from plan to plan. Of those workers in the Bureau of Labor Statistics study who were covered for disability, 53 percent would receive their normal retirement benefit in the event of disability, 15 percent would receive their normal retirement benefit plus an additional supplement until they become eligible for social security benefits, and 12 percent would receive less than their normal retirement benefit.

21. Mischo, Chang, and Kaston, *Corporate Pension Plan Study*, pp. 18, 20.
22. Ibid., pp. 345, 347; and Bankers Trust Company, *Study of Industrial Retirement Plans, 1960*, p. 16.

Survivor Pensions to Spouses

Before 1974 many plans made no provision for retirees' surviving spouses. The passage of ERISA reversed this trend by requiring that most pension plans offer protection for the retirees' surviving spouses through the provision of joint-and-survivor annuities. A joint-and-survivor annuity consists of a worker's pension payable over the life of the participant plus a survivor pension payable over the life of the surviving spouse. The extra protection offered by the joint-and-survivor option is usually purchased through reductions in the retiree's own pension and is provided automatically unless rejected in writing by the retiree. For example, a participant who would have received a pension of $100 a month in the absence of the joint-and-survivor option might instead receive a reduced annuity of $80 a month. After the worker's death, the surviving spouse might receive a pension of $40 a month. Alternatively, a plan may allow the participant to pay premiums for the survivor option rather than reduce his benefit.

Vesting of Benefits

Vesting refers to the provision that after an employee meets certain requirements he will retain a right to all or part of his accrued pension benefits even if his coverage under a plan terminates before retirement. An employee can collect vested benefits at normal retirement or sometimes, at a reduced rate, upon departure from the firm. Usually an employee's accrued pension benefits derived from employer contributions become vested only if he has worked for a specified period of time. Accrued benefits derived from the participant's own contributions are always fully vested, as are IRA and Keogh plans assets.

Prior to the enactment of ERISA, most plans were not legally required to vest employer-financed benefits before an employee retired. Many people, therefore, had to meet stringent age and service requirements before their accrued pension benefits became vested. As a result long-service workers who left a firm before retirement often forfeited their pension benefits. To assure that accrued pension benefits are vested after a reasonable period of service, ERISA established vesting standards for qualified plans, requiring that a company vest at least 50 percent of an employee's benefits after ten years of service and 100 percent after fifteen years of service. Moreover, an employee's accrued benefits now must be vested completely by the time he reaches the plan's specified normal retirement age.

To ensure the receipt of vested pension benefits ERISA created the Pension Benefit Guaranty Corporation. As discussed in chapter 6, this agency ensures the payment of vested pension benefits in private defined benefit plans that terminate with insufficient assets.

Portabilty of Pension Credits

Portability is a term that refers to the transfer of a worker's accrued pension credits when he changes jobs.[23] In the United States today there is no general mechanism for pension portability among private plans. Thus when a worker terminates coverage under a pension plan, his nonvested benefits are normally forfeited. Vested benefits are either held by the employer until the worker reaches retirement age or transmitted to the worker in a lump-sum payment. To increase portability, some have suggested the creation of a central clearinghouse in which the vested pension credits of all workers who terminate employment under a pension plan could be accumulated. Without such a centralized system, the limited portability available in the private sector is restricted to the continuous coverage provided by multiemployer plans and ERISA's provision for tax-free rollovers into individual retirement accounts.

The general lack of pension portability among private pension plans creates problems for both employers and plan participants. Under current practices, if a worker terminates employment under a company plan, accrued vested benefits usually remain with the plan until he reaches retirement age. By this time the real value of the worker's benefit may have been greatly reduced by inflation, since private pensions are not indexed between termination of employment and retirement. The higher the rate of inflation and the further the worker is from retirement age, the greater the erosion in the real value of the benefit.

The payment of benefits to mobile employees is also difficult for employers, who face the costly task of administering small benefit claims. To relieve employers of this administrative burden, ERISA permits them to "cash-out" employee benefits of $1,750 or less when a

23. The following discussion of portability is based on a more comprehensive treatment by Donald S. Grubbs, Jr., "Pension Portability," in *National Pension Policies: Private Pension Plans,* Hearings before the Subcommittee on Retirement Income and Employment of the House Select Committee on Aging, 95 Cong. 2 sess. (GPO, 1978), 529–65.

worker terminates employment. Although these funds can be reinvested until retirement, many workers (particularly low-income workers) use lump-sum distributions to meet current expenses.

Part of the limited portability available today is through multiemployer plans, which allow workers to carry their accrued benefits from one contributing employer to another regardless of whether they are vested. Many multiemployer plans also have reciprocity agreements that protect the benefits of workers who move among plans.[24] The 1974 Bureau of Labor Statistics pension study revealed that 53 percent of workers covered by multiemployer plans received reciprocity coverage.

Opportunities for pension portability have been increased somewhat by ERISA provisions for tax-free rollovers into individual retirement accounts. A worker who terminates employment under a qualified pension plan and receives a lump-sum payment of vested benefits can transfer these funds into an IRA. By doing so within sixty days he can take advantage of the rollover option, that is, defer taxes on the funds. Even though the rollover of lump-sum payments to an IRA can be useful—particularly to workers who receive lump-sum payments from several employers—only a small proportion of workers who receive lump-sum distributions exercise this option.

The question whether to increase portability in the private pension system by establishing a central clearinghouse for pension credits calls for careful consideration of the potential costs of such a plan. First, the implementation of a portable pension system could place a substantial administrative burden on private plans, forcing a greater number to terminate and discouraging new plan formations. Second, the costs of such a system—whether paid by the government or passed on to plan participants—could be significant. Finally, the payment of sizable lump-sum benefit payments to a central fund could create cash-flow problems for individual pension plans, since they currently tend to restrict such distributions to small benefit amounts. For these reasons, the voluntary portability provisions that were contained in the Senate version of ERISA were omitted by the conference committee.

Conclusion

The great variety of private pension plans complicates their classification; nevertheless, for purposes of discussion, it is possible to think in

24. See Maurice E. McDonald, *Reciprocity among Private Multiemployer Pension Plans* (Irwin, 1975).

terms of a plan prototype. Despite a growing trend toward defined contribution plans, most pension plan participants today are covered by defined benefit plans, of which the majority are single-employer plans that qualify for preferential tax treatment. Approximately three-fourths of defined benefit plans use unit benefit formulas, which relate a worker's pension to both compensation and length of service.

The benefit provisions of these plans also exhibit several distinct trends. To qualify for normal retirement benefits, most participants in defined benefit plans must be sixty-five and have completed some requisite service, usually ten years or less. Almost all workers in defined benefit plans are eligible to receive early retirement benefits, although these are usually less generous than normal retirement benefits. In addition, over 80 percent of defined benefit participants are members of plans that provide for disability retirement.

Thus the "typical" pension plan can be thought of as a qualified, single-employer, defined benefit plan with a unit benefit formula that permits full benefits at age sixty-five after five years of service.

appendix C Pensions and Inflation: A Model of Required Rates of Return

A simple model shows that full indexation with current contribution rates is possible only if the real rate of return on the plan assets is not adversely affected by inflation.[1]

Consider the most general case where an employee's benefit (B_j) is a proportion (α_i) of his past salary (S_i) over his work life (e), and the contribution rate (β) is set at such a level that the present discounted value of benefits (PVB) between retirement $(e + 1)$ and death (d) equals the present discounted value of contributions (PVC). That is,

$$(1) \qquad B_j = \sum_{i=1}^{e} \alpha_i S_i$$

$$(2) \qquad C_i = \beta S_i$$

$$(3) \qquad PVB = \sum_{j=e+1}^{d} (1 + r)^{-j} \sum_{i=1}^{e} \alpha_i S_i$$

$$= \sum_{i=1}^{e} \alpha_i S_i [(1 + r)^{-e} - (1 + r)^{-d}]/r$$

$$(4) \qquad PVC = \sum_{i=1}^{e} \beta S_i (1 + r)^{-i},$$

where C is contributions, and r is the interest rate.[2] Therefore, by setting PVB equal to PVC and rearranging, we have

$$(5) \qquad \beta = \frac{\sum_{i=1}^{e} \alpha_i S_i [(1 + r)^{-e} - (1 + r)^{-d}]/r}{\sum_{i=1}^{e} S_i (1 + r)^{-i}}.$$

1. To simplify the presentation, the annuity is computed from an average life expectancy rather than a distribution. Contributions are assumed to be paid on an annual rather than a monthly basis.
2. Simplification of equation 3 is based on the formula $\sum_{i=0}^{n-1} b^i = (1 - b^n)/(1 - b)$.

With this framework, it is possible to determine for four separate cases the interest rate required for the contribution rate (β), set in the noninflationary period, to yield sufficient revenues to cover benefits in the inflationary period.

Case 1: Career average plan with no post-retirement indexing. With a constant inflation rate (π) the benefit and contribution equations for a career average plan with no post-retirement indexing become

(6)
$$B_j = \sum_{i=1}^{e} \alpha_i S_i (1 + \pi)^i$$

(7)
$$C_i = \bar{\beta} S_i (1 + \pi)^i$$

(8)
$$\overline{PVB} = \sum_{j=e+1}^{d} (1 + r')^{-j} \sum_{i=1}^{e} \alpha_i S_i (1 + \pi)^i$$
$$= \sum_{i=1}^{e} \alpha_i S_i (1 + \pi)^i [(1 + r')^{-e} - (1 + r')^{-d}]/r'$$

(9)
$$\overline{PVC} = \sum_{i=1}^{e} \bar{\beta} S_i (1 + \pi)^i (1 + r')^{-i}$$

(10)
$$\bar{\beta} = \frac{\sum_{i=1}^{e} \alpha_i S_i (1 + \pi)^i [(1 + r')^{-e} - (1 + r')^{-d}]/r'}{\sum_{i=1}^{e} S_i (1 + \pi)^i (1 + r')^{-i}}.$$

With these plan provisions the preinflation contribution rate can remain unchanged ($\bar{\beta} = \beta$) if the following equality holds:

(11)
$$\frac{[(1 + r')^{-e} - (1 + r')^{-d}]/r'}{(1 + r')^{-i}} = \frac{[(1 + r)^{-e} - (1 + r)^{-d}]/r}{(1 + r)^{-i}} \quad \text{for all } i.^{[3]}$$

Thus when benefits are tied to average earnings and there is no post-retirement indexing, a constant nominal rate ($r' = r$) allows the contribution rate to remain unchanged. A constant nominal rate generates sufficient revenues because higher nominal benefits are exactly matched by increased contributions from the inflated wage base. Similarly, if interest rates were to rise in response to inflation, contribution rates could be lowered in career average plans with no post-retirement indexing.

3. To simplify the model, this equation is based on the assumption that the contribution in each year equals the present value of benefits accrued in that year.

Case 2: Final earnings plan with no post-retirement indexing. For a final earnings plan in an inflationary environment, the benefit and contribution equations become

(12) $$B_j = \alpha_e e S_e (1 + \pi)^e$$

(13) $$\overline{PVB} = \sum_{d=e+1}^{d} \alpha_e e S_e (1 + \pi)^e (1 + r)^{-j}$$

$$= \alpha_e e S_e (1 + \pi)^e [(1 + r')^{-e} - (1 + r')^{-d}]/r'$$

(14) $$\overline{PVC} = \sum_{i=1}^{e} \bar{\beta} S_i (1 + \pi)^i (1 + r')^{-i}$$

(15) $$\bar{\beta} = \frac{\alpha_e e S_e (1 + \pi)^e [(1 + r')^{-e} - (1 + r')^{-d}] r'}{\sum_{i=1}^{e} S_i (1 + \pi)^i (1 + r')^{-i}}.$$

In this case, the required change in interest rates can be determined by comparing $\bar{\beta}$ with the contribution rate for a similar plan during a period without inflation:

(16) $$\beta = \frac{\alpha_e e S_e [(1 + r)^{-e} - (1 + r)^{-d}]/r}{\sum_{i=1}^{e} S_i (1 + r)^{-i}}.$$

If the interest rate remained unchanged ($r' = r$), then the contribution rate would have to increase ($\bar{\beta} > \beta$). On the other hand, if the new interest rate fully incorporated the inflation premium, that is, $1 + r' = (1 + r)(1 + \pi)$, then the contribution rate could be lowered ($\bar{\beta} < \beta$). Therefore, to maintain the preinflation contribution rate, some inflation premium must be reflected in the discount rate. However, nominal yields need not rise by the full increase in prices, since with no post-retirement indexing the inflated yields on fund assets after the employee retires represents a gain to the pension fund that compensates for the inadequate financing of the final earnings plan over the employee's working life.

Case 3: Career average plan with post-retirement indexing. In pension plans with benefits based on career average earnings, but with provision of post-retirement cost-of-living adjustments, the present value of benefits and contributions are

(17) $$B_j = (1 + \pi)^{j-e} \sum_{i=1}^{e} \alpha_i S_i (1 + \pi)^i$$

$$(18) \quad \overline{PVB} = \sum_{j=e+1}^{d} (1+\pi)^{j-e}(1+r')^{-j} \sum_{i=1}^{e} \alpha_i S_i (1+\pi)^i$$

$$= \frac{\sum_{i=1}^{e} \alpha_i S_i (1+\pi)^i (1+\pi)^{-e}[(1+r')^{-e}(1+\pi)^e - (1+r')^{-d}(1+\pi)^d]}{(1+r')(1+\pi)^{-1} - 1}$$

$$(19) \quad \overline{PVC} = \sum_{i=1}^{e} \beta S_i (1+\pi)^i (1+r')^{-i}$$

$$(20) \quad \bar{B} = \frac{\sum_{i=1}^{e} \alpha_i S_i \dfrac{(1+\pi)^i(1+\pi)^{-e}[(1+r')^{-e}(1+\pi)^e - (1+r')^{-d}(1+\pi)^d]}{(1+r')(1+\pi)^{-1} - 1}}{\sum_{i=1}^{e} S_i (1+\pi)^i (1+r')^{-i}}.$$

For contribution rates to remain unchanged, the following equality must hold:

$$(21) \quad \frac{(1+\pi)^{-e}[(1+r')^{-e}(1+\pi)^e - (1+r')^{-d}(1+\pi)^d]}{(1+r')^{-i}[(1+r')(1+\pi)^{-1} - 1]}$$
$$= \frac{[(1+r)^{-e} - (1+r)^{-d}]/r}{(1+r)^{-i}} \quad \text{for all } i.$$

If the nominal interest rate remains constant, that is $r' = r$, then the left side of equation 21 would be greater than the right and the contribution rate would have to increase ($\bar{\beta} > \beta$). On the other hand, if the nominal interest rate increased to fully reflect the inflation, that is, $1 + r' = (1+r)(1+\pi)$, then the contribution rate could be reduced from the preinflation level ($\bar{\beta} < \beta$). Thus for cost-of-living adjustments after retirement in a career average plan, nominal rates must rise to maintain the preinflation contribution rate, but need not rise by the full rate of inflation.

Case 4: Final earnings plan with post-retirement indexing. In this plan, the most comparable to social security, the initial benefit is based on final earnings, and benefits are adjusted for cost-of-living increases after retirement. Benefit and contribution equations become

$$(22) \quad \beta_j = \alpha_e e S_e (1+\pi)^e (1+\pi)^{j-e}$$

$$(23) \quad \overline{PVB} = \sum_{j=e+1}^{d} \alpha_e e S_e (1+\pi)^j (1+r')^{-d}$$
$$= \frac{\alpha_e e S_e [(1+r')^{-e}(1+\pi)^e - (1+r')^{-d}(1+\pi)^d]}{(1+r')(1+\pi)^{-1} - 1}$$

(24)
$$\overline{PVC} = \sum_{i=1}^{e} \beta S_i (1 + \pi)^i (1 + r')^{-i}$$

(25)
$$\bar{\beta} = \frac{\dfrac{\alpha_e S_e e[(1 + \pi)^e (1 + r')^{-e} - (1 + r')^{-d}(1 + \pi)^d]}{(1 + r')(1 + \pi)^{-1} - 1}}{\displaystyle\sum_{i=1}^{e} S_i (1 + r')^{-i}(1 + \pi)^i},$$

whereas, the contribution rate in the absence of inflation is

(26)
$$\beta = \frac{\alpha_e e S_e [(1 + r)^{-e} - (1 + r)^{-d}]/r}{\displaystyle\sum_{i=1}^{e} S_i (1 + r)^{-i}}.$$

Therefore, if $1 + r' = (1 + \pi)(1 + r)$, then $\bar{\beta} = \beta$. In other words, for the pension plan to remain actuarially sound without increasing the contribution rate while providing benefits based on final earnings and post-retirement cost-of-living adjustments, the nominal interest rate must rise by the full inflation premium.

Index

Aaron, Henry J., 73, 189n
Accounting practices, pension, 161–68. *See also* Augmented balance sheet
Accounting Principles Board, 162
American Council of Life Insurance, 4n, 8n, 9n, 39n, 47n, 95n, 160n, 218n
American Express Company, pension plan, 3, 8
American Institute of Accountants, 161n, 162n
Andersen, Arthur, and Company, 163, 168n
Ando, Albert, 63n, 209n
Annuities, 71, 72; life insurance pension funding through, 92, 217
Arak, Marcelle, 189n, 190n
Archer, James G., 41n
Assets, pension fund: capital loss, 103; and corporate assets, 142–43, 146, 149; exchange of index bonds for accumulated, 193–94; illiquidity, 70; individual asset holdings compared with, 115–17, 119; inflation effect on, 187, 189–90; life insurance, 95, 96, 217–18; management, 120–22, 137–38; mortgages, 99–106; pension trust, 92–95, 96, 217; as percent of company net worth, 130; stocks and bonds, 96, 97–99, 104; total, 62–63
Auerbach, Alan J., 85
Augmented balance sheet, 141–44

Bagehot, Walter (pseudonym). *See* Treynor, Jack L.
Bakay, A. J., 127n
Baltimore and Ohio Railroad, pension plan, 8
Bankers Trust Company, studies of defined benefit plans, 172, 173, 184, 214, 223, 224
Banks, management of pension fund assets, 120–22

Barber, Randy, 110
Barro, Robert, 80, 84, 88
Bartell, H. Robert, Jr., 93n
Basic Steel Industry Fact Finding Board, 216
Bell, Donald R., 54n
Beller, Daniel J., 54n
Benefits, private pension: backloading, 135; cost-of-living adjustments, 178–79, 184–85; early retirement, 223–24; gift and estate tax concessions on, 38; inflation effect on, 170–71, 173–74, 175–77; as issue in labor negotiations, 11; lump-sum versus periodic payments, 36, 37–38; PBGC guaranty of basic, 138–39; as percent of total retirement benefits, 199; survivor, 225; tax treatment, 36–37, 43–46, 60. *See also* Vesting of benefits.
Benefits, social security: adjustments for inflation and productivity, 177–78, 185–86; gap between income requirements and, 16, 26; inadequacy, 12, 13; indexed, 29, 177–78, 180; measures for evaluating, 20–23, 26; "notch" problem, 16–17n; saving and, 78–79; tax exemption for, 50
Berkman, Neil, 125, 127
Bernstein, Merton C., 10n, 13n, 176n, 216n
Bixby, Lenore E., 83n
Black, Fischer, 143n, 146–48
Blackwell, Kate, 131, 132n
Blinder, Alan S., 64n, 77n, 86, 182n, 192n
Blume, Marshall, 127n
Bodie, Zvi, 192n
Bonds: advantage of pension fund investment in, 146–48; index, 191–94, 197; individual versus pension fund holdings, 115–17, 119; inflation effect on yield, 190; life insurance companies investment, 98–99, 128; pension fund growth

235